The Dreaming Road

3/2/18

Jam,

Words cannot express how grateful I am to you for introducing me to the powerful healing energy of the dolphins and for your ability to midwife those who come to dance with them on the sea.

With infinite love & gratitude ♡

Bette

The Dreaming Road

ELIZABETH MOORE

Elizabeth Moore

**TURNING
STONE
PRESS**

Cover design by Glen Edelstein (Hudson Valley Book Design)
Cover art by Amos Morgan and Nina Malyna | | Thinkstock
Author photo by Leila Grannis of Grannis Photography
Interior design by Howie Severson/Fortuitous

Turning Stone Press
8301 Broadway St., Suite 219
San Antonio, TX 78209
turningstonepress.com

Library of Congress Control Number
is available upon request.

ISBN 978-1-61852-120-0

10 9 8 7 6 5 4 3 2 1

Printed in the United States of America

The day her daughter died
Time stood still
Shattering the glass mountain
For the quest of a greater will.
Picking up the pieces
From a world fallen apart
She suddenly heard a whisper
In the night of her broken heart.

—"Dancing Down the Dreaming Road"
by Shawn Gallaway

Grain of Sand

I am a little grain of sand,
please hold me gently in your hand.
You may think that I am small, but I am vast,
and forever I will last and last.

—Cassandra Moore

Contents

Introduction

Dear Reader:

The Dreaming Road was conceived in the beginning as a diary. On the day of my daughter's funeral, a very kind soul suggested that I start a diary to record my thoughts and emotions after her sudden death. My friend implied that if I remained steadfast in my recording I could look back over the years and see how far I had progressed in my journey through what we, on this side of the veil, call grief and loss. And so, several days later I began to write, and I found that the writing was healing for me.

After about five years, I started to feel that something more needed to happen with my diary: perhaps I wasn't writing just for myself, but maybe for my family and friends as well. I turned it into a memoir of sorts, changing names and altering places and events to protect the anonymity of those involved. I planned to give my memoir to my daughter's friends and our family members as a Christmas gift when I was done, as Christmas was her favorite holiday.

After several months of writing in every spare moment, I started to hear a very insistent voice inside my head telling me in no uncertain terms that I was just writing half of the story. I tried to ignore the voice, thinking it was just a figment of my overwrought imagination.

At that time, I had communicated with my daughter in dreams and through several mediums but never thought that I would be able to talk with her directly while I was awake. As a scholar, a researcher, and an academic, as well as a nurse, I struggled continually with whether or not the extraordinary experiences I'd had since my daughter's death were real or just a product of wishful thinking.

But the voice was extremely persistent, and every time I sat down to work on my memoir I became utterly distracted by this voice in my head. One of the things that survivors of suicide often ask is what happened, why did my loved one not reach out to me for help, why did he or she feel that the situation was so hopeless that the only way to escape the pain was death? I had been mulling over these questions in my head, and the voice was getting louder and even more insistent. So, late one night I just gave up my resistance to the voice. I grabbed a yellow legal pad, sharpened a couple of pencils, sat down at my desk, and asked the voice what it would like to tell me. The words began flooding in faster than I could write them down. I lost all track of time, and I really didn't know what I was writing until I read it over the next morning and was completely blown away. The writing I had produced was my daughter describing her encounter with an angel in a life review wherein she was guided to confront all the emotions that led to her suicide.

After that, I decided to suspend my disbelief and write what I heard without trying to censor it or fit it into my logical, analytical view of the world. This was my "lived experience." I also realized that my book was no longer a memoir, because how could I objectively verify the events that happened to my daughter in this other realm that she called Summer Wind? I guess I will ultimately come to know the truth of her story when I cross the veil as well.

But my experience is what it is, and in my heart of hearts I do believe that my daughter has been communicating with me since the day she died; it's just taken me a while to "cowgirl up" and listen. One of the things that amazed me as I wrote her part of the story was how much she had retained her personality and her manner of speech, which could be pretty blunt at times. She always had that razor-sharp, sarcastic edge. But her spirit was much heavier when she was on earth, and in Summer Wind she seemed quite amused when she told me about her adventures. The predicaments that she managed to get herself into were told with such humor that I always looked forward to the times when I would pick up my pencil and let her tell me her stories. It was almost as if my daughter was off on an amazing, exotic adventure and writing letters home to tell me all about it.

For me it was quite a ride, and her letters from heaven helped offset some of the heaviness as I went through a period of prolonged and complicated grief, as do many suicide survivors, during which time I was continually racked with guilt. I saw all the red flags and warning signals in hindsight when there was nothing I could do to change the outcome.

It was at this point that I began to realize that there might be a larger purpose to our collaboration than just the writing of a novel based on a true story to share with family and friends. The novel was taking on a life of its own with two related but separate journeys. The first journey was my recovery from the sudden death of my precious daughter who meant the world to me, and the second was her experiences on the other side of the veil as she came to terms with what she'd done and its effect on everyone who loved her, as well as her growing understanding of her soul's intention in choosing such an abrupt and traumatic exit. So, I began, with the help of two wonderful editors, to weave the two stories together like braids in a lock of hair or plaits in a horse's mane so that the whole became more than the sum of its parts. The story is no longer a memoir, and it's not a fantasy either. This is the reason my book has ultimately become an inspirational novel and why I have decided to share my story with more than family and friends. For those of you searching for a lighthouse in the midst of a raging storm, it is my way of helping you navigate your own journey.

It is my hope that you, the reader, can get a glimpse of the enduring connections that exist between us and our loved ones who have passed on. The ties that bind us remain unbroken even in death, and when we understand the "soul" purpose of our journeys here on earth, we are set free.

And so, this is our story, mine and my daughter's. It has been a collaborative effort, between not just the two of us, but also a host of treasured friends both here and on the other side. We offer it to you with the most profound love and respect, hoping that in reading it you will understand that our connections are eternal and that love never dies.

Prologue

This is my story, the story of Callie Murray, and I'm sticking to it.

I'm telling it to you exactly as it happened to me.

I know that many of you readers are going to think, What a terrible tragedy. A beautiful (I admit I was beautiful) sixteen-year-old girl with her whole life in front of her . . . Well, in Summer Wind, we don't look at it that way at all. In fact, from the perspective of our side, it was perfect. Everything in my life as Callie unfolded exactly as it was meant to.

❦ 1 ❧

Diane—Nightmare

The morning my daughter died, I woke and sat bolt upright in bed, my heart racing, my breath coming in ragged gasps. In my dream, dark spirits were chasing Callie. Thin, black, and waiflike, they surrounded her, tearing at her clothing, mocking her as she struggled to pull herself free. I tried to fight them, but my fingers swept through them as if they were vapor. I could only watch as Callie suddenly jerked herself from their grasp, her feet pounding the ground, her arms pumping as she sprinted away, her long blonde hair within a breath of their reach. I could only watch as they drew closer, could only will her—*Run, my baby girl, run.* Lately, it seemed, we were all moving through water.

Across the bedroom, sunlight was filtering through the blinds, casting shadows on the bed. Outside, birds were calling in the warm spring morning, and a soft breeze swayed the curtains toward me as I looked out the window at the shoreline of the lake across the street. *It was only a dream.* Casting off the covers, I rubbed the heaviness from my eyes and padded barefoot to the closet, wondering what to wear. Like all parents, I had beat the morning routine into submission, finessed it into a precise science.

My eyes half open, my fingers fumbled through the racks of clothing with a blind efficiency—Anthony had a make-up math exam before school today—and landed on a short brown dress patterned with large pink lilies, which I slipped off the hanger and tugged over my head. It was one of Tom's favorites, and I knew he would be downstairs already, making coffee, laying slices of bacon in a hot pan, and mixing some eggs in a bowl. It may not have worked out with Callie and Anthony's father, but in Tom I'd truly found a man I knew I could spend the rest of my days with.

I was halfway down the hall when I noticed the light coming from Callie's bedroom. Ah, to be a teenager again, with no regard for things like electric bills. I swore I spent half my life following these kids around, shutting off lights in their wake. "Callie!" I shouted. "Time to get up!"

I cocked an ear as I sailed by, waiting for the familiar groan. Callie had become crankier and more withdrawn this year—at times downright nasty. Sometimes I couldn't help but think there must be something I'd done wrong. In these moments, I vowed to try harder. I turned and made my way toward my eldest's closed door. Callie had gotten into trouble again yesterday, skipping school, coming home drunk from an afternoon party by the lake. We'd fought, but Callie and I were always fighting these days. I switched tacks, raising my hand to knock softly.

"Cal?" Silence. "Come on, honey. Are you up? I don't *want* to nag you . . ." I listened intently for a moment, then tried the door. At least she hadn't locked herself in. Grasping the cool knob, I turned it slowly, waiting for an exasperated, "OK, OK, Mom!"

At first I couldn't make sense of what I was seeing.

Wearing only a red-and-white ribbed T-shirt and a red lace thong, Callie was lying on her back on the floor, legs stretched out straight, hands clenched in tight fists at her sides. Her blonde hair lay tangled around a face as pale as porcelain. Her eyes were wide open, staring at the ceiling, eyebrows arched, and her lips were a dark purple-blue.

"Oh, my God! Callie, wake up! What happened?" All sense left me as I fell to the carpet to pull her into my arms. "Tom!" I screamed, rocking her, shaking her.

I frantically checked for breathing and a pulse. Nothing. It was her face that frightened me most. Frozen in time was an expression of absolute wonder and amazement. I'd never seen a look like that before. She looked as though the gates of heaven had opened up and ushered her inside.

Tom rushed into the room, my son, Anthony, following close behind.

"Don't let Anthony in here!" I shouted frantically, waving my arms. "I think Callie's dead. Call 9-1-1."

I could vaguely hear Tom as he spoke to the emergency operator, saying something about a dead little girl.

"Diane!" His fingers gripped my shoulder to shake me out of my shock. "She wants to know if anyone can do CPR."

CPR! Tom was trying to startle me into action. Cradling my daughter, I was nothing but a mother. I somehow completely forgot that I was a registered nurse. I shook myself and lay her back down on the floor, rose to my knees, and placed my hands at the center of her chest, just above her breastbone. The danger with young kids is cracking their ribs. I pressed, one two three four five. I closed her perfect nose between my fingers, tilted her head back, breathed once, twice. Again and again, until the operator suggested that Tom help me. I tried to show him how to perform chest compressions, but the clinician in me knew he was not compressing Callie's chest deeply enough.

"Harder!"

"I'm afraid I'll hurt her."

"Goddamn it, Tom! Right now, a fractured rib would be the least of her problems!"

There was a loud knocking at the front door. "Anthony, go answer the door!" I yelled. An instant later, the paramedics rushed into the bedroom.

"I'm a nurse," I called to them. "I can help."

"No, ma'am," the man with the emergency kit responded. "You'd be best over there, if you don't mind."

I stood against the purple wall of Callie's bedroom, shivering uncontrollably and watching them try to resuscitate my only daughter. After a long moment, I felt Anthony come up beside me.

"Mom."

"Yes, baby?"

"Should I call Papa?"

"Yes," I sighed, pressing him to me. "Go, call Papa."

I watched as the paramedics gave Callie injections of epinephrine and attached portable EKG electrodes to her chest. They shocked Callie's heart. I watched the monitor with ferocity, willing the lines to spike, ordering them to come to life. Her body flounced but there was no response. I'd seen that flat line so many times. Sadly, it had never meant so much to me.

Anthony carried the phone into the room. "Mom, he wants to talk to you."

I took the phone and murmured into it, saying the words I would repeat over and over again, my eyes still glued to my lifeless child. For years afterward, the events of that day would remain burned into my memory like a red-hot brand seared onto bare skin.

"I found Callie lying unresponsive on the floor of her bedroom."

"What do you mean she's unresponsive?"

I described her appearance. "I started CPR. The paramedics are here, but there's no response, Dwayne, only a flat line." He knew what I meant; after all, we'd met in nursing school. He seemed unnaturally calm. "I knew something like this was going to happen. I'm leaving work now. I'll meet you at the hospital."

The police arrived as the paramedics rushed Callie to the waiting ambulance. Sirens blaring, they took off toward the hospital. The police gently escorted me, Tom, and Anthony out of Callie's bedroom so they could begin their investigation. Upstairs, I went into the bathroom, shut the door, and brushed my teeth over and over again. I had to get the taste of her lips on mine out of my mouth. I'd counseled patients on grief. I told them, "Grief makes you do the damnedest things, and that's OK." I stood there, numb and in shock, gazing in the mirror at my aging face. My auburn hair, pulled into a sloppy knot at the nape of my neck with a black scrunchie. An older version of the woman Callie would never become. I massaged the furrowed lines across my forehead. My hazel eyes seemed sunken into my face between thick, arched eyebrows and the dark circles that rimmed my lower lashes. I could see the crow's-feet starting to form at the corners of my eyes and the creases that etched the sides of my lips into a permanent frown. I pinched my cheeks to try to bring some color back into them and turned away from the mirror. In my heart, I hoped for some sort of miracle. The EMTs would bring her back on the way to the hospital. The doctors would save her. But the professional in me knew that this was not possible.

Callie was dead when I walked into her bedroom.

～ 2 ～

Callie—Summer Wind

I can't remember how long I lay there in the dark. After a while, I felt myself being lifted up, I felt myself twirling around and around, faster and faster. I knew I had one hell of a case of the spins. Sometimes, when I know I've really overdone it, I try to pretend me and Anthony are little again. We're taking turns climbing into Papa's leather recliner. I sit and Anthony takes a deep breath, gathering all of his puny strength to spin me around and around. We'd laugh and laugh.

I smiled in my half-sleep. Somewhere on the other side of my closed lids, I registered a faint humming noise that grew louder and louder. I must have gotten myself really fucked up this time.

What the hell—

A moment later, I was being jerked up into a dark, black tunnel that seemed like a tornado spinning around and around me. Images flashed at a sickening pace. Me playing "Captain and the Pirate" with Mama and Anthony in the swimming pool of our old house in California. Me climbing the fence in Tennessee, grabbing the saddle with one hand and the reins in the other, swinging one leg over Red's back and pulling myself astride.

Me laughing on the inner tube behind Papa's jet boat, begging him to go faster and faster as I flew on top of the water.

The sky above the tunnel became brighter and brighter, and suddenly I burst into the light, squinting against the brightness.

Where the hell was I?

I twisted around to find I was in a vast, emerald-green meadow strewn with purple wildflowers. I sat down, trying to remember what drug I'd just taken. Maybe it was one of those pretty sugar cubes laced with LSD or some of those magic mushrooms. Whatever it was, it looked like I was going to have a pretty good trip.

Ahead of me a stream dazzled with multicolored rocks just below the surface of the water. A pretty white bridge over the stream caught my attention, and as I got up to walk toward it, I spotted a furry little black creature bounding over the bridge toward me. *Could that be—no.* He was barking and yelping and, as I stepped onto the bridge, he practically leapt into my arms. My heart swelled and my breath caught in my throat as I lifted him. It was my little cocker spaniel, Boo! But he'd died when I was about six years old, just before we moved from California to Tennessee. I felt his cold, wet nose nuzzling my neck as his whole body wagged. "Oh, Boo," I said, "It's so good to see you." I held him to my chest, his curly black fur soft and reassuring. "Where are we, Boo? What's happening to me?"

My face was buried in Boo's fur when I heard a soft but unmistakable nicker, causing my ears to prick up of their own volition. *Red?*

I snapped my head up to see him standing at the other end of the bridge, his smooth mahogany coat glistening in the sun. Shaking my head in disbelief, I knelt to put Boo down and he scampered ahead as if leading the way. Across the bridge, Red pawed the ground impatiently with his hoof. He gave a soft whinny of pleasure as I reached him, and, putting my arms around his neck, I drank in his warm scent.

"Oh, Red, I've missed you so much," I whispered, salty tears flowing down my face and mingling with his mane. Suddenly I felt his body shift, and as he knelt down on one foreleg, I understood he wanted me to climb onto his back. Taking Boo under one arm and grasping a piece of mane in the other, I pulled myself astride and looked around me. The meadow was surrounded by a huge forest of oak, fir, and maple trees. In the bright afternoon sunshine, puffy white clouds scuttled across an azure sky on a gentle breeze. Ahead of me, several lanes led into the woods, and Red turned toward a sunlit path. I relaxed against his body and let the soft clip-clop of his hooves carry me into the forest.

I was so tired that the gentle rocking of his hind legs nearly put me to sleep, but after some time I noticed the lane was finally emerging from the woods. Squinting, I could see a pretty, two-story pink-and-white house with a pink Corvette convertible in the driveway by the front yard. It looked *exactly* like my old Barbie doll playhouse! From the pink shingled roof and hot-pink front door to the large bubble-gum-pink windows framed with lavender curtains, it was identical in every way, only life-size, which made me a little nauseous. Of course, pink had been my favorite color when I was little, but these days I preferred black. Multicolored flowers nestled in rectangular boxes seemed to pulsate with color as I walked up the front steps. I'd tripped out before, but I couldn't ever remember having such crazy visuals. Suddenly I'd had enough. I wanted out of this whacked-out dreamscape. I mean, I hadn't played with Barbies since I was six!

I pushed the unlocked door open tentatively. "Hello?"

There didn't seem to be anyone home. I stepped into a foyer covered in eggplant-purple tile where sparkling glass teardrops hung from an ornate brass chandelier. To the right of the foyer sat a cozy-looking parlor where a chunky vase filled with red roses was perched on a glass-topped table in the center of the room. Ahead of me was a staircase covered in pale pink carpet. Climbing the stairs, I found my way to a bedroom on the left and was instantly drawn to its pretty canopy bed with pink-and-white-striped sheets and a white lace comforter with pink rosebuds on it. The last of the afternoon sunlight streamed through a nearby window, and the room felt warm and safe.

Maybe if I just lie down, I'll sleep this off and I'll wake up back home. I was beginning to feel a little like Dorothy in *The Wizard of Oz*. Turning over on the soft bed, I was surprised to discover that afternoon had turned to evening. Outside, I could see twinkling stars and the shining sliver of a crescent moon. I let my tired body sink into the mattress as Boo hopped up on the bed and turned in circles until he felt he'd made an adequate nest among the blankets at the crook of my knees. As my eyelids began to drop, I let out a sigh I hadn't known I was holding in, and I drifted into sleep.

DIANE

The three of us were silent in the car on the way to the hospital. Glancing over at Tom, I could see his face etched with concern. He reached one hand to my knee, keeping the other on the steering wheel.

"You worried about Dwayne?"

"Yes," I whispered. "How on earth can I explain this?"

As we pulled up to the emergency room door, I could already see Dwayne pacing outside, a lit cigarette pressed between his lips. He was my second husband and often had dramatic mood swings. I never knew whether he was going to be kind and understanding or angry and accusatory, especially where the children were concerned. I took a deep breath and climbed out of the car to embrace him.

"I met the ambulance when it pulled up here. The doctors only worked on her for a few minutes and then ended the code. Jesus, Diane. What happened?"

"I don't know." I clasped and unclasped my fingers, trying to keep them from shaking. "Callie came home at noon yesterday from school. She'd burned her finger in cooking class. Tom was working from home so he gave her some Tylenol and antibiotic ointment and bandaged her finger. She was supposed to go back to school—instead she called some friends and went to a party down by the lake. She called me at about five and told me she was with Megan, who had to take her sister to the dentist to have two of her wisdom teeth pulled. Callie said she was helping Megan take care of her sister. When she came home with Megan at about seven, she stumbled up the steps to the back porch. I knew she was drunk, and I was so stupid. I was thinking, 'How did she get drunk at the dentist's office?' She fell into bed and I asked her, 'Callie, have you been drinking?' She didn't answer me; she just turned her head away and rolled toward the wall." Tears were coming now, and I fought to contain them, fought to keep my voice level enough to talk.

"Listen," Tom interjected, coming over from having parked the car, with Anthony in tow. "Why don't we go inside and sit down?"

"Good idea," Dwayne replied. We wandered in through the emergency room doors to find the ER mercifully quiet—there were only a few patients sitting in plastic chairs waiting to see a doctor, and most of the staff were congregated at the nurse's station, talking. Tom went over to let them know we'd arrived while Dwayne, Anthony, and I settled in a private corner of the waiting room.

"So what happened next?" Dwayne asked, leaning toward me. "After you saw what kind of state she was in?"

I leveled my gaze at him, daring him to challenge me.

"I left her. There was no point arguing with someone in her condition. Megan left a little while later. I saw her sneaking down the back steps. When I went back into Callie's room, she was asleep. I took her purse to the kitchen and emptied it onto the kitchen table, looking for drugs, but I didn't find any. I kept her cell phone. She'd already had her car and her driver's license taken away, so the only thing left was the phone. I went back into her room and put her purse on the floor and lifted Ruffy onto her bed."

"Ruffy is our new puppy," Anthony explained. "She's a teacup Chihuahua."

"You got them another dog? Without telling me?" Dwayne's face reddened a moment, but then he seemed to regret having said anything at all. "Please, Diane," he urged. "Continue."

"Um . . ." I tried to think back, remember every little thing. "Megan called Callie twice during the evening, wanting to talk to her. After I told Megan I'd confiscated Callie's phone, she told me she'd dropped Callie off at the lake party and taken her sister to the dentist. After Megan got back home with her sister, one of the boys from the party called asking her to pick up Callie because she was throwing up in the bathroom. Megan went straightaway, found Callie, and asked if she was OK. Callie told her that she was 'peachy fucking keen.' Those were her words exactly. Megan swore to me that Callie said she'd only had a few beers. I checked on Callie about ten p.m., but she had locked her door and turned off the lights. I decided I would deal with her in the morning and went to bed."

"How could she possibly die from a couple of beers?" Dwayne spat, shaking his head.

"I don't know!" I replied. "Maybe she had something else at the party—some pills, cocaine. Maybe some drug interaction killed her."

The detective who'd come to our house, Joe Rodriguez, appeared in the waiting room doorway with an apologetic look on his face.

"Ma'am, I'm sorry, but if it's OK, we'll need to ask you all some questions."

I cleared my throat. "That's fine, Detective, of course."

"Why don't we start with your son." His glance flicked down to the notepad in front of him. "Anthony."

I looked over to Anthony, who I knew must be in a horrible state of shock. "I'd like to be present," I said.

The officer shifted his weight from foot to foot for a moment but then agreed. "Yeah, OK. We can do that."

The three of us went to sit in a quiet adjoining room, and the officer took a soda out of a nearby mini-fridge. I studied my youngest's face as we pulled out the chairs to sit around the table. His mop of wavy brown hair hung down over his forehead and desperately needed a trim. In spite of the chaos, he'd managed to find his glasses, and his eyes were wide and apprehensive behind the large, thick frames. He'd thrown on a pair of old blue jeans that were too short, and peeking out from under the hems was a pair of mismatched socks. Now fourteen, he'd had a recent growth spurt that left him in dire need of new clothes.

Anthony had always been a quiet child, content to sit on the sidelines watching the world go by, whereas Callie always wanted to be the center of attention. Callie was very busy, into everything, a bundle of movement and energy. Anthony was cautious. I could almost see his little mind weighing his options before he took a chance on anything. Callie was reckless, plunging down the hill leading to our street one day on her roller skates, out of control, until she pitched forward and broke her arm.

Anthony was stoic at the pediatrician's office when he received his immunizations. He didn't want me to hold him. He would sit completely still on the examining table as just one tear slowly trickled down his face. Callie usually had to be held down by several nurses as she thrashed and screamed. Or she would hyperventilate until she almost passed out. Anthony was prone to migraines and asthma attacks. Callie was robustly healthy but took out her frustrations by trashing her room, emptying her bookshelves and closets and throwing all her books and clothing on the floor in fits of rage.

Three years behind her in school, Anthony always seemed to walk in Callie's shadow. They fought constantly over who would sit next to me in the car on the way to school, what radio station to listen to, and who would be dropped off first. As they grew older and developed different interests, the fights became less frequent. Anthony's teachers commented that he seemed very mature for his age, respectful, thoughtful, and conscientious about his homework. Callie tried, but she had difficulty keeping on task in the classroom. She would either daydream or fidget in her chair.

I remember coming home from work at the hospital one Valentine's Day when Anthony was about nine years old to find half a dozen red roses sitting in a vase on my dining room table. At first I thought they were from Dwayne, until I read the card and realized they were from Anthony.

After I hugged him, I asked, "How did you get these flowers?"

"Well," he said proudly, "I saved all of my allowance. I called a couple of flower shops until I found one that would deliver the flowers to our house and let me pay for them with my allowance money. I asked them to come today after I got home from school, and here they are!"

Anthony was small, shorter than most boys his age, and more interested in books, playing cards, and computer games than in sports. Callie was tall and slender. She blossomed early into womanhood and soon caught the eye of boys who were much older than she was. Anthony always wanted to do the right thing, but Callie wanted to do whatever she thought she could get away with. It seemed that I was always trying to haul her back from whatever cliff she found herself on.

Callie often asked if she could bring a girlfriend with her when we went on our annual summer vacations to the beach. Dwayne would relax at the hotel, drinking coffee and reading the newspaper. Callie would roam the beach with her girlfriend as the boys circled closer and closer, daring each other to be the one to speak to the girls first. Anthony and I would go bike riding, shopping, or bodysurfing or comb the beach for shells.

Although Callie was the reckless one, Anthony seemed to get into more accidents, usually through no fault of his own, and I had been in the very same emergency room with him just seven months earlier. I remember that evening well. I was out at a Garth Brooks concert with Tom, and Callie was home with Anthony.

"Now, if Dwayne calls while I'm gone," I'd told her as I made her write down my new cell phone number, "tell him I'm at a reception at the university. Don't tell him I'm out with Tom." Our divorce wasn't final yet, and I didn't want Dwayne to know that I was dating.

"Sure thing, Mama," she said with a conspiratorial wink.

We were waiting in line at the arena when the phone rang.

"Mama!" Callie exclaimed breathlessly, all in a panic. "Anthony's friend John hit him in the head with a golf club by accident when he was swinging."

I gasped. "Is he all right?"

"No, he's got a terrible cut just below his eye and it's been bleeding all over the place."

"Is his eye OK?"

"I think so. The cut's on his cheek."

"All right, get a clean towel and place it over the cut and put some pressure on it to stop the bleeding. I'm coming right home."

"I already did that, and I called 9-1-1; the ambulance just came and got him."

"I think you did the right thing. Did you call your dad?"

"Yeah, he was at work but he's on his way to the hospital now. He asked me where you were and I said you were at the university."

I heaved a sigh of relief. "Thanks. I'm going straight to the hospital; I'll call you when I get there."

My face must have turned sheet white, because Tom took me by the arm and said, "I'll drive you."

"No, I'll be OK. I'll call you." I started racing toward my car. Luckily, we had driven to the arena separately. The last thing I needed was for the two men to meet up at the hospital. How had my life suddenly gotten so complicated?

I rushed into the emergency room to find Anthony lying on a gurney in a private room, his eyes closed, with an ugly red gash that had just been sutured right below his left eye. The skin around the cut was quite swollen and was beginning to turn a colorful shade of deep purple-blue. He was going to end up with quite a shiner. Dwayne was sitting in a chair next to Anthony, still in his blue hospital scrubs, reading the newspaper.

He glanced up at me as I walked in, folded his newspaper, stood up, and leaned over Anthony, whispering, "Your mother's here. I've got to get back to work." And without speaking a word to me, he strode out the door.

"What took you so long?" Anthony asked, glaring at me accusingly.

"I'm so sorry. The traffic downtown was terrible, and I got here as soon as I could." I sat down in the chair that Dwayne had so abruptly vacated. "What happened?"

"I was practicing golf with John and he hit me in the face with his golf club. I basically collapsed. Callie put a towel over the cut and called 9-1-1."

I bit my tongue to keep from exclaiming, "Why wasn't he looking at where he was swinging? You both need to pay more attention to what you're doing!"

Instead I said, trying to be reassuring, "It looks like you're going to be OK, and the doctors and nurses are taking really good care of you."

"It took a long time for the ambulance to come," he grumbled, warming to his story and sitting up in bed. He was unusually talkative. *It must be the pain medication*, I concluded. "First a police car arrived, and I was thinking why did the police come; I need an ambulance!"

Probably to arrest me for child neglect, I thought glumly.

"They asked me what happened, if I was unconscious, and if I could see out of my eye. I wasn't unconscious, Mama, if I was talking to them."

"I know, Anthony." I reached over and patted his hand.

"Then they told me the ambulance was coming but it might be lost. After that they went off into their own world talking about their hunting trip last weekend. I thought I was going to die, and they're talking about their hunting trip."

"I'm sorry, Anthony."

He twisted the sheets in his hands. "Next the fire engine comes. They ask me the same questions and then start talking to the police officers. About twenty minutes after I got hit, the ambulance finally comes. They ask me the same questions, then drive me to the hospital. Apparently I wasn't a priority."

"Well, you're very important to me." I knew a gash that needed stitches wasn't exactly a life-threatening emergency, but how could I explain the intricacies of medical triage to a fourteen-year-old boy?

Detective Rodriguez popped open the soda can and handed it to Anthony, rousing me from my reverie. *I'm having flashbacks*, I thought, shaking myself back into the awful present moment.

"I'm sorry about your sister," he began. "We're trying to figure out what happened to her. Can you tell me everything that you saw or heard, starting with when you got home from school yesterday?"

"Well," Anthony began, nervously clutching the cola can in his hands. "Mom picked me up. I got home from school around four o'clock. She told me to clean my room and study for my math test before I went out to play baseball with my friends. I made spaghetti for dinner."

"You like to cook?"

Anthony nodded.

"Mom, Tom, and I had spaghetti together but Callie wasn't home yet. Then I went back to my room to watch TV. I took a shower and went to bed around ten. I didn't see Callie anywhere, but I saw Mom talking on Callie's cell phone when I went to say good night."

"Did you hear anything unusual during the night?"

"No sir, I didn't hear anything until this morning when my mom started screaming."

"What did you do then?"

"I ran into Callie's room and she was just lying there on the floor. My mom was telling Tom that she thought Callie was dead. I asked her if I should call Papa and she said yes."

"Do you know if there was anyone else in the house last night besides you, your mom, Tom, and Callie?" The detective leaned forward in his chair.

"No, I was asleep all night. I didn't hear anything until this morning."

"Was Callie involved with drugs?" I focused my attention on my son's face. I wasn't sure how much he knew about her recent drug problems. But I also knew that Anthony was wise beyond his years.

He squirmed in his chair and looked down at the floor.

"Anthony, I know you don't want to say anything negative about your sister, and I understand that. But in order to find out what really happened, we have to know what was going on in Callie's life."

"Yes, she was into drugs."

"What makes you think she was involved with drugs?"

"Well, lots of times late at night after Mom went to sleep these kids would show up at the house. The lights from their cars would wake me up when they drove into the driveway. Callie would go outside and I could see them through my bedroom window by the swimming pool, smoking and drinking beer. Once I went outside and her friend Ashley offered me a joint."

"Did you say anything to your mom about this?"

Anthony looked nervously from me to the detective before he answered.

"No, Ashley made me promise not to tell anyone. She said it would be wrong to snitch on Callie and that she wouldn't like me anymore if I said anything."

I felt a twinge of disappointment, but I knew that Anthony had a crush on Ashley. I wasn't surprised that he wanted to play it cool. The detective, sensing our discomfort, decided to switch his focus.

"Did she seem at all depressed to you?"

"No, she seemed fine. She had lots of friends."

"Thank you, Anthony. Listen, here's my telephone number." He handed him a business card. "If you think of anything else that might be important, please call me."

Then he turned his attention to me, handing me a yellow legal pad and pen.

"Mrs. Murray, what I'd like you to do, if you can, is write down everything you can remember about what happened last night."

"I'll try," I said, taking the pad and pen from his hand.

"Sometimes writing things down when they're still fresh in your memory will help identify details that may not have seemed important at the time but can help us with our investigation."

"Yes, I'll do everything I can."

"When you're through, make sure you give the information to me."

We returned to the waiting room, where the waiting seemed endless. I knew then that it was over. She wasn't coming back. The feeling of loss was indescribable, and in the blackness that opened up, memories flooded in. Callie in her little pink-and-white ballet costume after she had gotten into my makeup and smeared bright red lipstick unevenly all over her lips. Callie wearing her black riding helmet and jeans, on Red after they had just cleared a cross-rail, smiling, laughing, and patting his smooth neck. Callie racing up the back-porch steps after school, throwing her books on the kitchen table and jumping into my arms to give me an exuberant hug.

These fleeting images from the past were all that I had left. There would be no memories of Callie graduating from high school, going to college, getting married, and having babies of her own. I covered my face with my hands and started rocking slowly back and forth in my chair, trying to keep from sobbing out loud. Tom wordlessly placed his arm around me, pulling me gently toward him as we waited.

When the police finally let me in to see Callie, she was lying pale and motionless on a gurney, eyes gently closed, her long blonde hair framing her heart-shaped face.

The sobs I'd been holding at bay burst from me, and I reached out to her.

"Oh, Callie!"

The officer in the room took a step toward me.

"I'm sorry," he said. "I can't let you touch her, Mrs. Murray. We're still conducting our investigation."

I retracted my fingers and nodded, numbly. My body ached to gather Callie in my arms, take her to the wicker rocker in her bedroom, just to rock her to sleep one last time.

I sat there, gazing at her motionless face for what seemed like forever, even as it dawned on me that I was looking at a shell. A shell that had contained her, made by me and Dwayne—but my daughter, and her spirit, were gone.

We took our turns saying good-bye. It felt so wrong to leave her there. But finally the staff urged us to head home and try to get some rest. As we were leaving the emergency room, Detective Rodriguez stopped me. "Mrs. Murray," he said, "I promise you, we will find out what happened to your daughter."

CALLIE

I woke feeling like I'd slept for a hundred years. What day was it? Why hadn't anybody pounded on my door to wake me up? Slowly I blinked open my eyes. Sunlight was striking some clear crystals hanging in the window, creating rainbows on the bed. I watched them dance, transfixed by their beauty. I felt so much better than I had the night before—so light. The horrible feeling of darkness that always seemed to be within me was gone. I stretched and sat up.

Shit! I was still in that goddamn Barbie house!

Suddenly I was aware of a presence by the edge of the bed, and I turned quickly to see an elderly woman knitting an afghan in a rocking chair I hadn't noticed before. She had short, snow-white hair and was wearing a tan skirt and a fluffy pink mohair sweater, her wire-rimmed glasses secured around her neck with a gold-beaded eyeglass chain.

She gave me a disarmingly warm smile. "How are you feeling this morning, Miss Callie?"

"I—much better," I managed. "But who the hell—I mean, who are you?" There was something about this woman that made me want to be careful not to cuss.

She laughed softly. "I'm your great-grandmother Eleanor. But you can call me Ellie," she answered, her blue eyes sparkling.

"Ellie? But you've been dead for years." I rubbed my eyes, trying to make her disappear. Was I one of those freaks now? I thought of that creepy scene in *The Sixth Sense: I see dead people* . . . God! Get me out of here!

"I want to go home now. My mama's going to be worrying about me. She doesn't know where I am, and I've forgotten to bring my cell phone. I can't call her."

Ellie looked at me with concern. "Callie, I need to explain something to you." She paused, putting aside her knitting. "You're in Summer Wind now. I'm so sorry, but you can't go home. Not ever again."

"*What?*" I shouted, throwing off my covers and jumping to my feet. "Where the hell is Summer Wind, and what do you *mean* I can't go home?"

"Callie." Ellie sighed. "Please sit down."

I assessed her for a long moment, then sat. She reached out to take my hand, then continued.

"I know this is all very new to you. Please try to listen to what I'm saying. Summer Wind is a part of the angelic realm. You're *here* now, Callie. You're not dreaming, you're not on . . . drugs," she said, with some contempt. "Your human body is dead. You killed it. That's why you can't go home. This is your home now."

I shook my head in disbelief. "No. No! I'm not dead! I'm sitting here talking to you, so how can I be dead? I—I'm going to get my things." I stood and looked around for my purse, car keys, cigarettes. *God, do I need a cigarette!* "I'm going home," I said determinedly.

"Sit down, Callie," Ellie said again, more firmly. "Let me show you something."

My legs buckled completely without my permission. "This is completely fucked up," I said. "Sorry," I added quickly, blushing, reading the shock on Ellie's face.

She reached behind her with impressive agility and pulled out a little screen—it was like a laptop screen without the computer.

"Here, press this button. Then ask a question. This will tell you anything you want to know."

"OK, screen," I said, secretly impressed with the angelic realm's cool technology. "Where's my mama and what's she doing now?"

The screen blinked a few times, and suddenly I saw my mother. She was wearing her rumpled old yellow pajamas, curled up on her bed with her hair in what used to be a bun. It was hanging out all over the place. My heart lurched in my chest. *Did I even have a heart?* I could still feel it breaking. She was clutching Ruffy in her arms, crying and crying.

"Why is Mama crying?" I whispered, beginning to understand.

The screen flashed again and I saw something horrible, something I immediately wished I would never have to see again. It was my mama, on her knees on the floor of my bedroom. She was bent over my body, and it was me, but I was completely white. My lips were a hideous purple-blue, and she was frantically trying to breathe air into my lungs. Trying to pound the life back into my chest.

"Oh, my God." I whispered, my fingers to my mouth. "What happened?"

One more scene flashed before I could handle no more. Me, sitting on my bedroom floor. A shot glass in one hand, a bottle of pills in the other. I was swallowing them, tears streaking down my face, one by one by one. Then I saw myself lying in a coffin.

I dropped the screen and it clattered to the floor, a sob rising in my throat. "Oh, my God. What have I done?"

Ellie left me alone. I sat on my bed, motionless, roiling with regret, stunned. Hours passed, as I sat staring out the window and watched the gathering dusk bring the night sky alive. I lay down again and tried to go back to sleep. I still had the faint hope that this was just a mirage, an illusion. *I'll go to sleep. When I wake up, I'll be back home with Mama, Anthony, and all my friends.*

I missed them; I missed them more than anyone will ever know.

❦ 3 ❧

Diane—Requiem

Back at home, I made sure Anthony brushed his teeth, and then I went to his room to say good night.

"I'd like to go to school tomorrow to see my friends."

"We'll see how you feel in the morning," I said. "Try to get some sleep now."

He looked at me for a long moment, then closed his eyes. I gently tiptoed out of the room, turning the light off behind me.

Tom was waiting for me in our bedroom, and when I entered he wrapped me in his arms. I couldn't even cry. I felt dead inside, as if any life that beat within me had ended the moment I found Callie motionless on her bedroom floor.

"Put these on, honey," he said, offering me a pair of yellow pajamas.

I nodded numbly, letting him help me undress. I crawled wearily underneath the quilt and, curling up in a ball, heard him standing over me. After a moment, his footsteps retreated and I welcomed the soft click of the door. Holding Ruffy to my chest, I cried myself to sleep.

〜

A soft knock on the door awakened me. For a split second, I didn't remember Callie was gone. When it hit me, the pain shot through me like a knife, and I was bewildered to see it was morning. I couldn't believe I had slept. How could I, when she was dead?

"Hi, sweetie," Tom murmured. "I'm sorry; I didn't want to wake you. But the detective is downstairs. He wants to see you."

I wrapped a sweater over my pj's, then made my legs move down the sturdy wooden stairs. Detective Rodriguez was standing by the front door.

"Were you able to get some sleep last night?" he asked.

"I was so exhausted that I finally slept."

"I'm sorry, but I have to ask you a few more questions."

"That's OK." I gestured toward the kitchen. "Why don't we go have a seat?"

He followed me down the hallway and settled into a chair across from me at the rounded table. "Did you and Callie argue the night of her death?"

"No," I replied. "Not really. I mean, I'm sure she knew I was angry. I asked her if she'd been drinking, that's all. There was no point in arguing with her when she was drunk."

He pursed his lips for a moment and nodded. "I wanted to ask because . . . we've found something. We think Callie may have committed suicide," he said slowly.

"No, no," I exclaimed, shaking my head. "She would never do anything like that."

He didn't argue with me. Instead, he silently handed me a note written on a sheet of loose-leaf notebook paper. I stared down at it, disbelieving, trying to focus on the words.

May 10

Mama, I love you. You are the best mom I could ever have. I wish I could've been a better daughter. But I'm not. I'm a fuckup. Please forgive me. You've done nothing wrong. I don't deserve to be on this earth. I love you; please tell my friends I love them. Please forgive me for what I am about to do. Please take care of Ruffy. I know I don't deserve her, but I love her. I love you, and Papa, and Anthony. Please forgive me.

Love always, Callie

"We found this note in her jewelry chest. She must have put it there so you would find it. Is this Callie's handwriting?" Detective Rodriguez asked.

"Yes," I managed, my hands shaking, blurring the writing on the page.

"Do you have another example of her handwriting?"

I shook my head as if to clear it. "Ah, yes. There's a note she wrote here on the kitchen table. Telling me she was going to the mall after school last week. It's around here somewhere." I fumbled through the pile of bills and reminders until I uncovered her familiar scribble.

He stretched out his fingers to retrieve the paper from my hands.

"Thank you. I'll get back to you."

I looked up at Tom, who had been listening to our conversation, ready to intervene if I became too distraught, as the detective showed himself out. The whole world, as I knew it, had just fallen apart.

I stood there immobilized for a moment before a fierce rage welled up, sending me up the stairs to Callie's room two at a time. How could she have done this? There must be something, some clue in that room that could tell me what sent her over the edge. I tore through her belongings almost frantically, emptying bureaus and bookcases, searching through purses, jackets, jean pockets, school folders, and books, throwing them recklessly to the floor, looking for something—anything—that could tell me what had gone wrong. Tom stood in the doorway silently watching me, his strawberry-blonde hair tousled around a square, tanned face and firm jaw, blue eyes full of compassion and concern. He was wearing his standard at-home attire, a rumpled flannel shirt and jeans, and his hands were shoved deep into his pockets. He was such a kind and gentle man, but even in my agitation I could feel his hesitation and uncertainty. He didn't know what to say or do to help me. Racing to my tool chest, I grabbed a pair of carpet scissors and started to rip the carpet up from the floor of her room, tearing at it with my bare hands until they bled. Exhausted at last, I collapsed on the floor, hysterical in my grief.

Tom knelt down and gently touched my shoulder. "Diane," he said. I fell into his arms, clutching his shirt in tight fists, hanging on for dear life. With him I had always felt safe, but I wondered if this violent maelstrom that had engulfed me unawares would rip us both apart.

Pulling myself together, I raised my head to inventory the room, now in total shambles. Schoolbooks, clothes, and shoes were scattered on the floor, mingled with the used supplies left by the paramedics: the cartridge from a syringe, an EKG electrode, oxygen tubing. Numbly, I walked through the room, picking up a blouse here, a pair of socks there. I retrieved a twelve-pack of empty beer cans from the back of Callie's closet, one or two joints, and some rolling papers. I also found a box of notes passed to and from Callie during class at school, and a notebook of poetry. But I couldn't bring myself to read them just then, so I piled them into a cedar chest in my bedroom closet. Returning to Callie's room, I spotted the small perfume bottle on the bureau, the one she'd saved up for weeks to buy, the one that was so sickly sweet I'd ragged on her every time she wore it. *I always hated that perfume*, I thought, reaching for the bottle. Before I'd even touched it, the plunger depressed and the perfume misted my face.

"Jesus!" I shrieked. Then I froze a moment, looking around the room. I knew I hadn't touched the plunger.

I walked gingerly over to Callie's antique gold mirror above her washbasin.

"I think maybe we should cover this mirror with a sheet," I mused, looking over at Tom.

"Why?" he asked bewildered.

Gently I stroked the beveled edge of the mirror, which was covered in gold leaf trim. "It's an old tradition," I told him, "to keep lost souls from becoming trapped in the mirror and unable to find the light."

"Well," he said, placing his arm around me, gently leading me out of the room, and closing the door firmly behind him, "I think we should just leave this room alone for a while."

He thinks I'm going crazy. My imagination was running wild. What if I saw her face materialize in the mirror? What if she reached out of the mirror with her hand? Would I go with her? Would I let her pull me in?

～

I met Dwayne in the parking lot of the funeral home the next morning to pick out a casket. His dark brown eyes were red-rimmed and swollen.

"You OK?" I asked him.

"I am right now," he replied. "But I have these crying jags where I just collapse and can't control myself. My heart starts racing and I can't seem to catch my breath."

"You should see a doctor," I urged, thinking of his history of heart problems.

"Well, I have some Valium at home. Last night I took an Ambien and was able to sleep for a few hours." Then he changed the subject abruptly. "Let's get this over with." He opened the front door of the funeral home.

"I really think Callie should be cremated," I said tentatively. "Then we could take her ashes to the ocean. We could rent a boat and scatter them near a group of dolphins. She would like that." The idea of her body lying there rotting in the ground was repulsive to me.

"No, I think we should bury her in the cemetery," Dwayne stated definitively. "That way her friends can visit her."

I didn't have the strength to argue with him. I never had.

The funeral director escorted us into his office, guiding me to a soft, comfortable armchair and placing a glass of water in my hand and some tissues beside me. "I'm sorry for your loss. Do you feel ready to discuss some of the funeral arrangements?"

"I guess so." I nodded tentatively.

"One of the first things we need to do is decide what to put in Sunday's paper." He pulled a yellow legal pad out from a drawer in his desk.

"What activities was she involved in at school?" He prodded gently.

"She was in the chorus," I said. "She loved to sing."

After we sketched the details of Callie's short life, I asked, "Can you say something about how she was an angel to her family and friends and how much we will miss her?"

"Of course we can," he replied, his smile radiating sympathy.

He took us to look at caskets. Most of them were revoltingly dark, sinister mahogany chests straight out of a horror movie. I couldn't imagine Callie lying in any one of them, and my stomach lurched. *Oh, God,* I thought, *I don't want to be sick.*

Another strange thought entered my head. Maybe I could take her home with me frozen in a clear block of ice. I could put her in a glass freezer in her room. I could fix the room back up exactly the way it was when she was alive. Just like the mountaineers who perished in the death zone on Mount Everest, she would remain frozen in time forever, and she would always be with me.

I touched Dwayne's sleeve.

"Maybe we could . . ." I started to say, but then I realized just how bizarre my words would sound. "Never mind. I don't like the mahogany caskets. How about this one?" I walked over to a light blue casket with a pale pink velvet interior lined with red rosebuds. "I think she would like this."

Next we walked through the cemetery looking for the right place to bury our daughter. The whole thing seemed so surreal, like some crazy dream. Surely I would wake up soon.

After we had finalized the arrangements, the director asked, "Would you like the casket to be open or closed during the service?"

"I don't think it's a good idea to expose Callie's friends to seeing her lying there dead," I said, horrified at the thought.

"But she's beautiful," he replied. "There's not a mark on her."

I let that sink in. "All right," I said, quietly.

~

The morning of the visitation, I stood in Callie's bedroom trying to decide what to bring to the funeral home for her to wear. I wanted her baby-blue prom gown, but the funeral director told me the autopsy scars would show if Callie wore a dress with spaghetti straps, so I decided on a blue turtleneck top and tan pants. When I insisted on going to the funeral home to help dress Callie, nobody thought it was a very good idea.

"I think you should let the funeral home take care of her," my mother stated firmly.

"Callie was my only daughter!" I was insistent. "This is *my* responsibility." Callie had always been meticulous about her appearance, never leaving the house without her hair fixed and her makeup on. I had to make sure she looked the way she'd want for her funeral. I even arranged to have my hairdresser, Sherry, meet me there.

"After several of my lady customers died, I fixed their hair for their funerals, but they were all older," Sherry said, twisting her hands nervously by the door of the funeral home. "Lots of times their deaths were expected. Callie's death has been a shock for all of us."

She'd done Callie's hair just a few short weeks earlier for prom. "Callie told me as I hugged her good-bye, 'Thank you for making me beautiful,'" Sherry told me. "That was the last time I saw her."

We were interrupted by a kind, matronly woman who greeted us and showed us to a private room. "You two can wait here while I go get her," she said, motioning to a set of chairs, but I couldn't sit down.

A few moments passed before Callie appeared on a metal gurney. Her eyes were closed, and she had a serene expression, as if she were only sleeping. I morbidly reminded myself that all her body parts were probably placed in a plastic bag in the center of her chest after the autopsy; there was no way she could wake up. Her long blonde hair, newly washed, hung beside her face.

"Callie's hair was really tangled," the woman explained. "It took me a while to wash it and comb it out. I talked to her as I washed her hair. I talk to all the people I take care of; I don't know why, I just do."

"Thank you." I was holding back tears.

"How would you like me to fix her hair?" Sherry asked.

"Let's try a bun at the top of her head."

We dressed her, applied some light eye shadow, outlined her lips with a dark-red lip liner, and filled in with pink lipstick. Callie was wearing yellow nail polish. "That won't go with her blue turtleneck," I said. Sherry removed the yellow polish and carefully applied a pale silver-blue. Somewhere outside myself I realized that this felt right to me, being able to tend to her, having another woman to help me; since time immemorial, women have prepared their dead for passage into the unknown, I told myself.

Small pearl earrings went into her ears, and the tear-drop necklace she'd worn to prom was clipped gently around her neck.

"She looks so forlorn, lying there all alone," I said. "I'm going to pick out some things to place in the casket." I went home and brought back her Beanie Baby collection, her stuffed dolphins, and her little red heart-shaped pillow, and I placed them around Callie. I put one of her favorite romance novels in one hand and her car keys in the other. The key chain read, "Don't drive faster than your angels can fly." Satisfied, I stepped back. Now Callie looked less lost among the white sheets and pillow.

~

I put off going to the visitation as long as possible, until Dwayne called me.

"The funeral home is packed with Callie's friends," he said. "They're asking for you."

I entered to find a room full of heartbroken children. Slowly they made their way to me. "We're so sorry," they said, sobbing, not knowing what else to say.

"It's all right," I said, embracing them one by one. "I understand." I had seen many people die, but Callie's friends were just children. What did they know of death? And how awful for them to find out in this way.

The funeral was held late on Tuesday afternoon. White lilies surrounded my daughter's small body, and their heavy, sweet scent hung in the air in the church like a pall. Callie had always loved lilies.

I walked unsteadily into a private room just outside the chapel, Tom by my side. The funeral director immediately spotted me and escorted me to a chair. *He's probably wondering how I'm going to hold up*. After what seemed an eternity, he motioned for me, Tom, Anthony, and Dwayne to enter the chapel. I could feel the eyes of everyone on me, looking at me sympathetically. I stared steadfastly at the floor. I had promised myself that I would be strong and not break down. Callie wouldn't like that. She would be embarrassed if I flung myself at the casket and sobbed hysterically until I had to be escorted out of the room and sedated.

Finally, the ceremony began. Anthony sat next to his father, and I sat between Tom and Dwayne, holding their hands. Under better circumstances, I thought ironically, it would be *inconceivable* that I could be sitting between my ex-husband and my boyfriend, holding both their hands.

"Blessed are they that mourn," the minister began, "for they shall be comforted."

As he intoned his reading from the Bible, I willed myself to detach emotionally, if only for a moment, to see the service as though I were merely an observer looking down, surrounded by Callie and the angels. I could hear the sobs of my daughter's friends floating toward me as if from far away.

"Callie, at the end of her life, made some wrong choices," the minister continued. "Children in pain sometimes try to numb themselves with drugs. Callie was looking for something; Callie was looking for real love, the love that only Jesus and God can give you. Life is mostly painful. Life is uncertain; none of us have the promise of tomorrow. People may betray you, but Jesus will never let you down. You can dwell with Jesus for eternity.

"Obedience to God is the only route to heaven," he preached. I wasn't so sure about that. *Why do people feel that everything is so black and white, right and wrong, good and evil?* For me, God wasn't some all-knowing father in the sky. *God dwells in each of us, in our own hearts,* I thought as I reminded myself that the only way to know happiness was to know sorrow, and the only way to know hope was through despair. *I'm just getting an overdose of sorrow and despair right now.*

The next part of the service consisted of bits and pieces of memories of a girl whose life was interrupted much too soon.

"Callie had a crib full of stuffed animals," said Callie's aunt, "and she stuffed the hearts of all who knew her with love. Callie loved the water, waves, and sand and wanted to be a little mermaid."

Her friends stood bravely to talk about what Callie had meant to them, or to tell a little story, like the time she nearly set her room on fire. "I remember when Callie, Ashley, and I decided to have a séance with a Ouija board to try to contact Princess Diana," her friend Jenny said, smiling. "We turned off all the lights in Callie's bedroom and lit candles, which was really spooky, until one of the candles fell over and caught the carpet in Callie's room on fire. We all panicked but managed to put it out before we burned the whole house down!"

A little laughter was such a release, and I looked down at the program on my lap, tracing the words of a poem my daughter had written with my fingers.

I Am Truth

I am the truth so I can see
that there is nothing that exists but me.
I am truth so I can hear
the sound of the enchanted sea nymphs singing near.

I am truth so I can touch
the stars sparkling above the beach soon after dusk.
I am truth so I can taste
the salt from sea foam on my face.
I am truth so I can smell
the ocean's breath rising up from a very deep well.
I tumble in the ocean's arms,
and know that I am safe from harm.
Resting gently in the sea,
I am at peace and I am free.

"Diane . . . Diane!" Dwayne whispered, nudging me gently. I looked up to see everyone waiting expectantly. Standing, I took a deep breath, then made my way haltingly to the podium.

"First, I want to thank all of you on behalf of Callie for coming to her celebration of life. There is one thing I want to tell you about her," I continued. "Every time we said good-bye, when she hung up the phone, when she went to sleep at night, or when she left for school, she would always tell me she loved me. And she would always make sure that I said 'I love you' back. Even if I was angry with her, even if she had done something wrong, she would always make me tell her that I loved her. Once, I asked her why, and she said, 'You never know what's going to happen, so I always want to leave you by telling you that I love you.' In our last telephone conversation, before she died, she ended with 'I love you, Mama,' and I said, 'I love you too, sweetheart.' Her message to you, to all of you today, is just that. No matter what happens or how hard things are, please hold this in your hearts: Only love is real."

The last time I told Callie I loved her was the evening before she died, during the last conversation we would have on this side of the veil. But, of course, I hadn't known it was that at the time. I had spoken those words with such emphasis from my office chair, and after hanging up, I couldn't help but lean back and wonder why. Of course, I loved my daughter, but this was just an ordinary evening conversation. Now I realized that in some deep, dark recess of my mind, I must have known what was coming, known that the dice had already been cast and that there was no turning back.

CALLIE

I woke up with a start. Boo was jumping up on the bed, pulling my covers off with his teeth, and then licking my face with his rough, pink tongue. "Boo, yuck! Don't do that!" I laughed. Holding him at arm's length, I sighed. "Looks like I'm still in Summer Wind, wherever the hell that is," I muttered.

Ellie appeared with a big pot of tea and some delicious-looking raspberry and apricot scones on a tray. I was surprised to realize that I was hungry. Ellie set the tray down on my bed.

"Today," she announced, "we're going to visit your guardian angel, Seraphiel."

I was tired of asking questions and decided that maybe it was best to just relax and try to go with the flow for once. "Right, my guardian angel. And where does he live?"

"Look out the window," Ellie replied. "See that magnificent castle in the distance?"

Sure enough, far away I could see a large, gleaming white fortress with ornate, spiral-shaped towers and high, pointed blue roofs.

"Great!" I told Ellie. "What do you think about taking that pink Vette in the driveway? I'll drive."

"Oh, no, it will be much faster if we just imagine ourselves there."

Damn. No matter where I go, nobody lets me drive.

"OK, I'll just close my eyes, and when I open them I'll be there." I laughed to myself. *Yeah, right, this is really gonna work.*

I opened my eyes to find my nose a quarter of an inch from a thick wooden door. It was covered in intricate metalwork in a rose pattern and looked worn from what must have been centuries of use. "Oh, my God," I said for what seemed like the zillionth time. Ellie was beside me. She took my hand and the door opened as if by magic. My feet found their way to a marble floor, and as I moved through the doorway, I found we'd entered a massive library. The high, arched ceiling was painted a sky blue, and huge gold-and-white angels with their wings outstretched looked like painted frescoes from a distance. But when I looked more carefully at them, I could swear that their wings were moving. The walls were covered with rows and rows of bookcases filled with volumes of all sizes, shapes, and descriptions. A huge spiral staircase circled the library, and there were multiple levels with tables, chairs, and comfortable-looking leather recliners on each level by the windows. Ellie led me to a reception desk in the center.

"We're here to see Seraphiel."

"He's on the sixteenth floor," replied the lady seated there, dressed in a gold suit.

"Let's go," Ellie urged. Before I could protest, she bent slightly and jumped, and her body hung in midair. Her hand tugged on mine from above. Squeezing my eyes tight shut, I launched myself up, repeating, *don't look down, don't look down.*

The next thing I knew, I was standing in front of this really hot guy who was sitting with his feet propped on one of the tables. His sneakers lay in a heap on the floor. He was wearing baggy blue jeans, a white T-shirt, and a baseball cap turned backward. I could see his muscles rippling underneath that tight white T-shirt. He looked like he worked out—a lot. He had piercing blue eyes.

"Callie," he said, jumping up from his chair. "I've been waiting for you."

"I'm very pleased to meet you," I exclaimed, giving him my coyest smile and arching my eyebrows slightly. I could wrap any guy, even the really cute ones, around my finger in a New York minute. "But you sure don't look like an angel to me."

I watched in awe as he began to melt and change his appearance before me, becoming a tall, regal-looking man with long white hair that streamed back from his chiseled face, even though no wind was blowing. T-shirt and jeans had become a royal-blue robe. Huge white wings encircled his body, and at the tip of each feather was a golden eye. I stared at him, flabbergasted, speechless for once in my life, or maybe more appropriately for once in my death.

"Do you like this better?" he asked with a twinkle in his eye.

"Not really," I said, recovering. "I'll take the young, hot one, if you don't mind."

He smiled and instantly changed back into young Seraphiel.

"You can call me Raphael," he said. "So, Ellie tells me that you crossed yourself over."

Uh-oh. For the first time since landing in Summer Wind, the thought came to me: In killing myself, what if I'd broken the rules?

"I hope this doesn't mean I'm going to Hell," I exclaimed, suddenly afraid. "I didn't know what I was doing and I'm sorry, truly sorry, for all the trouble I've caused."

Seraphiel just looked at me expectantly.

"I mean, I took these pills, but I really didn't know if they would work," I tried to explain. "Besides, I thought dying meant going to sleep and never waking up, but here I am, somehow still alive, but in a very strange place. It was all just an accident." I placed my hands on my hips, trying to look much more confident than I felt, and attempted a bright smile.

"Callie." His blue eyes pierced mine, reading everything that had lain, long-buried, in my heart. All I wanted to do was run away or scream. "Tell me, why did you overdose yourself on those pills?"

I suddenly realized that I couldn't bullshit him, I couldn't lie. I felt the emotions surge up like a raging torrent, the ones I'd been trying to stifle for so long, and a sob escaped as they pushed themselves up and out of my throat. "I felt so alone," I said with a wail. "I felt like nobody really knew me anymore, like nobody truly loved me. I was always getting into trouble. I tried, I really tried, but everything I did just turned out all wrong. I felt like everyone would be better off without me," I said, dissolving into tears.

"Callie," he replied gently, "I want to show you something."

He held up a mirror. I looked inside the mirror and saw all my friends crying as they wrote little notes telling me how much they loved me; how they were sorry, oh, so sorry, if they had ever done anything to hurt me. I saw them writing these notes and slipping them into my coffin. I saw my three best friends in the whole world—Megan, Ashley, and Jenny—crying and telling each other that they would always love me, no matter what I'd done. I saw my mama, my papa, Anthony, and all my relatives. I could see inside their hearts, and I knew they all loved me. I watched for a long time, and then I slowly put the mirror down.

My throat ached from crying, and I wiped the tears off my face with my palm. "They really did love me, didn't they?" Seraphiel nodded. "But it's too late now. I can't go back."

"No, you can't."

I looked at him pleadingly. "What do I do now?"

"First, there is something I think you should know. And then, there's someone I think you should meet."

He pulled two large books covered in gold leaf from one of the bookcases under a section entitled The Covenant of the Red Rose. The first was called *The Book of Diane*; the second, *The Book of Callandra*.

"This is your mother's book of life," he explained, pointing to the first, "and here is yours," he said, handing me *The Book of Callandra*. "It contains all the agreements you made before entering your last life as Callie, and all the events of that life until the day you died.

"Here," he said, his long, gold-ringed fingers pointing to a page in the book. "Here is the agreement you made with Diane. You made a contract with Diane to be her daughter and to die young. We all, on this side, knew you would die in your teenage years; we just didn't know how. That was your choice."

"But why would I ever choose to die young?" I argued. "I haven't even finished high school. I wanted to go to college and become a marine biologist or psychiatrist. I wanted to get married and have children!"

"Yes," he replied calmly. "Life is the most precious of gifts. It would seem we would all want to live for as long as humanly possible. But for the answer to your question, there is someone else you must meet."

DIANE

It was Mother's Day, despite how hard I'd tried to ignore it. The house was so still you could hear the soft click, click of my Labrador retriever Beau's nails on the hardwood floor as he anxiously paced behind me. He knew that I'd been upset. Anthony stayed in his room all day, Tom in his office, while I wandered aimlessly through the messy house. Absentmindedly, I started dusting the bookshelves in the family room—I just didn't know where to begin. The front doorbell rang, startling me. Wearily, I made my way to the door. Ashley, Jenny, and Megan were standing on the front porch holding bouquets of flowers.

"Oh, Mama!" Jenny exclaimed, as she embraced me. "We're so sorry about Callie."

Megan handed me a bouquet. "It's Mother's Day, and we wanted you to have these."

Ashley wordlessly handed me a large, orange and black paper butterfly, a monarch, on a tall wooden stake. Then, as quickly as they had come, they were gone.

The four girls had been friends since junior high school, and I knew their mothers well. I adored Megan, Jenny, and Ashley, and we'd spent so much time together I felt more like a big sister to them than a mother. I often baked marshmallow Rice Krispies Treats and sat down on a barstool at the kitchen counter to talk to them about their problems. All three girls had boyfriends and were experimenting with sex. One day, I caught them thumbing through one of my maternity nursing textbooks.

"Girls, what are you looking for?" I asked.

"We were . . . just looking up the symptoms of pregnancy," Jenny replied vaguely.

An alarm bell went off at once. *OK, who's pregnant?*

I gave them a look to let them know I was on to them. "Well, the symptoms of pregnancy are in the chapter on prenatal care. But why do you need to know? Just curious?"

"We think one of our friends might be pregnant," Jenny said evasively.

"Well, if that's true, she needs to go to her doctor or to Planned Parenthood for a pregnancy test right away. Girls, you can tell me. Is it one of you?"

"Oh, no!" they said together, shaking their heads emphatically.

"Are any of you having sex?" I looked at them expectantly.

They all got quiet and stared down at the brownies I had just baked for them on the counter.

"Well, I make Jimmy wear a condom," Jenny said.

"What happens if the condom breaks?" I asked.

"I guess I'd be in trouble," Jenny replied as the other girls began to laugh.

I took a deep breath, hoping their mothers wouldn't mind, and decided to give them the birth-control talk that I gave to my teenage patients before they were discharged from the hospital with a new baby.

I showed them pictures of IUDs and diaphragms, told them to always use foam with condoms, and advised them to use another form of contraception if they missed a birth control pill. I warned them that there was a chance they could become pregnant even if they had just finished their menstrual period, and that birth control pills would not protect them against HIV.

The girls listened intently, hanging on every word. "Always use a condom," I said. "Remember, you're not just having sex with them, you're having sex with every girl they have ever had intercourse with."

At this, I saw their eyes start to glaze over with information overload.

"Thanks, Mama," Callie said, smiling. "But I think we've learned enough for now."

After that, the girls came to me with all kinds of questions.

"It burns when I pee," Megan complained one day, and I suggested she might have a urinary tract infection.

"Sometimes it hurts when Jimmy and I make love," Jenny stated on another occasion. I gave her suggestions about how to make intercourse more comfortable.

Callie sometimes seemed to enjoy the fact that I was popular with her friends, but at other times she appeared a little jealous. I would catch her eye as she stood with a slight frown on her face, hanging back from the girls who were clustered around me.

"Just because I like to spend some time with your friends doesn't mean I love you any less," I said to her one day. "The girls don't have an adult they can talk to about these things."

"I know, Mama," she replied, but she still looked hurt as she walked away.

Megan told me later that after Callie died, the three of them made a pact. They would take care of me and help me in any way they could.

～ 4 ～

Callie—The Meeting

Seraphiel led me outside to a lovely courtyard enclosed by towering arched columns of white marble. In a gigantic gold fountain with a fluted rim, water cascaded from an urn down into a turquoise-blue basin where angelfish with beady black eyes and pearl-gray bodies swam. Trellises hung heavy with pink and red roses whose scent perfumed the air. And there, standing in the center of the courtyard, was . . . *Jesus?*

He was wearing a brown habit of undyed wool, and his rich ebony hair was covered by a brown cowl. His beard was cropped close to his chin, and his mustache was full and luxuriant. But what struck me the most were his eyes. They were the color of polished black obsidian and radiated kindness and all-knowing. Several small bluebirds fluttered around his head, and as he reached out his hands one bird landed in an upturned palm.

He turned to face me. "Hello, little Callie. I'm glad to see you're home again." Love seemed to radiate off him. I knew instantly there was no judgment, only acceptance. I was in the presence of Jesus Christ.

"Sit down next to me," he urged, patting a long stone bench as he made himself comfortable on it. "I will tell you a story."

Overwhelmed, I sat.

"Before your last life as Callie, you were one of my followers. You were a member of the Covenant of the Red Rose," he explained, taking a crown of red roses and placing it on my head. "On earth, you wore the crown of thorns. Here there are no thorns, only red roses," he said, and I felt his smile warm the heartache I'd been feeling earlier, making it disappear.

"You see, Callie, earth is a very difficult school. You learn about all that is by experiencing what it is not. For example, you learn about joy through sorrow, love through loss, and hope through despair. How else can you truly understand what these things are, if you cannot experience what they are not? You, little Callie, wanted to help the suffering children, to comfort them in their despair, to assist them as they crossed over, to be the light that would guide them home. But you asked, before you took on this task, if you could become one of them for just a little while, to know loss, sorrow, and despair, so that you could better serve them. And so, I let you go to earth, as God did with me, knowing that you would suffer, but also knowing that it was not only your choice—because you chose it to be so—but your destiny."

"Oh, but you're Jesus," I said, swallowing hard. "I don't know if I can do this."

"Yes, you can," he said, placing his hand on my heart. "Look."

I looked down as the ground opened up in front of me. Through the whirlwind that had brought me to Summer Wind, I could see the earth. There were little children with no food to eat and no one to comfort them; sick children in hospitals, frightened and alone; desperate teenagers with guns pointed at their heads or needles in their veins.

I took a deep breath. I looked at Jesus, at Seraphiel, and then at my great-grandma Ellie. "OK," I said softly. "I'll try, but first you have to help me get a message to my mama. I have to let her know that I'm all right."

"You can do this yourself," Seraphiel told me. "It's simply a matter of lowering your vibration and imagining a silver cord connecting you to your mother. Here," he said as he lightly touched the center of my forehead between my eyebrows with a forefinger. I felt heat from a sudden flash of light.

"Imagine a movie screen inside your head. Connect to her with that silver cord while she is sleeping and you will be able to watch her dreams unfold. When you find a good place in her dream, a place where logically she might be dreaming about you, slip some of your soul essence down that cord. You can enter her dream and become a part of it. She will see an image of you in her mind and will be able to hear your voice inside her head. Her logical mind won't be trying to understand or analyze things while she's asleep, and she will be more receptive to your being there and to your message."

"This is just too hard," I protested.

"Well, you're the one who chose a scientist for a mother."

Seraphiel went on to tell me I couldn't visit too often. "They have to move on, although they can still hold you in their heart," he explained. "You can visit them, but they have to move forward in their life on earth without your physical presence, and you have to move on with your work here on this side. This is the way it must be, for the greatest good of all."

DIANE

I plucked three vases from the cabinet and had just finished placing the girls' flowers around the house when I looked out the window and noticed how tall the grass had grown. A task! I leapt on it as though it were a life raft, found my water bottle and the baseball cap that read "Living well is the best revenge," and headed out to my lawn tractor in the garage. I mowed for several hours in large rectangles, watching the area of cut grass grow larger and larger. The sun warmed my back, birds fluttered in the dogwood trees, and several small yellow and white butterflies dipped and rose in the air above the tractor.

Maybe, just maybe, I will survive.

Sweaty and covered in grass clippings, I felt invigorated and eyed a patch of weeds by the side of the house. It had once been a flower and vegetable garden but had become utterly overgrown and was now a waist-high tangle of blackberry canes, thistles, onion grass, and wild mustard. I decided to make it into a memorial flower garden for Callie. Rake, shovel, pitchfork, and an old tiller came out of the back recesses of the garage as I got to work.

I used the pitchfork to loosen the roots, then pulled up the weeds with my bare hands and carted them to a large fire pit behind the horse barn. After a while, I paused to catch my breath. Looking down at my hands, I noticed that my once beautifully manicured nails were now a jagged mess, the polish chipped, the once smooth ends rough and ragged with dirt caked underneath them. Several large thorns had embedded themselves into my bleeding fingers. I went to an outdoor water spigot by the house to wash the first layer of mud from my hands, then sat down on a rock in the sun to rest and to pull out the thorns from my aching fingers.

As I sat, I ruminated. When had everything started to go wrong? Callie was always endlessly curious and, like a puppy, would hurl herself into every activity until she collapsed. She was Mary in her kindergarten Christmas play because she couldn't sit still on the bleachers. Her teachers thought that she might be able to stay in one place if she was standing next to Joseph at the front of the stage rocking baby Jesus in his cradle. Their strategy didn't work particularly well because as soon as she saw me and Dwayne in the audience, she ran down the aisle laughing joyfully to greet us. One of the teachers would patiently fetch her and haul her back onstage, where she would stand uncertainly for a few minutes and then scamper merrily down the aisle once again.

She seemed so full of exuberance and joy as a child, but early in her teenage years the light began to fade, her moods became darker, the sparkle in her eyes dimmed, her wan smiles seemed insincere, and sometimes a chill would seem to come upon her and she would be distant and remote. At other times, she would cling to me and we would talk late into the night about her problems and I would try to reassure her that tomorrow would be a better day. She got involved with boys and dove in too deep too fast, and it seemed I was always trying to help her mend a broken heart. Occasionally she almost seemed too bright, like a diamond sparkling on the sun-swept snow, but she was much more fragile than that and her moments of elation burned up very quickly.

She began to act out almost from the first day of high school. Older boys started showing up in our driveway. I smelled cigarette smoke in her bedroom. When I emptied the garbage, I'd find bags full of beer bottles tucked into the outdoor trash bin. Callie became even more secretive and moody. Late one Saturday night, I found her bedroom empty. Frantically, I called her friends. She'd sneaked out of the house to go to a party.

Dwayne and I started fighting. We didn't know how to deal with Callie, and we had opposite ideas of what needed to be done. Dwayne claimed Callie needed structure, rules, and discipline—she should be grounded and lose privileges like talking on the telephone or watching TV. I, on the other hand, wanted to understand Callie and be her friend. I felt that if I just loved her enough, somehow, she would straighten herself out.

We were both wrong, it occurred to me now. The problem wasn't the alcohol, the cigarette smoking, or the drugs that came later. How could I have been so blind? They were merely symptoms of a far bigger problem: Underneath it all she was depressed and was medicating herself to feel better. Neither Dwayne nor I had a clue about what was really going on.

One Super Bowl Sunday, Dwayne found cigarette butts Callie had thrown out her bedroom window littering the ground in my garden. He was furious; he slapped her and called her names. Callie was terrified. She ran upstairs looking for me. I flew into a rage; I called the cops on Dwayne and stayed with Callie in her bedroom that night. The next day I sent her to stay with Ashley and her family for a while, and I filed for divorce.

Now, I looked up at the setting sun, an orange ball of fire sinking slowly below the horizon, the sky next to it a pale yellow, the clouds purple and edged with a vibrant red. I watched until the clouds faded to a deep blue-gray, until dusk pulled its dark mantle over the earth. It was getting late. I wearily made my way back into the house.

For the next few days, I got up early in the morning, threw on a raggedy pair of blue jeans and a T-shirt, pulled my hair into a ponytail, dropped Anthony off at school, and headed out to the garden. Mercifully, my supervisor at the hospital had granted me a two-month leave of absence from work. I knew I was in no shape to take care of patients. After I'd pulled up all the weeds, I began to dig up piles of limestone rocks buried in the soil as I extended the edges of the garden to make it bigger. Removing each rock occupied all of my attention, and as I worked, the accusing voices inside my head would cease temporarily. But when I collapsed on the grass, they'd come flooding back to haunt me. *I should have gotten divorced from Dwayne sooner. I shouldn't have taken her cell phone away—maybe she would have called one of her friends that night instead of killing herself. I should have checked on her during the night instead of assuming she was OK.* The voices went on and on.

After the divorce, things got hard. People chose sides and I lost some good friends. I was working, going to graduate school, and trying my best to take care of Callie and Anthony, but I was gone so often I left Callie with plenty of time to get into trouble. She learned to lie. She could look me straight in the eye and tell the most outrageous lies. I believed her because I wanted to. After all, Callie was my little girl.

I joined a dating website and had several misadventures. The most memorable was with a local doctor whom I met online. After several weeks of e-mails and telephone calls, he asked me out.

"But Mama!" Callie protested over breakfast that morning. "You don't know anything about him." Irritated, she stabbed at the scrambled eggs on her plate with her fork. "He could be an ax murderer. Or a serial rapist!"

But I just laughed. "I'll be careful," I promised.

He took me out to dinner and then dancing downtown at the Blues and Boogie bar. I should have anticipated trouble when he asked me if I would like to see his office on the way back to my car, which was parked at the restaurant. Once we arrived, he turned on some slow jams and proceeded to make a major move on me, pinning me to the wall, kissing me with such force that it left my lips bruised.

"See, I told you that was a really bad idea," Callie said reproachfully the next morning as I gave her a blow-by-blow description of the evening's activities. "These guys online are only after one thing."

I could tell she thought I was naive and didn't know anything about men.

"Well, I'm done with dating and with men. They're all worthless."

And then I met Tom. I remember the day I first saw him at the university like it was yesterday. I was working on my PhD in Nursing Science, was a teaching assistant in a research course for master's-level nursing students, and was working part-time as a nurse at the hospital. There had been complaints that the teaching assistants weren't attending the lectures, and the dean had decreed that we be present for each class. The topic of that day's lecture was descriptive and inferential statistics, my least favorite subject. I groaned as I slumped in a chair in the back of the room, tossing some articles that I planned to read during the lecture onto the desk. I glanced at the podium as the course coordinator announced that a new faculty member from the biostatistics department would be presenting the day's lecture.

Then Tom strode up to the microphone. He was lanky with wavy, strawberry-blonde hair. Immediately mesmerized by the fluidity of his movements, I sat up slowly, leaned forward in my chair, and cupped my chin in my hands. Everything else forgotten, I gazed at him, enraptured, as he spoke. *My God, where have you been all my life?* I muttered.

During a break in the lecture, I nudged another teaching assistant. "He's an excellent speaker, but I can't place that accent."

"He's from Australia."

"Oh. Do you know anything else about him?"

"He just recently arrived at the university. He said he spent the summer hiking to base camp on Mount Everest."

"No wonder he looks so fit," I sighed.

"Apparently, he's traveled all over the world. He told me he's dived the Great Barrier Reef, trekked through India, went skydiving in New Zealand, and climbed the Great Wall of China."

After Tom's lecture, I kept running into him at research presentations that I attended with my adviser. Several times I caught him gazing at me during the presentations, and when I looked at him I would feel a spark of electricity jump between us, but then he'd smile shyly and immediately focus on the papers in front of him. *Maybe he's interested in me.* But then I'd remind myself that I was just a lowly graduate student.

Then one day several months after I'd sworn off all men, I was sitting down with my adviser discussing a workshop she wanted me to attend to learn how to analyze the data for the results section of the systematic review and meta-analysis I was planning to conduct for my PhD qualifying paper. I was in a foul mood. My life felt like it was disintegrating into chaos. Callie kept getting into trouble. Her latest misadventure had been a curfew violation in early September. Callie and her friends had gone searching for a haunted house but had ended up getting lost in the projects. A policeman called me to report that he had found them around midnight in a bad section of town. I was getting really concerned about her behavior. The last thing I wanted to do was attend the conference in Baltimore.

"You should ask Tom if he'd like to go with you," Dr. Weakley said as she handed me the latest version of my qualifying paper, covered with red ink from all the comments she'd made. "You're going to need some biostatistics support for the meta-analyses."

"I don't think Tom is going to be interested in attending a conference with a student," I replied wearily as I gathered the papers in my arms.

"Oh, you'd be surprised. Faculty are often willing to assist an exceptional student, and I've mentioned your paper to him already."

Damn, what the hell am I going to say to him?

I shot off a brief e-mail giving Tom the details about the conference, not expecting to hear anything back. But a half hour later I heard a knock on my office door. I looked up from my papers and there he was, smiling down at me, looking devastatingly handsome in a navy-blue shirt and yellow tie.

"I got your e-mail about the conference."

I blushed and my heart started to race.

"My adviser suggested that I send it to you. I know it's really short notice. You probably are very busy. I really don't expect you to try to squeeze it into your schedule."

"Oh, but I'd like to go. It sounds like a really interesting conference. I've been wanting to learn more about meta-analysis techniques. I'll see if my teaching assistant can take over my classes while I'm gone. I'll get back to you."

Then he strolled out of my office. *Oh, my God,* I thought as my heart rate slowly descended back to normal. *What an attractive man!*

When we got back from the conference, I kept hoping he would ask me out. I stopped wearing slacks and tailored shirts to work and took to wearing nice dresses, jewelry, and just a touch of makeup. But nothing happened.

Finally, I came up with what I thought was a brilliant ruse.

"I would like to take you out to lunch," I said at our next meeting, "to thank you for all the help you've given me with the meta-analyses. We can go to your favorite restaurant. It will be my treat."

He looked up at me then and smiled. "Lunch would be great, but you don't have to treat me. I really haven't done all that much to help you. The review is coming along so nicely because of all your hard work."

Our first date started out none too auspiciously. After much debate, we decided on a cozy little Italian restaurant for lunch just a few blocks from the university. I spent the evening before trying on numerous outfits, Callie sitting on my bed, swinging her legs and critiquing each one.

"That red dress is too short and too tight. You don't want to look too sexy, Mama, or you will give him the wrong impression. Oh, I don't like that gray suit either;

you don't want to look too businesslike. Wear that little black crepe skirt with the ruffled hem. It's not too form-fitting but will look very pretty on you."

She strode into my walk-in closet in her black leather boots and pulled a tan scoop-necked blouse with small white pearls and chrysanthemums scattered across the front from its hanger. She held it up over the skirt. "Put this one on."

"This is perfect," I exclaimed, spinning around so I could see myself from all angles in the mirror.

"Here's how you should do your hair," she said as she ruffled it in front of the mirror. "Put it up in large hot rollers, then finger-comb it out just a little, flip it forward then toss it back to give it that tousled look."

"Oh, you mean that slightly-disheveled-after-good-sex look."

"Yep, that's the one," she laughed.

So I dressed up for our first date. Tom, who always wore a long-sleeved shirt and tie to work, dressed down in a short-sleeved blue-and-white striped shirt, open at the neck.

When I got to his office, I said, "Let's take your car instead of walking; it's really humid and hot outside and it looks like it could rain any minute."

"I rode in on the bus this morning. Let's just go over to that little deli across the street. I only have an hour, then I have to get ready for my next class."

Oh, no, I thought. I had just made a noon reservation for a quiet little corner table at the restaurant, explaining over the phone that this was my first date with a very special man.

"Then we'll take my car; you can drive if you like," I blurted out. Suddenly I remembered the CD with the big red heart on the cover, titled *How to Find Your Soul Mate*, which was lying on the passenger seat; the mud-encrusted riding boots in the back; the tattered riding helmet and gloves on the floor. *God, I hope my car doesn't smell like a horse barn.*

"Oh, no, I could never drive your car."

"Then I'll drive, but you'll have to direct me. I have a terrible sense of direction."

When we got to the car, I quickly picked up the CD and threw it in the backseat before he could sit down on it. He gallantly handed me my riding helmet and gloves and said, "I keep all my tennis gear in my car."

Then I looked up with horror at the rosary beads and other trinkets from my last trip to New Orleans that were dangling from the rearview mirror. I quickly scooped them up and shoved them into the glove compartment, hoping he wouldn't notice.

"I'm Catholic," he said, smiling. "My mom has some rosary beads around her car mirror too."

I started the car and one of Callie's favorite TLC songs, *Red Light Special*, started blaring from the radio. I turned it off. When we got to the restaurant, a car that was backing out of a parking space almost rear-ended us.

Then, when I told the hostess my name, she winked. "You're the one who requested a quiet table in the corner."

I blushed and nodded. *What more can go wrong?*

I had memorized a list of questions to ask Tom in case there were any uncomfortable silences. "Tell me about Australia and all your travels," I said, after the waiter took our orders.

Then he was off. He told me about Monkey Mia, where the dolphins were so tame they would swim right up to you in shallow water; about Ayres Rock, which was thought by the aborigines to contain magical powers—how it changed colors from red to gold to deep purple with the setting sun; about the Great Barrier Reef, with its crystal-clear water, vividly colorful coral cays, whirlpools of spinning zebra fish, and beyond it the Coral Sea, with sheer limestone rock walls that plunged into the depths of the ocean.

I sat there mesmerized by the man and his adventures. The lunch crowd finished their meals and dispersed, leaving us alone at our tiny corner table. He finally glanced down at his watch. It was almost three p.m.

"Oh, my God, I've got to get back to work," he exclaimed. After we made our way back to the university, he told me how much he had enjoyed lunch, then raced up the stairs to his office.

After that we started to go downtown occasionally on Saturday nights to listen to a country band play at a local bar. Callie told me that I needed to give her some idea of when I'd be home, so she wouldn't worry about my being out late downtown. But as I'd find out later from Megan, as soon as I left, Callie would call her friends.

"Mama just left and the party's going down at my house right now," she'd say. Pretty soon there'd be a least a dozen kids at the house. They even devised a plan in case I came home early. The boys would park their cars a little way up the street. They'd put all the empty beer cans in their car trunks and post someone on guard at the window around the time I was supposed to come home. As soon as they saw my red car turn into our street, one of the boys would yell, "Red alert, red alert." They'd cut the music, turn off the lights, and head into Callie's bedroom, closing the door. The boys would escape out her bedroom window to their cars, and I'd walk in to find the house utterly quiet. Little did I know the girls were all in Callie's bed, laughing, burying their faces in the pillows to keep me from hearing them.

Occasionally, I'd call Callie to check on her. I'd remind her that she could have one of her girlfriends over so she wouldn't be all alone, but no parties, or boys, or alcohol. "Yes, Mama," Callie would say. "Me and Megan [or Jenny or Ashley] are just watching old movies on TV and eating popcorn." Of course, the party was probably already in full swing, and Callie was frantically waving her hands at her friends to make them stay quiet until she got off the phone so I wouldn't hear anything.

Several weeks after the Garth Brooks concert, Ashley's mother couldn't find her at home. She started calling all her daughter's friends and decided to stop by my house on her way to the grocery store to see if Callie knew where she was. Ashley was at the party at my house. I, as usual, was out with Tom.

Ashley's mom phoned me. "I'm at your place," she began. "And I just broke up a couples party and sent all the boys home. I found Callie and her boyfriend Rusty half-naked in her bed. Ashley was with Troy in Anthony's bed, and Jenny and Jimmy were both upstairs in your bedroom. Where's Anthony tonight?"

"Oh, no!" I exclaimed. "Callie said the girls were just planning to rent some movies. Anthony's with his dad this weekend. I'm on my way home."

"Well, just for your information, the house reeks of marijuana smoke, and there's an unopened twelve-pack of beer on the kitchen counter. Apparently, the kids were too preoccupied with other things to get to the beer."

"I'm so sorry," I replied. "It won't happen again."

"My house is turning into a brothel," I said to Tom after I told him the story.

His grown daughter had been unruly as a teenager, and I knew he'd want to help me keep Callie out of trouble. He, in typical male fashion, heard me out and then suggested the perfect solution to my problem. "Perhaps we should stop going downtown for a while." I instantly agreed, and the Saturday night parties at my house were over forever.

Callie seemed to get along well with Tom, as long as he didn't try to tell her what to do. He complimented her on her outfits and her hair, and she loved that. When Callie tried to have a drunken party on Halloween night, Tom helped me order all the boys home. He gave me good advice on how to set limits with Callie. I remember thinking then that maybe now, with Tom, life was going to get better, that all of my troubles might be behind me. But in reality, they had just begun.

That thought stirred me from my reverie. Wearily I pulled myself up from the grass and went back to my garden project.

Slowly my work progressed. When I was unable to lift a rock by myself, I would trudge back inside the house and appear at the door to Tom's office, dirty, smelly, sweaty, and unkempt, insisting that he come outside right away to help me move the rock. Tom, looking up from his work and probably deciding that he had better not mess with me in my current state of mind, would obligingly trudge out to the garden to help me. In the aftermath of Callie's death, he had become my haven from the sad and perilous struggle that my life had become.

I guess it was the previous Christmas when I finally realized that I was hopelessly in love with him. The day before he was to leave for Australia for the holidays, I hung around my office wistfully praying that he'd stop by to say good-bye. Final grades were due at the university registrar that day and I knew he'd be incredibly busy. When six o'clock rolled around, I gave up and was just about to leave when I heard those now-familiar footsteps in the hall. I looked up and there he was, standing by the door of my office, winter wool jacket on, briefcase in hand. He put down his briefcase and held out his arms to me. I gently melted into them.

"I hope you have a wonderful Christmas holiday," he said as he hugged me quickly. Then he let go and picked up his briefcase.

He backed away smiling as I said, "You too—please stay safe with all your travels." Then he turned and was gone.

I sat down heavily in my chair. I felt I would burst into tears at any moment, the sense of loss was so overwhelming. If only I could tell him what was in my heart! How could I explain this irresistible force that pulled me toward him? Being with him felt like coming home.

Back at the house, the girls consoled me as they made hot chocolate and popcorn. Megan insisted that we huddle together in front of the big-screen TV, crocheted afghans across our knees, watching *Casablanca* and clutching tissues in our hands for all the sad parts of the story.

"It's only two weeks," Callie reminded me.

"But I know it seems like forever," Megan sympathized as she patted my hand.

"It will be over before you know it."

"I hope so," I snuffled as I blew noisily into a tissue and dropped it on the floor to rest beside all the others.

I'd clean up in the morning. *What will the New Year bring?* I snuggled down further into the warmth of the afghan. Would he fall madly in love with me, if he wasn't in love already? Or would he come back from Australia and act like nothing had ever happened between us? I had such hope for the future then.

I bought him a biography about George Mallory, the English climber who had disappeared on the northeast ridge of Mount Everest just below the summit in 1924, over the Christmas holidays and stewed about whether it was appropriate, at this stage of our acquaintance, to give him a present. I wrapped the book in gold paper and tied it with a huge red bow. I talked his administrative assistant into letting me leave it on his desk a few days before the winter semester began.

The first day of classes, he appeared in my office door, book in hand. He knocked softly and I spilled the papers scattered across my desk to the floor as I rose to meet him. He smiled, bent down to retrieve them, and gathered me into his arms. At that moment, all the feelings I tried to suppress over the holidays came rushing back into my heart and I was head over heels all over again.

Finally, in late January he began to let his guard down, and I discovered he had a secret life. One evening when the kids were with Dwayne for the weekend, I asked him over for dinner, and when I went to meet him in the driveway he pulled an old, battered guitar case out of the trunk of his car. I knew he liked country music but hadn't realized that he was a closet songwriter and musician. He had the lyrics to the most beautiful music on sheets of notebook paper stuffed into his guitar case.

"Sing me one of your songs," I begged as we were sitting by the fire after dinner.

"Oh, I don't know, Diane; I don't sing very well. I just like to play music."

"Just one—sing me your favorite song."

He then started to play a melody about love and loss with such harmony and grace that it carried me on its wings to a place in my heart that, like a rose, was just beginning to unfold. When he sang, I could feel, in the softness of his voice and the way his fingers caressed the guitar strings, his gentleness and his vulnerability, the pain hidden beneath an exterior of polished calm. In the flickering firelight, his eyes became the color of the midnight sky caught between the brightest of stars, but like all men who are attracted to the wildness of the dolphins and consider themselves untamed, he was afraid to open his heart to love. I had never met a man who wanted to be cared for so much but in whom the fear ran equally deep.

We slept together for the first time that night. His fingers felt like spun silk the way he moved them from the base of my spine up my back to finally ruffle my hair, and oh, how much I loved him.

The sharp sound of a siren in the distance jerked me out of my reverie. It seemed that every time I heard an emergency siren I was immediately back to that moment when I found Callie lifeless in her bedroom. Back to work.

Once the weeds and rocks were gone, I pulverized the soil with a tiller, going back and forth over the dirt until all the large clumps of clay were ground into the soil. Then I smoothed it with a rake. As my work progressed, I went to the house only to eat or use the bathroom until dusk had settled on the garden and the early spring air had grown too cool. Then I would wearily take a shower, collapse into bed, and immediately fall into a dreamless sleep.

After the tilling, I spent the next several days driving back and forth to a nursery across town in my truck, to make sure I didn't run into anyone I knew. With Ruffy at my side, I purchased pots of flowers and shrubs—crepe myrtle, rose of Sharon, lilacs and lilies, chrysanthemums, peonies, columbines, snapdragons, and iris tubers. After digging holes and filling them with water, I lovingly placed the plants in Callie's garden. If these flowers could live and grow, maybe, I thought, just maybe, in a still summer twilight, with the fireflies twinkling in the soft, jade-green grass, my daughter could walk barefoot into my garden and see all the flowers that I had planted for her after she was gone. I couldn't think of anything else to do to feel close to her again.

I couldn't avoid going out in public in my neighborhood forever, despite how much I wanted to. Anthony was running out of sandwich meat, and we'd had pizza three nights in a row. Grudgingly, I disguised myself in a knee-length gray cardigan and blue jeans, hiding my unwashed hair under a baseball cap. I slipped on a large pair of sunglasses to hide my red-rimmed eyes and jumped into my truck to pick up a few groceries at the store. I was standing idly by the canned dog food when one of my neighbors passed by, pushing her shopping cart, and almost collided with another shopper who was apparently one of her friends. Neither of them noticed me, and they stopped at the end of the aisle and started chatting.

"Gina, oh, my goodness! I didn't mean to run you over!"

"That's OK, Sue. How are you?"

"I'm OK, but I guess I'm a little distracted. There's been a lot of commotion in my neighborhood recently."

"Why? What's happened?"

"Well," she said, glancing left and right before leaning in conspiratorially, "an ambulance showed up at my neighbor Diane's house on a Friday morning around six a.m. two weeks ago. About a half hour later, I saw her daughter being wheeled out on a stretcher."

"Oh, no!" The other woman lifted her hand to her mouth in horror. "I hope she's OK."

"Unfortunately, no. She passed away. No one knows how she died, but a bunch of police cars arrived at the house soon after the ambulance, and they didn't leave until around noon."

"Goodness. That's very strange."

"Yes, there's been lots of unusual things going on at that house. A bunch of teenagers have been hanging out there at all hours of the day and night. Sometimes my husband and I heard loud music coming from the open windows until the wee hours. The obituary was in that Sunday's paper and we went to the funeral. It was very sad."

"Wow. Well, I'm sorry to hear that, but I've gotta run. My son's baseball practice is just about over.

"Of course, see you soon."

They moved toward the checkout counters while I stood there wishing I could shrink myself down like Alice in Wonderland, so I could crawl into the shelves behind the cans of pet food and disappear forever. Was everyone in the neighborhood talking about what had happened to Callie? I stood there, frozen, for what seemed like an eternity. Shaking myself at last, I adjusted my purse on my shoulder, returned my empty cart, and found my way back to the car.

I started having thoughts of suicide about a week after the incident at the grocery store. I often took Ruffy and my Labrador retriever Beau across the street to an old, abandoned, one-story ranch house with yellow vinyl siding and a disintegrating shake roof covered in green mold. It had once been owned by a retired physics professor at the university who kept a beautiful rose garden in his front yard. He wore a perpetual frown as he went walking down the street, bent over an old cane that he clutched in his right hand. The house had been vacant since he died. The garden was now a tangle of weeds and thorns.

One afternoon, the dogs sniffed out an old path leading down through a maze of rocks to the lake, and I followed wearily behind them.

An underground stream ran through the property, opening onto a small rock ledge and cascading to the lake below. I stood on the ledge, watching the dogs run down to a dilapidated boat dock leaning precariously on its side. The rusty chains on the dock made an eerie clanking noise when the wind blew across the lake. Hanging from one of the beams on the ceiling of the dock was a thick rope. I bleakly imagined making myself a noose from it and hanging myself and wondered how long it would take for one of the passing boaters to notice me. A chill swept through me and I whistled, quickly summoning the dogs back on the path toward home.

～

That night, I opened the medicine cabinet and looked at the bottle of sleeping pills Dwayne had given me after Callie's wake. I remember thinking, *there are probably enough pills in this bottle for me to check myself out if I take them all at once. I'll just save them. If the pain gets too bad, I will take all of them and go to sleep.* I morbidly imagined myself putting on Callie's blue prom gown, fixing my hair the same way she had worn it, putting on Callie's makeup and jewelry, and taking one of her blankets and pillows, a bottle of Southern Comfort, and the "check out" pills to Callie's grave late one night after Tom had gone to sleep. But then I remembered Anthony, realizing I could never abandon him like that, and so I changed into my pajamas, brushed my teeth, and tucked myself in under the covers. Tom, half asleep, pulled me toward him, my back pressed into his chest, his arm around my waist.

"You OK?" he murmured into my ear.

I heaved a shivering sigh. "I am now," I replied as I relaxed into his embrace.

When sleep came, I dreamed of Callie. It was a bright spring morning and I walked into my kitchen to find her sitting on a barstool by the counter, munching on a piece of toast. She was wearing her new cotton pj's with the yellow moons and stars scattered on a bright blue background, her hair pulled into a ponytail.

As I walked into the room, Callie looked up at me with a sly half-smile on her face and said, "I got a parking ticket last night and it's really expensive."

I reacted instantly. "What do you mean you got a parking ticket?" I exclaimed. "You're not supposed to be driving!"

She dismissed this unwelcome comment with a wave of her hand and a self-satisfied smile. "But I'm going to get my driver's license back really soon," she continued.

This moved me from mild exasperation to outright anger. I leaned forward on the counter and glared at her until something struck me. Puzzled, I said to her, "Callie, no, you're not. You're dead!"

She dropped her toast and started laughing, her head tilted back and her chest heaving, as though this were the funniest thing she'd ever heard. I reached over to touch her, but under my fingers her body disappeared. In her place was a luminous silver globe that hung in the air for a moment, suspended. I watched as it flew up into the air with sparks trailing behind it, circling around my kitchen faster and faster, before it vanished and I was left standing alone, awestruck.

I awoke to find the house dark and very still. Tom lay asleep by my side, and Ruffy lay curled against my arms. *It was only a dream. Callie is dead. We buried her just three weeks ago.* Tears filled my eyes and I softly cried myself back to sleep.

The next evening, I made some coffee and found myself sitting in front of a blank document on the computer. Several relatives had suggested that I write down my thoughts and feelings as a form of therapy.

Where do I begin? How can I make sense of any of this? "My daughter killed herself," I started to type, "or at least she thought she did."

I was startled by a knock on the front door. Megan, Jenny, and Ashley were standing on the front steps.

"Come with us," they said. "Come to a meditation down by the lake." Anthony was at a friend's house and Tom was buried in a grant proposal, so I just slipped outside.

We drove several minutes in the twilight along the main road until we pulled in at a small cove. A group was standing along the shoreline in the gathering dusk, and searching among the crowd I recognized Megan's mother, Ruth, and some of her friends. Several of the first fireflies of summer twinkled in the grass or lit the soft gray sky. Megan, Jenny, and Ashley talked about Callie, and everyone did a silent meditation, sending love and light her way.

I listened to the soft lap of water, the muffled quacks of ducks settling in for the night, and the low chirp of crickets. I imagined Callie up there somewhere among the stars in the distant sky, and I longed to reach her. We used to talk by phone several times every day, though now I knew that when she told me where she was, she was lying half the time. Now her cell phone was silent, confiscated by the police and tucked away in some deep, dark evidence box covered with tape. A man at the edge of the group pulled out a flute and began to play a low, mournful tune that hovered above the dusky water.

"I feel so lost now that Callie is gone," I heard myself say aloud. Tears fell, and I hastily brushed them away.

The man with the flute turned his head, locking eyes with me. "She's not gone," he said softly. "You're just going to have to find another way to communicate with her."

He gazed at me somberly for a moment that seemed to extend into eternity as I lost all sense of time, his long mahogany hair framing a chiseled face, eyes the color of black pearls. Then he turned away and appeared to melt into the trees behind the lake.

"Who was that man?" I asked Ruth as we made our way back to the cars.

"He's a full-blooded Cherokee; some people think he's a shaman. He has this strange habit of showing up where he's needed, and then he just evaporates. I don't think anyone really knows him or where he lives."

"That's very strange." But it seemed I'd had quite a few unsettling experiences since Callie's death.

After dropping the other two girls off, Megan dragged me to a little local hangout, a diner on Gosling Creek. It was a squat brown building with a flat tin roof, and *Whistlers* was painted in large letters on a sign above it. A gnarled, split-rail fence lit by a streetlamp separated the asphalt of the parking lot from the grassy shoreline of the creek. Mallard ducks swam lazily in the gray-green water, which rippled gently on a soft breeze. We sat at a square card table covered with a cream canvas cloth by the window, underneath a signed photo of a country music star. It was late in the evening but they served breakfast all day, so I ordered scrambled eggs, bacon, biscuits, grits, and gravy. Megan only wanted the silver-dollar pancakes. I knew I was eating to make myself feel better; somehow the food made me feel a little less empty inside.

Megan was distracted, gazing pensively out the window. Her heart-shaped face was framed by loose honey-brown strands, and her hazel eyes were large and troubled. Turning toward me, she picked up a spoon and stirred cream into her coffee, watching it swirl around in her cup.

"Meg? How are you doing?" I reached out to touch her hand.

She tossed me a weak smile. "Oh, I have my good days and bad days. I just can't believe that she's gone . . . and everyone is mad at me."

"I can't understand why anyone would be mad at you," I said, surprised.

"Well, I was the last person to see Callie alive. I *took* her to that party. I wanted to spend the night at your house but my mama told me I had to come home to clean my room and finish my homework." She brushed an errant strand of hair from her face. "If I hadn't gone home, maybe Callie would still be alive. She tried X and cocaine, and she wanted to try heroin. I told her I thought it was a really bad idea and that she needed to talk to you about her problems. I knew I should have come to you myself!"

My mind flashed back to the day Callie had confided in me. "Megan thinks I'm depressed," she'd said.

"I'm seeing a really nice woman who is a psychologist," I'd offered. "Cal, why don't you let me take you to see her?"

I was in therapy to help me cope with Callie's rebellious behavior. Like many children of the 1960s, I was too lenient. I wanted Callie to be able to express herself, but was trying to learn ways to set boundaries when she was acting out.

She went once, and never again. "I don't want to talk to that psychologist anymore," she'd said obstinately, slamming the car door shut after her first visit. "I don't want to talk to a stranger about my problems."

I discussed the situation with the pediatrician she'd been seeing since she was six years old. He decided to start Callie on an antidepressant. She seemed happier about taking pills than talking. A month later, Callie was gone.

"Meg, it's not your fault," I said forcefully. "You can't blame yourself! I wish I had taken Callie more seriously when she told me that she might be a little depressed."

But Megan shook her head. "I've been going over and over in my mind what could've happened at that party. I thought she just drank a few beers. But one of the boys has been bringing lots of pills to the parties. I don't know where he gets them or what they are. She might've taken a few pills and had a bad reaction. Oh! I should have stayed with her that night." She dropped her head to her hands.

"Megan, listen to me. You can't beat yourself up about this." *After all*, I thought, *there's more than enough guilt to go around.*

For the first time, her eyes locked on mine. "You know, I'd been picking Callie up every morning to take her to school, ever since her driver's license was taken away. She used to call and make sure I was up, but that morning my cell phone never rang. I figured she wasn't feeling well after getting all sick at the party." She paused a moment, then shook her head. "I stopped my car at the turnoff to your street that morning. I had the strangest feeling that something was wrong. But I ignored it and just decided to go on to school."

"What happened when you got there?"

"Well, at the beginning of second period, Jenny, Ashley, and I were told by our English teacher to go to the principal's office. We looked at each other and sat down, wondering what kind of trouble we'd gotten ourselves into this time. The principal, Mr. McGowan, instead of sitting all stuffed up behind his desk, sat down in a chair next to us. I remember thinking that something must be really wrong. He said, 'Girls, I have some very bad news. Your friend Callie was found unresponsive in her bedroom this morning.' He told us the paramedics had rushed Callie to the hospital and every attempt was made to save her life, but she was already gone when they got to the emergency room."

Megan's eyes filled, and she looked out toward the water for a moment, struggling.

"I remember I screamed and made a dash for the door, but a school counselor stopped me and I collapsed in her arms. Jenny fell to the floor on her knees sobbing hysterically. Ashley's face turn sheet-white, and she put her hand to her mouth, just staring wild-eyed at the principal."

"Oh!" I exclaimed, reaching for Megan's hand once more. "That must have been terrible for you girls."

"Yeah." She nodded. "It was the worst day of my life. The principal called our parents and Mom finally came to pick me up and take me home. We were holding onto each other and crying as we walked to our cars. Some of our friends in the hall stopped us to ask what was wrong. 'Callie's dead!' was all we could say. Then they all burst into tears too.

"I didn't go back to school after that horrible day. I shared a locker with Callie and I just couldn't deal with all the stares from kids who knew that we were best friends. My sister went to the school and brought me my books. I had trouble studying for my final exams. You know, everything just seemed so pointless."

"Well, maybe Callie's death will help us all realize what's most important in life, like friends and family and helping people in need. Callie would want us to be brave and strong. You have a lot of courage, Megan. Just hold onto that. You'll get through this. We all will."

I remember thinking at the time that I sounded a lot more certain than I felt.

"Yes, you're right, Mama," Megan replied, reaching in her purse for a Kleenex to dry her eyes. "I've enrolled in another school for next fall where no one knows me. I'm going to try to put all this behind and finish high school."

∾

I attended a class on adolescent depression a few years before Callie died, concerned about some of the teen moms that I saw in my clinical practice. When I got home from the meditation and the diner that night, my conversation with Megan got me thinking. I never thought that Callie was significantly depressed, certainly not suicidal. I thought her problems were with drugs.

I changed into my pj's and, after pouring myself a glass of wine, popped the cassette recording I'd purchased of the psychologist's presentation into the player.

"These kids often experience feelings of helplessness and hopelessness," the psychologist explained. "They have low self-esteem and feel that they are worthless. They believe their problems are overwhelming and can't be resolved. They may seem isolated and alone and can be the victims of bullying and physical or sexual abuse. Or they can be the overachievers, children who have a tremendous fear of failure. Unfortunately, they feel that they are only loved for what they do, not for who they are."

Did Callie feel helpless, hopeless? Why didn't she talk to me about her problems?

"It's very common for kids who are depressed to self-medicate with drugs," he continued. "The drugs often make them feel better temporarily. The drug use is a symptom, not the underlying problem. We need to find out why these kids are using drugs and what drug use does for them. Only then can we can guide them to more appropriate ways to help them alleviate their pain. We need to focus more on why the child hurts, not on their drug use."

Had I done that, focused on her drug use rather than on her pain?

At the end of the lecture, a high school teacher brought up a situation that had troubled everyone at her school.

"One of our sophomore girls recently committed suicide," she said. "We've been racking our brains trying to figure out what clues we might have missed."

"Did you observe any changes in her behavior?" he asked.

"Well, her parents were recently divorced. Her grades had been slipping, and sometimes she fell asleep in class. We had some concerns that she might be using drugs. Marijuana is an issue at our school. One of the teachers had confiscated the student's purse when her cell phone rang during class. She found an infant's pacifier in the purse. The student swore she only used it when she was babysitting."

The psychologist interjected, "Pacifier use is often associated with a drug called ecstasy. Users often suck on pacifiers to prevent their teeth from grinding, which is a common side effect of the drug. Go on," he urged.

"She didn't seem like a typical drug user and she didn't appear depressed. She always wore nice outfits to school, although sometimes I felt that they were a little too provocative. She seemed to have lots of friends. She wasn't a child whom we would have labeled suicidal. We were more concerned about the social outcasts, the goth kids, or the ones obsessed with dark, heavy-metal music about death and destruction."

This girl sounds just like Callie, I thought as I listened to the recording.

"Well that's the problem," the lecturer said with a sigh. "The vast majority of teen suicides are just baffling. The kids are more often than not well liked and from good homes with attentive parents. Sometimes, I think, their decision is tragically impulsive and caused by a crisis they feel that they just can't deal with at the time."

"It's so sad," the teacher remarked.

"I'll tell you what's sad," he replied. "Once someone has decided to commit suicide, there may not be a lot we can do about it. They may appear calm, even happy, and completely deny their suicidal intent. These kids often shut down emotionally before they do so physically. The kids we call the suicide ideators don't usually die; they just talk about it. They'll open up about their feelings and are receptive to counseling. The kids that really mean it won't tell you a damn thing."

I sat there on the couch, transfixed, the tape player whirling silently in front of me as I slowly began to put the pieces together. So, Callie had probably fantasized about her own suicide, planned it over weeks, maybe even months, but never told a soul about it. She kept her feelings buried, refusing to trust anyone, not even her own mother. Yet her case didn't appear to be unusual. *What makes these kids turn away from the whole world and from everyone who loves them?* Silent tears of salt-tinged regret and despair started to fall as I sat there, motionless. Out in the dark, I could hear the faint rumble of thunder in the distance, heralding an early-summer storm. The wind suddenly picked up, rattling the windowpanes and scattering the first drops of rain across the glass. She knew that I loved her more than my own life itself.

Why hadn't she allowed herself to open her heart to me?

❧

The autopsy report I received the next day stated that Callie had died from an overdose of her antidepressant medication. The medicine that was supposed to make her feel better had, in the end, taken her life.

It was so cold, so clinical. It described Callie as a sixty-three-inch tall, 117-pound, well-nourished, well-developed sixteen-year-old white female. It included the condition of her organ systems, as well as urine, blood and gastric toxicology reports. *A sixteen-year-old white young woman was found unresponsive in her bedroom by her mother and was taken by EMS to the emergency room. Advanced cardiac life support was continued in the emergency room but was unsuccessful. A suicide note was found in her bedroom at home. No internal trauma was identified. No pregnancy was seen. The cause of death was a drug overdose. The manner of death was suicide.*

In Callie's room, I sorted everything into piles: the few things I couldn't bear to part with, things Callie probably would want her three best friends to have, things to give to Goodwill. The last thing I moved was Callie's little refrigerator, which sat on top of a bookshelf. Behind it was a perfectly round, spiral seashell. I had a shell just like it in my jewelry box, and I realized it was from our last trip to the beach together, when we'd run away to Nag's Head. I had a conference to attend, and Callie wanted to get the perfect natural suntan for prom, so I decided to take her with me. "She's going to miss several days of class," the high school principal had reminded me. "She's going to get behind in her schoolwork."

"Well, then, I'll make sure she gets her assignments from her teachers before we go," I assured him. After all, she would be leaving for college soon. I wanted to be able to spend some time with her at her favorite place, the beach.

The weather was unseasonably warm for April. Callie and I strolled barefoot along the sand. I'd always loved the ocean, but even the bright blue sky, gentle salt-tinged breeze, and rhythmic lap of waves couldn't shake the feeling of dread and impending doom that had come over me. I felt as if something awful was going to happen but couldn't imagine what it might be. The first months of the year had been filled with small crises and mishaps. Anthony had been involved in a car accident, resulting in a cut on his head where the car window broke. Then the pipe to our septic tank burst, causing water and sewage to back up in the pipes and flooding poor Anthony's bedroom. The carpet and part of the subfloor had to be replaced. One of Callie's boyfriends totaled her Mustang by driving it into a tree, but luckily no one was hurt. Another one of Callie's friends, who was looking for money to buy drugs, stole my purse out of our house. A monster thunderstorm blew a bunch of shingles off my roof, and half the roof had to be replaced. There had been so many red flags that I had somehow managed to ignore, being consumed by work, school, and a new romance. Additionally, Tom and I were having a few problems, probably the result of his moving into my home and having to deal with two rambunctious teenagers. Since his divorce ten years earlier, he'd been on his own in a comfortable two-bedroom apartment near the university. I'd had a hard time persuading him to even go out on a date with me.

He had been so elusive at first that I was floored when he suggested we move in together after his lease expired on his apartment in early March. So, when Callie and I were in Nag's Head, I was uneasy. *Maybe Tom will move out while we're gone*, I thought. *Maybe I will come back home and find that he has taken all his stuff, left no forwarding address— only a note stuck to the door of his office saying that he's sorry, but he just can't do it anymore.* That's when I looked down and noticed the spiral shell lying in the sand next to my feet. I picked it up and looked at it closely. *I'll take this shell home with me*, I thought, *to remind me that no matter what happens, I will be OK.*

Tom was still there when I got home and had made an elaborate dinner to welcome us back, but the feeling of dread persisted. How strange to find that exact same shell while cleaning out Callie's room months afterward—as though it was there to remind me now, when I needed it most, that everything, somehow, *would* be OK.

The days passed slowly. Every morning I woke up and remembered all over again that Callie was dead. I finally gave up on the idea that it was just a bad dream and that I would someday wake up, find Callie standing there, and be able to say, "Oh, Callie, I just had the most awful nightmare."

I dragged myself out of bed day after day to do whatever had to be done to survive. At night, I would close my eyes with relief, grateful for the oblivion of sleep and the escape from the unrelenting pain that accompanied my days.

Over and over again, I wondered what had happened to Callie. But there were no answers; there was only silence.

⮞ 5 ⮜

Callie—What Really Happened

After my conversation with Jesus in the courtyard, I spent some time holed up in my bedroom at that damn Barbie house. Ellie brought me pizza and macaroni and cheese but I refused to eat. I wasn't hungry. Our bodies actually don't need food in heaven anyway, but eating is a habit that's hard to give up. Kind of like cigarettes. I still sneaked outside late at night to smoke a cigarette, looking carefully in all directions before I lit up to make sure I wasn't being watched. I kept thinking that Ellie would kill me if she caught me smoking—until I reminded myself that, lucky for me, I was already dead.

I moped around during the day, mostly doing nothing. I'd lie on the floor gazing at the ceiling, or watch the new world go by outside my bedroom window. Sometimes I could feel my Barbie house lift slightly off the ground and start to spin around in a very slow circle like an old vinyl record on one of those turntables. If I was wondering about where the hell were all the angels that are supposed to be in heaven, they'd start to glide by my window gently flapping their wings and carrying trumpets, French horns, harps and other assorted musical instruments God knows where.

If I was remembering my mama's flower gardens and all my favorite butterflies, the orange monarchs, tiger swallowtails, and painted ladies, they'd start fluttering around too. I'd ask myself if they'd keep spinning around my house for eternity or eventually keel over from sheer exhaustion. I sighed; it really didn't interest me all that much. I'd wonder if it rained in heaven, and the sky would instantly turn a sickly gray-green and tiny drops would appear outside my window and, as I thought about the rain, they would turn into big gray globs that fell faster and faster until all I could see outside were huge sheets of sodden rain. It was all very depressing.

Almost every night, I picked up that awful screen that Ellie gave me. I didn't like the things that I saw happening on earth but they held some kind of morbid fascination for me. One evening, I saw my body on the autopsy table and even watched the doctor cut my chest open with a nasty-looking knife. I saw him toss his gloves into a trash can, disgusted, after he finished with me. Turning to that detective, Joe Rodriguez I think his name was, he said, "Well, there's no evidence of physical trauma except for that small cut on her head. She wasn't pregnant. All her organ systems look normal. She was a perfectly healthy kid who just threw her life away. How stupid can you be?"

I saw the boys sitting around my grave at midnight the night after they buried me too. They were passing a joint and speculating.

"Maybe Callie was all pilled up. Maybe all those pills she was taking just did her in."

"Maybe she was high on X; you know when you're flying on X, you're capable of doing anything."

They all thought it was the drugs that killed me. Not that, had I been there, I would have told them anything about the black hole I'd been running from for so long.

I watched that nice lady who washed and combed my hair at the funeral home. She said to my lifeless body as it lay there on a cold metal table, "Poor little girl. What happened to you?"

I watched the scenes over and over again until Ellie took the screen away. "There's no point in torturing yourself about what happened on earth after you left your human body," she said. "You have a whole new life ahead of you now in Summer Wind."

Finally, Ellie must have reported my deteriorating condition to Seraphiel, because he summoned me to his office at the library. The office was just like a sunporch. It overlooked a beautiful rose garden with a pond full of koi and large goldfish in the center. The garden was ablaze with color. Hundreds of roses were in full bloom, their large, broad or fluted petals outstretched to greet the shimmering sun. The windows were open slightly and I could smell the sweet scent of roses wafting into the room on a soft breeze.

Seraphiel sat me down in a white wicker chair across from him and poured me a glass of sparkling ice water. I had actually dressed for the occasion instead of wearing my pajamas all day. I put on my favorite pair of boot-cut blue jeans and a sleeveless red satin blouse with a plunging V-neck to impress him, but he didn't seem to notice my outfit at all.

He's an angel, I reminded myself. *He's not going to care what you wear.*

"How are you adjusting to Summer Wind?" he began.

I attempted to look bored. "Oh, as well as can be expected," I replied evasively. "Say, you wouldn't happen to have a cigarette on you that I could borrow?" He probably wouldn't like my smoking cigarettes any more than Ellie, but at that point I really didn't care.

"Afraid not."

Then there was this long silence while I looked down at the ivory tile floor and he stared at me with those piercing blue eyes.

"You know," I began, "I would have liked my house better if I were six years old and still playing with Barbie dolls."

"Ellie thought you would be more comfortable in a house that was familiar to you."

"Oh," was all I could think to say, scuffing my heel on the floor.

After another long silence, he said, "Let's start from the beginning. When was the first time you can remember feeling . . . depressed?"

I sighed loudly and shifted uncomfortably in my chair. "Do we have to talk about this now? It's too early in the morning and I'm not really awake. I haven't even had any coffee yet."

"Tell you what: I'll get you some coffee." He snapped his fingers and a cup of steaming-hot coffee appeared in front of me. "Sooner or later, we have to talk."

Shit! So, I wasn't going to be able to get out of this. I sighed again as I reached out and picked up the cup.

"Well, believe it or not, I was really shy when I was younger, but I don't think I was depressed or anything. On my first day of kindergarten, I hid in the closet that was used for all the kids' hats and coats. I remember that my teacher had to coax me out. I could feel the eyes of all the other kids on me, laughing at me."

"You felt different, like you didn't fit in."

"I guess you could say that. I did have a boyfriend when I was about five, though. His name was Jordan and his parents were friends with mine. Every Saturday afternoon we would watch TV together and eat popcorn or ice cream. We'd talk about how we were going to get married when we grew up." I smiled, remembering.

"What happened to Jordan?"

"Well, my family moved across the country from California to Tennessee when I was six years old. The last time I saw him was when Mama took me to his house to say good-bye. I really didn't know what to say. Then we just drove away."

"Do you think you had trouble coping with loss? Maybe you felt that you were too vulnerable or too tenderhearted?"

"I don't know. Whatever you say." I didn't like this. I didn't like it at all. I sighed again, miserably.

"What happened after you moved to Tennessee?"

"Well, I had to start all over again at a new school and make new friends in Tennessee. My best friend was Sara. She lived next door. I remember that we would play for hours on the floor of her bedroom with Barbies and her mama's makeup. But she moved away too."

"How did you feel when she moved away?"

"Well, I remember that my mama took me to her house to say good-bye and I started to cry. I was still crying when I got on the school bus and all the other kids laughed at me. I wrote a will on a scrap of paper after that and left everything I had to Sara." I could feel just one tear threatening to slide down my cheek. I didn't want to cry in front of Seraphiel.

"So you felt that you might die from a broken heart."

"I guess so. I had a dog named Piddles, too. We called him Piddles because every time we scolded him he piddled on the floor. One day, I wasn't looking where I was going and I fell over Piddles. He bit me on the nose, right here," I said, pointing at the spot. "Papa got all mad, took Piddles, and threw him in the car and drove away. I never saw him again."

"You sound really sad. You must have felt as if you wore your heart on your sleeve and it was always getting broken. You must remember that part of the earth experience is to learn wholeness through separation. To learn that you have all you need right here." He reached out and placed his hand over my heart.

Instantly I felt an explosion of warmth in my chest and that burning-hot sensation of tears just about to fall.

I averted my eyes and started picking at a hangnail at the side of my thumb to distract myself. "You wouldn't happen to know anyplace around here where I could get my nails done, would you? See?" I said, showing him my nails. "I need to get them filled in." I had been wearing acrylic nails on and off ever since I was thirteen and used to buy them with my babysitting money. My own nails were a wreck because I chewed them to the quick.

"Well, that problem is easily remedied." Seraphiel snapped his fingers again and a round, white bowl filled with a frothy, pale-pink liquid appeared in front of me. "Dip your fingers into the water."

I gave him a sly smile as I slipped my fingers into the bowl. The water was fragrant like honeysuckle, warm and slippery, and it made me instantly relax.

"What color would you like your fingernails to be?"

"Smoky lavender," I replied, trying to think of something exotic.

"OK, close your eyes."

I squeezed my eyes shut.

"Imagine that your nails are now a beautiful color of smoky lavender."

This was a fun little game, much better than talking about all the shit that happened to me.

"Now, open them."

I did, and as I removed my fingers from the bowl, I saw they were now perfectly filled in, and just the color I had imagined.

"Smoky lavender, Callie, is the color of amethyst," Seraphiel explained as he took a huge, pyramid-shaped rock from a shelf. It looked like it had been cut in half to reveal the inside. The outer core was a smooth, pale gray, but the hollow inside was filled with small, irregularly shaped and pointed purple crystals. Brilliant silver sparks burst from them when the sunlight hit them, like sparklers on the Fourth of July.

"Here." He placed the gigantic crystal in my hands. "Amethyst quiets and calms the mind. It has a very high spiritual vibration. Take it home with you and place it in your bedroom. It will help you. But now, let's get back to what we were talking about."

I put the pretty crystal down on the table with another sigh.

"What happened to you when you became a teenager?"

"Well," I remembered, thinking back. "I met Andy when I was thirteen at summer camp. He was sixteen, a camp counselor, and I was just a camper. He taught me horseback riding. He told me how much he liked me and would ask me to meet him in the woods during naptime or after lights-out at night. We would talk about just about anything. He gave me my first kiss. In the fall after camp was over, he started to show up at my house."

"How did your father feel about this?"

"Well, Papa didn't like him. He thought that I was much too young to be dating. He wouldn't let me go out with Andy. But one weekend when Papa was out of town on business, Mama let Andy take me downtown. We went to a really nice restaurant and on a carriage ride in the park. It was a beautiful night. The moon was full and the stars were just sparkling in the sky. He kissed me and told me that he loved me. But somehow Papa found out about it and he was really mad. He told me that I couldn't see Andy ever again. Andy broke up with me because he was afraid of my father."

"How did this make you feel?"

Damn, I just hated therapists. They were always asking me how I felt; it was so boring. Couldn't they think of anything more interesting to say? But I concluded that the sooner I talked, the faster I would get out of there.

"Like my heart had been shattered in a million pieces," I said. Seraphiel handed me a handkerchief, and I twisted it around and around in my hands. "I guess I cried myself to sleep for weeks after that."

"People are often placed in our life path to show us the places in our heart that we have yet to heal. How did you feel about your father?"

"I guess I was angry. I started hanging out with some older kids at school and stealing Papa's cigarettes and smoking them. I broke into the liquor cabinet and drank

Papa's good wine, and sneaked out of the house late at night to be with my friends."

"You started acting out."

"Yeah. At first it was all rebellion, but then I found out that the alcohol made me feel better. It took the edge off the things that were bothering me. Oh!" I exclaimed, trying to steer him off course and get him to talk about anything but my wrenched feelings. "I have to tell you this!"

I sat up in my chair and gave him a conspiratorial wink. "One time, we actually stole Mama's truck. It was her prize blue Chevy Silverado pickup truck. A famous country music star owned it before Mama bought it. We sneaked it down the driveway late one night without turning on the ignition. Then we went cruising down Main Street around two in the morning.

"We were going about ninety when we got stopped by the police for speeding and a curfew violation. The cop asked Ashley as he sauntered up to the driver's window, 'Do you know, young lady, that you were going about forty miles an hour over the speed limit?'

"They called Mama and I could hear her arguing with Papa over the phone. He wanted to let me spend the night in jail. 'It'll teach her a lesson' he said. Mama came and fetched me from the police station. She was really mad, but I insisted that we were just going to Blockbuster to pick up some old movies to watch on TV. 'Yeah, right' was all she said as she dragged my ass to the car." I started laughing then and looked at Seraphiel, but he wasn't laughing at all.

"It sounds like you were in a lot of pain," he said, refocusing the conversation. "Did you feel like you were sliding into a black hole?"

"I guess so."

"Why was your life so painful?"

"I hope you don't mind my saying this." I was really getting fed up with all the talk about my feelings. "But this is really a waste of time. Talking about how I feel isn't going to change anything."

Seraphiel pondered my response for a moment. "That's true," he said, surprising me. "It isn't going to change anything. But this is a journey of self-discovery. You have to acknowledge your pain before you can free yourself from it."

"Oh."

"So, tell me. What was the source of your pain?"

I surprised myself by knowing the answer to this right away. "I felt like I was living a lie. I mean, everyone said how *together* I looked. I always had makeup on, my hair just so, and I was really into fashion. But it was just a sham. Deep down, I didn't like myself much, and I was sad a lot of the time because of that. But every day I would drag myself out of bed, put on my happy face, and try to suck it up and deal with another day."

"Beauty doesn't lie in how the human body manifests itself. It lies in the fullness of your being, in your compassion, and in your ability to overcome the challenges that life on earth presents to you. So, you didn't feel that anyone would love you for who you truly were?"

"No, I didn't—that is, until I met Rusty."

"You felt that Rusty would fill the hole in your heart that only your connection to source can fill. Tell me about Rusty."

"I think Rusty was the love of my life, short as it was. I thought he was my angel coming to rescue me from my darkness and despair. We would spend hours on the phone, just talking. We wanted to get married. We would live in my bedroom. Rusty would help Mama with the pasture, the horses, and the dogs. I would get pregnant and have a baby."

"Those are big plans, indeed. So, what happened?"

"Well, we fought a lot of the time, too. All the girls liked Rusty. He was really cute and someone was always trying to steal him away from me. One night, I was riding with Rusty in his truck and we were arguing over some girl, and Rusty crashed the truck just a couple of blocks from my house. He managed to call Mama on his cell phone, and she just flew to the scene of the accident. I can still see her frightened face peering into the truck window as the firefighters cut me out. Rusty and I were both bruised and cut up, but otherwise all right. But things only got worse after that."

"When you view the world from lack of love, rather than from the wholeness that you are, you will keep being presented with challenges like this until you finally realize the truth. How did your life get worse?"

"It was Rusty who got me into drugs, I guess. First we just smoked dope, but then he introduced me to cocaine. I loved the way coke made me feel."

"There are many forms of escape that you humans try to distract yourself with." Seraphiel stood up and started pacing the floor in front of me, gesticulating emphatically. "Drugs, ambition, money, sex, beauty, even exercise and health of the physical manifestation. Tell me about your escape."

"Well, it sounds terrible when you talk like that, but I felt so happy and alive. Cocaine made me feel like everything was gonna be all right. But the coming down was hard. Life was so beautiful when I was high on cocaine.

But when I came down, it just turned into darker shades of gray. Pretty soon I tried X. It was even better than cocaine, but the coming down sucked. I felt like I was taking a freight train straight to hell."

He stopped right in front of me, locking eyes with me. "So, in reality, the drugs *didn't* help you in your journey of self-discovery."

"No, they just made everything worse. Rusty finally met a girl he couldn't resist and broke up with me. Then the darkness swallowed me. The only times I felt good were when I was high; the rest of the time I was barely hanging on. I guess it was then that I began to think seriously about suicide."

"What was the appeal of ending your life on the earth plane?"

"I guess I felt like it would be the ultimate escape. All my problems would instantly disappear."

"But your problems haven't really gone away. You've just removed yourself from your human body. These feelings remain inside of you, and they will follow you into your next physical manifestation unless you release them." He sat back down and immobilized me with his penetrating gaze.

I sighed heavily. He was right; I just hated it that he was right.

"So, tell me, what happened next?"

"Well, Mama bought me a cobalt-blue Mustang for my sixteenth birthday. I think she did it to help cheer me up. I loved that car, and it made me feel better for a while. It was such a feeling of freedom." I closed my eyes for a moment and leaned back in my chair, remembering.

"I would get into that car, pop in a CD, turn up the volume on the stereo as high as it would go, and just fly down the road. Everyone knew my car. 'There's Callie,' they would say. 'Her car is so awesome.' And the boys would say, 'There's Callie. She is just so tight.'" I sat up, opened my eyes, picked up the amethyst crystal, and stared at the sparkling purple center, sighing again.

"But then, one of my so-called friends drove my Mustang into a tree and totaled it when he was high on X. Mama was just furious. She refused to buy me another car and wouldn't let me drive. 'Take the bus to school,' she told me, 'or get one of your friends to take you.' She just didn't understand. Nobody in their right mind would be caught dead on the school bus.

"I ended up in juvenile court for underage drinking. The judge took my driver's license away. He looked me straight in the eye and said, 'This is the first time you have appeared in my courtroom, young lady, and I don't like the look in your eyes. Too many young kids your age have died in this county. I don't want you to be next. I'm taking away your driver's license for a year, and I'm ordering weekly drug screens.'"

Seraphiel leaned back in his chair. "Your judge was very perceptive. Cars are another form of escape as well." He picked up a pencil and stated tapping it on the yellow legal pad he had in his lap. He hadn't written anything down. He probably knew everything I was going to say before I said it anyway. "How did you feel about having your license taken away?"

"I was walking around all the time with this red-hot ball of rage eating away at the insides of my stomach." I shuddered. "But I also felt like things were starting to close in on me. I mean, my car was gone. I couldn't drive, and if I did any drugs, I knew I might end up in juvenile detention. Poor Mama was at the end of her rope. But

I couldn't tell her how depressed I felt because I didn't want to cause her any more trouble, and I certainly didn't want Mama to send me away to some stupid camp for troubled teenagers."

"Trust is an issue that many struggle with on the earth plane. You didn't talk to anyone about how you were feeling?"

"Well, Mama sent me to see her psychologist, and she asked me about my depression. But I lied and said that I really wasn't all that depressed. I didn't want her to lock me up in some nuthouse. I talked about how I was thinking of becoming a marine biologist, because I loved dolphins, or a psychiatrist, because I liked to help my friends with all their problems. In the end, I think I convinced her that there was nothing much wrong with me. I sure could put on a good show. I told her I wanted to stop smoking. 'It's a nasty habit,' I said. 'It makes my clothes smell bad and makes me cough. Mama is worried that I might get lung cancer.'"

"What advice did the psychologist give you?"

"Well, she told me she would get me some great medicine that would help me stop smoking and would also help me feel better, if I got a little down in the dumps occasionally. I admit, that sounded great to me. In the car on the way home, I told Mama that I really didn't like talking to that psychologist all that much. But I didn't tell Mama I was afraid that, if I kept on seeing her, she might find out some of my secrets."

"So, you were afraid of that which you most needed. It sounds like you didn't trust anyone very much. How did you feel about taking an antidepressant?"

"Well, the day Mama gave it to me, I felt like she had given me the key to my salvation. You know, I was a lot smarter than everyone thought. I read the instructions for taking the antidepressant. I read that it could cause seizures and heart problems if it wasn't taken correctly. I thought maybe it could even kill me. I said to myself, if things get too bad, I'll just overdose myself on these pretty little pills."

Those red-hot tears were brimming over my eyelids now and rolling down my cheeks, making a mess of my makeup and staining my pretty satin blouse, but I didn't care.

"Tell me about the weeks leading up to the day you left your human body."

"Well, I went out with a few guys, but they always dumped me after a couple of dates. I didn't trust them and I wasn't happy. I was always expecting them to break up with me, and so I guess they did. I went with Mama for a week to the beach. I said it was to get a nice suntan for prom. But that wasn't the real reason. I had already decided to kill myself; I just hadn't decided when. I thought this would give her a nice last vacation with me, something to remember me by. I went to prom because I wanted all of the boys to have one last dance with me. I didn't tell anyone about my plans, not even my very best girlfriends. I didn't want anyone to try to stop me."

"How were you feeling during this time?"

"Well, I felt like I was just . . . done with this life," I blurted between hiccupping sobs. "I mean, nothing had turned out the way I'd planned. I had lost all hope. I knew that I was hanging out with the wrong kids, still getting into trouble, still doing drugs, hoping no one would catch me on my next drug screen. I knew it was wrong, but I couldn't stop myself. I lied to myself. I lied to everyone. My life was a charade, and I was disgusted with myself. I started to think that everyone would be better off without me."

I stopped talking for a moment to blow my nose noisily into the handkerchief. Seraphiel handed me another one.

"Tell me about the day that your human body died."

Everything started tumbling out in a flood. "I didn't plan to kill myself that day. I left school after I burned my finger in cooking class. I did my usual thing. I decided to go to a party down by the lake and get drunk. I vaguely remember Megan bringing me home around dinnertime. I fell asleep and woke up a little after midnight, stone cold sober. I was totally and completely fed up and disgusted with myself, and with life. I just wasn't gonna do this anymore. And I was so tired. I just wanted to go to sleep and never wake up. I listened to a few CDs while I sat on my bedroom floor. I decided that tonight was as good a time as any to die. I was a little scared, but I was almost beyond caring if I lived or died. I wrote a note to Mama and hid it in my jewelry chest. I didn't want anyone else to find it, but I knew Mama would. She was always tearing my room apart looking for alcohol or drugs. I had no privacy. In case it worked, I wanted my mama to know what happened to me. Ruffy was in my bedroom. For some stupid reason, I didn't want Ruffy to see me take the pills. I didn't want Ruffy to see me die, if I was actually going to die."

"So, what did you do with Ruffy?"

"I locked her in my bedroom closet. I put all my pills in a shot glass. I thought that this was very fitting. I swallowed them all down as fast as I could with bottled water. Then I lay back, waiting to see what would happen."

"And what happened next?"

"After a while I had to pee. I made it to the bath-room, but on the way back to my bed, I got very dizzy, fell, and hit my head on the glass table at the end of my bed. I grasped my bureau to pull myself up to look at my head in the mirror to see if it was bleeding. Then I fell again. I saw this darkness, like a black wave, coming toward me, and then I was just gone."

I clutched my stomach, rocking back and forth, racked with sobs by now. My breath was coming out in ragged gasps. Seraphiel waited for me to calm down a lit-tle bit and then handed me a glass of water.

"Drink this," he said. "It will make you feel better." His knit his brows thoughtfully before he continued. "I think this is probably enough for today. You've done very well, Callie, actually much better than I expected. You should be very proud of yourself—I know this isn't easy to talk about. But I need you to remember that you must acknowledge your pain so that it will die in this rebirth. This may be a little difficult for you to understand, but humans often think there is a past, a present, and a future. In reality there is no such thing as time, there is only right now. And as you discovered, perhaps the hard way, what you choose to do with your right now is everything."

He led me outside to a grassy knoll by the rose garden. With a snap of his fingers a fluffy, white cloud appeared before me.

"You'll start to feel sleepy soon. Why don't you lie down on this little cloud?"

I gave him a quizzical look as I gingerly lowered myself onto the cloud, but much to my surprise, it was fairly solid and I sank into it as if it were a featherbed. Closing my eyes, I let the scent of roses on the gentle breeze slowly lure me into sleep.

⇌ 6 ⇋

Callie—She's Not Gone

"**Y**ou all don't know how difficult it is to get a message back to earth," I grumbled to Seraphiel the next day. "Everyone is just so damn clueless. They can't see me, hear me, or sense my presence standing right there next to them!"

My communication problems with Mama annoyed me the most. Somehow, my energy got into the perfume bottle Mama was holding in her hand the night after I died, and I made the plunger go down. I didn't know I could do that. It was just an accident. I guess that's what Mama gets for hating my perfume. Next, I planted a special seashell in my bedroom, knowing that Mama would find it.

But mostly I tried to contact Mama through music. We loved the same music, believe it or not. Mama was an old-school person, and I was always introducing her to new artists. "Mama," I would say as she drove me to school, "I got this new CD, and I want you to listen to this song." Then I would pop in a CD by Brandy, TLC, Destiny's Child, or Usher, and Mama would love it. She even started stealing some of my CDs to listen to in her car on the way to work. Whenever one of my favorite

CDs was missing, I knew just where to find it. Of course, I took Mama's jewelry and makeup without asking. So the score was really even.

Anyway, I got the idea that I would let Mama know I was with my dog Boo by whispering in some poor DJ's ear, "Play Nelly and Kelly; play 'Dilemma.'" I loved that line in the song about being with my boo but still being crazy over you. But Mama never really got it; she just couldn't understand why she kept hearing that song over and over again. I tried the same thing with "I Can Only Imagine," the song they played at my funeral, but it was just hopeless.

I tried making my CDs disappear and reappear. One day, Mama would be listening to one of them—I think they helped her feel close to me. The next day, it would be gone. Mama would tear the house apart looking for it. But then it would turn up a few days later, just where she'd left it. It drove her crazy, I could tell, but she never thought it was my spirit moving things around. She thought she was losing her marbles from all the sorrow and the stress. I would even make her radio turn on and off by itself. It didn't work; Mama just thought the radio had a short circuit. I was beginning to think it was truly hopeless.

The first time I entered Mama's dreams, of course, she tried to explain me away by telling me that I was dead. I tried to show her just how alive I really was by flying around the room as a big, sparkling, silver ball, but Mama still didn't understand. She just thought that I was a figment of her overwrought imagination.

"Why not enter one of your mama's and one of Rusty's dreams on the same night?" Seraphiel suggested. I'd been watching Rusty and once or twice stepped into his dreams, but he felt so guilty for getting me into drugs, he really didn't want to see me.

The second time I decided to enter one of Mama's dreams was the night before she was going to take Anthony to summer camp. In the dream, Mama was stopped in her little maroon sports car at a red light at the corner of Greenville and Old Summer Island Road near our house in Cassville on a sunny spring afternoon. She glanced over to the passenger side of the car, and there I was sitting next to her, looking out the window. I was wearing sunglasses, black jeans, a white V-neck shirt, and my long, white sweater with the furry-trimmed collar so she would be sure to recognize me.

"Rusty and I watched *Moonwalker* last night."

"That's nice," Mama said absentmindedly. Then she suddenly remembered that I was supposed to be dead. "Oh, my God, Callie, you're here! You're not dead?"

I turned my head, slowly looking at Mama and shaking my head no.

Mama's hands started to shake as she grasped the steering wheel. Her eyes became so wide I thought they would pop right out of her head. She leaned over and squeezed my leg through my jeans as if she were afraid that I would just disappear, but I was very solid, and I could tell Mama felt that I was really with her.

I smiled, then laughed and said, "Mama, you had better concentrate on your driving."

She turned her head back to the road and said, "Oh, sweetie, is it really beautiful there?"

I nodded. "Yes."

"I'm so happy for you!" she said, smiling, tears in her eyes.

When I disappeared, Mama woke up.

DIANE

I jumped up out of bed and threw off the covers, searching for my slippers in the dark. This was no accident, no strange dream. Callie must really be trying to communicate with me from beyond the grave. It was four a.m., and I had awoken abruptly to the distant sound of thunder. Flashes of lightning flickered just outside my window. My daughter had always loved a big thunderstorm.

I rushed downstairs to my office, fumbled for the light switch, and sat down at my computer. *Come on, Diane, this is no figment of your tortured imaginings; this is real. Write down everything exactly as you remember it, so you will never forget.* The thunder grew louder, rumbling over the roof above me as I typed the words as fast as my hands could fly across the keyboard. I had no sooner finished, saved what I had written, and turned off my computer than I heard a loud clap of thunder coming from directly overhead as if for emphasis. Then the lights went out.

I sat there for a long time, listening to the thunder and the rain slamming against the windowpanes. As the thunder receded, the lights flickered back on, and I wearily made my way back to bed, emotionally spent.

The next morning was very busy as we loaded Anthony's gear into the truck and then headed down the highway toward a campground several hours south of town. It had been a hard decision to send Anthony to camp that summer, but he insisted that he wanted to go. I thought that being at the camp he had attended since he was seven years old might help restore some sense of normalcy to his shattered life.

Anthony was such a quiet and introspective child. He was content to spend time in his room assembling intricate dragons with Lego blocks, or banished down in the basement banging away on his drum set, about the only time he really made a racket, or embellishing my recipes to concoct strange desserts that were occasionally edible. Dwayne and I felt that at camp he would benefit from socializing with other boys his age. He stayed in a ramshackle cabin in the woods with about a dozen other campers and a counselor. He earned some money for camp fees by clearing tables after meals, and when one of the cooks discovered his blossoming culinary talents, he was occasionally allowed to help out in the kitchen. He wrote us the most exasperating yet endearing letters, and I saved them all.

Dear Mom and Dad,

How are you doing? Camp is OK; it's fun so far and there are two people I know in my cabin. Where's my care package? You forgot some stuff in your last package. Please put it in.

Love, Anthony

He hadn't talked to me about Callie's death since the funeral. He kept to his room and was quiet and withdrawn at dinner. I couldn't seem to reach him. He was so distant that I started to worry that I would lose another child. When I mentioned camp to him, he seemed to perk up a bit. The youth pastor at our church had called me a few days after the funeral. I was in such a distraught state of mind that I couldn't remember much of the conversation, but his gentle reminder about Anthony sunk in.

"I know you're grieving over Callie," he said softly, "but Anthony is still here and he's grieving, too. He's going to need your love and attention now, more than ever. Don't let your sorrow consume you so much that you shut him out too, because if you do he will lose both a sister and a mother."

I'd had a friend in college whose brother had drowned in a boating accident when they were both in their early teens. The brother was the family's superstar and his parents never recovered from their loss. My friend suffered from anorexia and was constantly trying to excel at everything he did, but he felt that no matter how hard he tried, he would never measure up to his brother's idealized accomplishments. He felt that his parents were constantly disappointed in him. He was always walking in his dead brother's shadow. Sometimes, he told me, he wished he had died instead of his brother. I wasn't going to let this happen to Anthony.

A few days before camp began, I found him sitting on the floor in his bedroom with most of his clothes scattered around him in disorganized heaps or overflowing from his laundry hamper. His open bureau drawers were completely empty.

"What are you doing?"

"None of my clothes fit me anymore and I have nothing to wear to camp." He threw a pair of smelly, dilapidated sneakers into a pile of old shoes that he had dragged out of his closet.

"Oh, it can't be as bad as all that." I sat down next to him racked with guilt. I couldn't remember the last time I had taken him shopping. Callie had been a clotheshorse and we frequently went to the mall together.

"Are all these clothes dirty?" I asked as I pointed toward the hamper.

"Of course they're dirty. Why would they be in the hamper if they weren't dirty?" he replied sullenly, scowling at me.

I ignored his rudeness. He was supposed to be washing his own clothes and putting them back where they belonged every week.

"OK. Why don't you sort them and put the darker-colored clothes in the washer first?" I suggested. He got up, emptied the contents of his laundry basket onto the floor and stood there eyeing the pile balefully. "Here, I'll help you."

After we started his laundry, I proposed, "Let's sort the rest of your stuff into three piles. The first will be for the clothes that you can still wear to camp, the second for clothes you've outgrown that we can donate to Goodwill, and the third for rags or to throw in the garbage. Anything you're not sure about, you can try on."

These instructions seemed to get him moving, and it wasn't long before our task was accomplished. I stood there examining the small pile of usable clothing and the one pair of navy blue sneakers that still fit him. "Now let's go shopping."

We got into the car and headed to the mall. As we shopped, Anthony became more animated, and I realized how little time I had actually spent with him doing something he enjoyed since Callie's death.

He sat next to me happily examining his new deck of Magic of the Gathering cards, drinking a soda, and playing with the radio dial on the way home. He liked classic rock, and it wasn't long before he located one of his favorite Beach Boys songs. He turned up the volume, rolled down the car windows, lay back, and closed his eyes with a contented sigh.

"I had fun today, Mama."

"Yes, I did too."

That evening I sat down on his bed next to his neatly packed trunk of camp clothes. "I'm sorry I've been so preoccupied and upset. I should have taken you shopping a long time ago."

"That's OK, Mama."

"You know, just because I feel sad about Callie sometimes doesn't mean I love you any less."

"I know."

"Callie's gone to heaven, but you're right here. You're the most important person in my life right now and I love you very much."

"I know that too, Mama."

"Do you think you'll be OK at camp?"

"Don't worry, Mama, I'll be fine. I'm the opposite of Callie."

He smiled and closed his eyes as I tiptoed out of the room.

Tom stopped me in the hall as I gently closed Anthony's door. "Are both of you ready for camp?" he asked with a smile.

"We are now."

Tom and I stopped for pancakes on the way home from camp. Sitting across from him at the restaurant, I decided to tell him about my dream. I watched his face cloud over with a mixture of skepticism and concern as I related my story. Finally, he reached for my hand across the table. "I know it felt real, honey. But it's not Callie, Diane. It's just your brain trying to make sense of what's happened to you. She's gone; no dream is going to bring her back."

Tom was such a warm and caring man, but on rare occasions his logical and analytical mind made me want to shake him. Why couldn't he allow himself to be open to alternate realities or magical possibilities that science might not be able to explain?

I shook my head impatiently. "I wish there was some independent, corroborating evidence that I could show you. I've read about people who've just died coming to their relatives in a dream to let them know they've passed on before anyone knew they were dead. And I never mentioned this before, but I had the most awful dream the night Callie died. I think it was a premonition."

Tom sighed. "Look, Diane. I know you really want that to be true. But it's OK, you know, if it's just you, dreaming about your daughter. Sometimes that's all it is. Sometimes it's just wishful thinking."

I was silent on the way home, but as we turned into the driveway, I saw Rusty's white pickup parked by the garage. I hadn't seen Rusty since the funeral. As he moved to get out of the truck, I could see that he'd been crying.

"Rusty, hey . . ." I began, alarmed. He fell into my arms. "I saw Callie last night."

I patted his back, a little stunned. Could it be a coincidence? "Yes," I said carefully. "She came to me in a dream as well. Last night, actually. She, uh . . ." I paused, wondering if Rusty would think I was crazy. "She told me you watched *Moonwalker* together."

He nodded; he didn't seem surprised. "Yeah, I almost fell asleep on the couch while I was watching it on TV late last night. Katie, in the movie, became Callie. Then she walked right out of the TV set and sat down next to me. She told me that she was OK, then she vanished."

"She said the same thing to me."

"Would it be OK if I went into her room for a while?"

"Yes, sure." I waved him in. He sat on the floor in her walk-in closet where all her clothes still hung from hangers and her scent still lingered in the air. I backed out of the room and gently closed the door. After about a half hour, he came back into the hall and started for the front door.

"Hey, Rusty, wait a sec." I ran back into Callie's bedroom and pulled her favorite stuffed animal from her bed. Clutching the little brown dog, I came back into the hall. "Here, take this. Callie would want you to have it."

Rusty gratefully took the dog and raced down the steps and into his truck. I stood there on the porch and watched him drive away. Maybe Callie's little dog would give him some of the same comfort that Ruffy had given me. Was it just a short month since I had taken Rusty and Callie to lunch together after school? They had already broken off their relationship, but decided to remain friends. It seemed like a lifetime ago.

That night I lay in bed thinking about my encounter with Rusty. Was this the proof of life after death that I had been searching for? Could Callie have found us both on the same night, appearing to each of us in a dream and telling us essentially the same thing? Believing that made sleep come more easily. *Maybe there is more to all of this than meets the eye*, I thought as I drifted away. Maybe all of it would make more sense in the light of morning.

⁊ 7 ⁊

Diane—Refuge

After my dream encounter with Callie, I started doing some pretty strange things. I would leave my word processor open on my computer at night, hoping I would find a few words from her on the screen in the morning. I turned my radio dial between stations when I worked in my office because I'd read somewhere that spirits could talk to you through the white noise on the radio. On the night of a full moon, I would sit by the side of the pool waiting for her face to materialize in the water. Tom found me late one night and hauled me back inside, wrapping a warm blanket around me.

"You're going to catch your death of a cold," he scolded gently. I knew he was worried about me.

Several weeks later, after endless internal debates about whether I was really losing my mind this time, I was sitting at the kitchen table, still in my pajamas, when I abruptly decided to contact a medium. Callie wasn't dead, I reasoned as I fortified myself with a third cup of coffee. She was out there somewhere; I just had to find her. I jumped up and grabbed the yellow pages. Now what was the name of Ruth's New Age bookstore? Oh, yes, I remembered: The Sacred Bridge. I quickly dressed, searched impatiently for my purse and car keys, and hurried out the door.

The Sacred Bridge was located in a cluster of stores that looked just like the Victorian houses I used to admire in San Francisco, with steep pitched roofs, slanted bay windows, and small canopies over their entrances. Painted in various shades of tan, green, dark orange, and red, many had second-story balconies that overlooked the street below.

Right beside the entrance of the store was a large golden statue of Hecate, the Greek goddess of the three realms, the earth, sea, and sky. Her shoulder-length hair was pulled back by an ornate headband, and she had an expression of fierce determination on her face. Her bare breasts were draped with a shawl, and she wore a knee-length skirt girded with a heavy chain belt with anchors at both ends. In one hand, she was holding a lit torch with a serpent encircling it, and in the other she had a large knife. Two hounds pressed against her hunting boots. She was standing at a crossroads marked by a human skull. I warily climbed the steps to the front porch, wondering what I was getting myself into.

The bells of the shop door jangled loudly as I stepped inside. Ruth was standing behind the counter, bent over a pile of invoices. She straightened too quickly upon recognizing me.

"Diane," she said, recovering herself and giving me a warm smile. "What brings you in this morning?"

"Oh, I . . . you know," I said my courage flagging. "I just figured . . . I've never been in here before. Thought I'd have a look around."

"Sure. Let me know if you need anything." She smiled again and turned back to her invoices.

Gingerly I made my way to the front room on the left side of the store, past a steep winding staircase that, according to a sign on the wall, led up to second- and third-floor rooms used for psychic and Tarot card readings, Reiki, and massage therapy. Wind chimes hung in the front windows, and a rack of clothing next to the far wall contained velvet hooded capes, Battenberg lace, batik and paisley dresses, long tiered and paneled skirts, and crushed-velvet tops. I thumbed through the clothing, wondering when I would work up the courage to actually talk to Ruth. Two greyhounds, one pure black and the other white, appeared as if from nowhere and began nuzzling my legs. I reached down to let them sniff my hand and then carefully patted them on their heads. Incense permeated the air; I could hear the faint sound of Indian drum and flute music coming from a speaker on the wall and water cascading from a two-tiered fountain with a mermaid on top in a walled garden behind the store. Swallowing my anxiety, I strode back to the counter, my gaze fixed on Ruth.

She seemed almost expectant, as though she could read my mind. As though she already knew what I was going to ask.

"So . . . Ruth . . . I was wondering . . . do you know of any spiritual healers in town who could help me or any mediums who might be able to contact Callie?" I managed.

She didn't seem at all shocked by my question. "Sure. There's a woman named Joy. She's really good; I recommend her to everyone." She smiled. "I can give you her number."

"Yes, please." I let out a small sigh, relieved. "That would be great."

Joy lived in a tan, one-story bungalow down a winding, tree-lined gravel road just outside of town. Her front yard was scattered with angel statues, gazing globes, and wind chimes among patches of flowers that bloomed happily in the June sunshine. I stepped up to the porch and knocked hesitantly on the front door, and a moment later a tall, middle-aged woman answered, a warm smile on her face. She was wearing a long blue-and-gold dress with monarch butterflies scattered across the fabric, her long, straight black hair secured at the back of her neck by a turquoise barrette.

She escorted me to a back room lined with tall shelves filled with milky-white and cream-colored moonstones, long, pointy clusters of rose quartz, and other crystals of all description. Another wall was filled with small brown bottles of flower essences: rosemary for vitality (Joy explained), lavender for stress, Saint-John's-wort for depression, and bleeding heart to soothe a loss. Across the room, a fish tank was filled with guppies and zebra fish. Some exotic perfume, tuberose with a hint of spice and fresh citrus, permeated the air. A portrait of an angel with long, flowing white hair, huge wings that looked like peacock feathers, and piercing blue eyes riveted my attention as I walked into the room. Just outside a large picture window was a butterfly garden filled with lantana, purple phlox, and red cardinal flowers.

Motioning to a small table with two comfortably cushioned chairs next to the window, Joy said, "Diane, I'm glad you've come. Please, sit."

I dropped my purse to the floor and nervously folded my hands in my lap.

"So, tell me why you're here today," she urged.

I explained in halting words the reason for my visit, after which Joy closed her eyes a long moment.

"Callie is in the spirit hospital," she began. "Souls go there when their crossing has been traumatic, or after a long and difficult illness. There they rest and are tended by the angels. My nephew went to the healing chamber for quite a few months, in earth time, after he was killed in a motorcycle accident ten years ago. Callie will contact you when she's ready. You may start hearing her voice in your head, or you may hear a song on the radio that she loved, or she may move things around in her room."

"I've been hearing this song that we played at her funeral, 'I Can Only Imagine,' over and over again on the radio every time I turn it on."

"Yes, that's what I mean. Did Callie call you Mama?"

"Yes, she usually did, unless she was mad at me. Then she called me Mother."

Joy chuckled. "I'm hearing a voice saying, 'Tell Mama I love her.'"

I was silent for a moment, trying to keep the tears from starting to flow. Finally, I asked, "More than anything, I need to know why this happened. Why did Callie take her life? She had everything going for her. She was beautiful, she was smart, she was creative, she wrote beautiful poetry, she had tons of friends, she was the life of the party, and she had her whole life in front of her."

"Callie was meant to die young. Did you notice how active she was and how she tried to cram as many experiences as possible, both good and bad, into her life? On some level, she knew that her time here was short."

"I can see that. She was diagnosed with ADD as a child. We never put her on any medication. She wasn't disruptive, but she certainly was into everything. She was a handful even as a young child."

"You and Callie contracted for this experience before you both came over to this side," Joy continued. "You knew that you were the stronger one. So, you chose to remain behind, and Callie chose to be the one to pass over."

"Why would I ever choose something like that?" I asked, not comprehending.

"That's for you to find out. Only you will be able to find the gifts in this experience. But I can tell you, remaining locked in grief will prevent you from hearing Callie clearly. The heaviness of your pain only makes it more difficult for Callie to contact you."

After a moment of silence, Joy asked, "Would you like a healing?"

"Yes," I told her. I certainly needed healing, but I hadn't been sure where to go. I had seen a number of psychologists in my teenage years, but none had been very helpful at the time, probably because I was so emotionally closed down. I didn't like to explore my feelings. And it seemed that just talking about my problems never made them go away, and taking antidepressants seemed even less helpful. No amount of talking, crying, screaming, pounding pillows, or taking drugs would make this pain go away. It was so vast, it consumed my whole universe, but, perhaps, I could try this.

"You'll lie down. I'll count back from ten to one to put you into a state of deep relaxation. Then I'll ask you questions that will make no sense to your logical mind. You'll answer with colors or letters. Pick the first one that comes into your mind. In this way, we will bypass your ego, your conscious self, and go to the heart of the issue that's concerning you."

I lay down and was able to relax for the first time in weeks as Joy began. "Travel in your mind to a beautiful meadow filled with wildflowers swaying gently on a soft breeze. Butterflies that are all the colors of the rainbow alight on the flowers and drink their sweet nectar. You lie down on the soft green grass and gaze up at a cloudless sky, and a large blue morpho butterfly alights on your chest over your heart. The butterfly tells you that it will take you on a healing journey to a place where you will change all the false beliefs that no longer serve you for your awakened truths."

Joy then counted down from ten to one. I could feel my body becoming heavier, and the constant chattering inside my head abruptly stopped. She asked me to choose a series of letters and colors to answer the questions that she asked.

She started by saying, "When you think of the core issue or belief that you wish to release, its color is? And its number is? The color of the emotion you feel when you think about this belief is, and its number is? Let go of this emotion and place it in a box; the color of the next emotion that you feel is?"

And so it went on. I could feel myself drifting somewhere between wakefulness and sleep, and sometimes she would call my name quietly to rouse me from my dreamlike trance. Finally, she placed earphones on my head and started playing a CD of dolphins dancing in the ocean. I heard the rush of waves breaking on the shoreline and the high-pitched whistling of the dolphins. I saw myself walking alone at midnight along the beach, feeling the cool waves break slowly over my bare feet. A dolphin swimming near the shoreline whistled to me softly as if he were asking me to ride the ocean waves with him. I waded out to him and climbed on his smooth, soft, rubbery gray back. We flew across the ocean waves. I stretched out my arms to touch the full moon, and in that magical moment, I was set free.

I could faintly hear Joy's voice talking in the background. The music gently faded away and Joy removed my earphones. I sat up and rubbed my eyes. The whole room was shimmering, brighter. I stared in amazement at the crystals on the shelves; they seemed to be vibrating from an inner light. Gradually the brightness receded and the room started to look normal again. I shook my head, trying to clear it.

"Well, you chose the colors for emotional strength and understanding," Joy said. "They will bring you the gift of fortitude."

"What does that mean?"

"The butterflies are telling you that you are whole, complete within yourself. They will help you see your world and your experiences through your own centered space rather than through the trauma and drama that you are creating now."

"But how can I do that?"

"You will eventually understand that all you experience is really your own creation. You will learn to face each challenge that you encounter in life with joy, for you are your own strength, and each trial will bring forth that gift."

Joy gave me a slip of paper with an affirmation written on it.

I am capable of being and doing all that I desire. I am my own strength. I am capable of taking care of myself and honoring all of my commitments. I am the answer to all of my dilemmas and I can do all that is required of me.

"Tape it to your mirror," she told me. "Say these words every morning upon waking and every night just before you fall sleep. Don't try to analyze this," she said, as if she could read my mind. "Just this once, let your heart be your guide."

I dreamed that night that it was Christmas Day. I hadn't put up any decorations or even a tree. I didn't want to do Christmas with Callie gone. Anthony came into my bedroom asking about presents. I'd managed to buy him a few video games but hadn't wrapped any of them yet. I told him I'd get his presents ready and bring them downstairs. Wearily I began searching the recesses of my bedroom closet for wrapping paper.

Suddenly, I heard the clatter of high heels on the hall steps. It was Callie. She was wearing her long white sweater with the rabbit-fur trim and was loaded down with bags of presents. Everything—bags, boxes, wrapping paper, ribbons, and bows—was silver, and there were little silver bells, jangling merrily, attached to all the bows. She was full of exuberance and joy. She darted into her bedroom, and I got only a glimpse of her before I abruptly awoke. I lay in the darkness of a midsummer night. *Maybe this coming Christmas won't be as awful as I thought it would be*, I mused as I drifted back to sleep.

The next morning, I opened the front door to find Megan, her finger poised on the doorbell.

"Hey, Mama," she smiled, but the expression on her face was far away. "I wanted to stop by this morning because the craziest thing happened last night."

"What, Meg? What is it?" I asked, concerned.

"Well, I saw Callie." She shifted her weight from one foot to the other, looking at me expectantly.

"What do you mean, you saw Callie?"

"This was not a dream," Megan insisted, "and I'm not making this up. I was driving late last night and I saw Callie, all of a sudden, sitting next to me in the car. She was kind of misty looking but I could tell it was her. She was looking through my CD case and saying to herself, 'Now, this is my CD,' like she didn't know I had gotten a bunch of her CDs. I stopped at a gas station and went inside. I was pretty freaked out. When I got back to the car, Callie was gone. I told Ashley about it but she doesn't believe me."

"Well, I do." But in reality, I didn't know what to make of this. After all, I had returned to school to work on my PhD. I was supposed to be a budding scholar and a scientist. My dissertation was a randomized controlled trial evaluating an intervention to help new mothers breastfeed more successfully. None of this fit into the world as I knew it. And now I was encountering things that were completely outside of my logical, and what I considered rational, view of the world. But as a scientist, I reasoned, wouldn't it behoove me to keep an open mind? These experiences were not like anything I had ever encountered before, but they felt so real.

Megan sat down on the front porch steps and fumbled around for her cigarettes and lighter in her purse. "Everyone thinks I'm going crazy."

"You're not crazy, Megan. Strange things have been happening to me, too." I sat down next to her and described my dreams as she pensively smoked her cigarette, watching the gray curls lazily disappear into the air as she exhaled.

"So do you think it was really Callie, Mama?"

"Yes, it's Callie. I think she wants us to know that she's OK, and maybe she's wondering what happened to some of her CDs. Here, Megan, let me walk you to your car." I got up and reached for her hand, pulling her to her feet. "You don't want to be late for summer school." She was trying to finish all her classes by the end of the fall so she could graduate in December. "I'm leaving in a few minutes to go to work. It's my first day back."

She dropped her lit cigarette to the pavement, ground it out with her heel, and climbed into the car. She was so much like Callie in every way.

"I hope you have a good day, Mama."

"Me too," I said as I watched her drive away.

My nurse manager had called me several times to see how I was doing and to find out when I might feel ready to return to work. The unit was perpetually understaffed, and it was difficult to find someone to replace a nurse who was out sick or on maternity leave or vacation. I really didn't know how I'd cope at work, but I couldn't afford to stay home any longer unless I obtained some sort of psychiatric disability compensation. But that diagnosis might follow me, I knew, making it impossible to find a job anywhere.

So, I put on my scrubs and duty shoes, climbed into the car, and made my way to the hospital. The staff parking lot was filling up rapidly as I drove in, and the elevator to my unit was jammed with visitors, nurses, residents, and medical students, carrying steaming cups of coffee and chattering all at once. A new father was toting a bouquet of pink and white carnations and a big brown teddy bear tucked under his arm. I made my way down long halls in the glare of fluorescent lights. Labor and delivery was busy as always, I noted as I passed by the nurses' station. Opening the door to the office I shared with several other staff members, I saw a huge bouquet of white lilies on my desk next to a sympathy card. I put my purse in a drawer and picked up the lab coat I'd hung so thoughtlessly on a hook beside the door a little more than two months earlier. There was an old grocery list in one of the pockets, along with a reminder to pick up some tampons for Callie. Remnants from another life.

When I reached my unit, I paused to steel myself for the ordeal. The night shift was just reporting off at the nurses' station. Breakfast carts were being wheeled down the hall, and a group of residents and medical students in their lab coats clustered around their attending physician outside a patient's room, talking quietly among themselves. When they looked up and saw me, everyone momentarily stopped what they were doing. The charge nurse immediately left her group and came up to embrace me.

"I'm so sorry about your daughter," she murmured, "but I'm glad to see you back at work. Are you going to be OK today?"

"I hope so; I think I'll be all right."

"I've given you an easy assignment. I'm going to have you make breastfeeding rounds in the NICU to see if any of the mothers need help."

"OK." I managed a smile.

"This is the first patient I want you to see." She handed me a referral form from the NICU. "The baby had a Norwood procedure a few weeks ago and isn't eating very well. The doctors are talking about inserting a gastrostomy tube."

I sat down at a computer next to the nurses' station to read the baby's chart. As I sat there, the staff started coming up to me, one by one, to hug me or touch me on the shoulder. All of them told me how sorry they were about Callie. And then they asked if there was anything they could do to help me get through the day.

After I finished, I made my way across the sky bridge that connected the main hospital to the NICU. Windows lined one side of the bridge, overlooking some of the other hospital buildings and the street below. I paused to collect myself; *I can do this,* I kept repeating. Then I made my way to the NICU.

The mother and baby were in the step-down unit in a private room. Bunny rabbit wallpaper lined the walls, little brown bunnies cavorting in the lush green grass next to a flower garden full of pansies. The scrawny little boy with tufts of light blonde hair lay in an Isolette in the back of the room. His eyes were scrunched tightly shut. Small prongs in his nose were attached to tubing that delivered extra oxygen from the wall. An intravenous line in his arm for extra fluids was connected to an arm board by several layers of gauze and tape. Small electrodes were attached to his chest, and a round band connected a pulse oximeter to his foot. Three lines scrolling across a monitor at the end of his Isolette documented his heart and respiratory rate and the oxygen saturation of his blood.

His mother stood anxiously by. One round window of the Isolette was open, and she'd inserted her hand into the opening so she could softly stroke his arm with her fingertips.

I reached out to touch her shoulder. "I'm Diane. I'm here to help you feed Jason. How is he doing today?"

"I think he's a little better. About a half hour ago, I saw him open his eyes and suck on his fist for a minute or two, but now he's gone back to sleep."

"Let's see if I can wake him up a little bit."

I carefully opened the door to the Isolette and started to massage the baby's legs. I gently sat him up and rubbed his back. The baby yawned and stretched out his thin little arms and legs as I picked him up to remove him from the Isolette. When he opened his eyes, he looked just like a wizened old man with a wrinkled forehead. An expression of acute anxiety crossed his face. "There, there," I murmured. "Everything's going to be all right."

I lifted him out of the Isolette and placed him in his mother's arms. He gazed at her as she stroked the sides of his little face with her fingers, and I could see his expression become more peaceful.

"Let's see if we can get him to nurse."

I helped her unbutton her blouse and undo her bra strap, then guided him gently into place next to her nipple. "See if you can express some milk and then gently stroke his lips with your nipple," I suggested.

As the mother did this, he started to lick, and then a light bulb seemed to go off in his little head. He latched on to her nipple and started to suck.

"Oh," she exclaimed, startled. "He's never done this before."

"I think he's getting the hang of it."

We silently watched him nurse on and off for several minutes before he fell asleep. His mother leaned back in her rocking chair and heaved a sigh of relief.

"He did very well," I stated, smiling. "Ask the nurses to call me if you need help with the next feeding." I slipped out of the room and brushed a few tears from my cheeks, glancing back. The mother had closed her eyes and was gently rocking the baby in her arms, her face now serene.

After that, the nurses in the NICU asked me to see patient after patient—mothers who were so stressed that their milk had almost dried up, sleepy premature babies who wouldn't wake up to eat. I saw a baby with Down's syndrome and a heart murmur, another with a cleft lip and palate. At the end of the day, I wearily made my way back to the office. I sat down at my desk and opened the sympathy card, and read all the little notes that the staff had written on it, and my heart broke all over again. But it was then that I realized that I was not the only mother who suffered. Some of those mothers I had seen in the NICU were in for a world of heartache too.

～

That summer seemed endless. Anthony spent most of it at camp, except for occasional weekends at home.

One afternoon in mid-July, he called me on the camp phone. "Is it all right if Brandy comes home with me this weekend?"

Campers weren't supposed to use the staff telephone, but because he helped out in the kitchen, he got special privileges.

"Yes, but who's Brandy?"

"She's one of my friends from camp."

"Well, I'll have to talk to her mother first."

Her mother, when I called, seemed quiet and preoccupied. Her speech was slightly slurred and she seemed to be more than happy to have me take Brandy for the weekend. I sure wouldn't have been very comfortable letting Callie spend the night at a stranger's house, I mused as I made my way down the familiar road toward camp.

As soon as I stopped the car in the parking lot, Anthony came trudging toward me carrying two laundry bags full of clothes across his back. Behind him was a breathtakingly beautiful girl of about sixteen in a lime-green smocked sundress. She had long auburn hair that hung in little ringlets almost to her waist, porcelain skin liberally sprinkled with small freckles, and large aquamarine eyes.

"Mama, this is Brandy," Anthony stated as he shoved the clothes bags into the trunk of the car. She solemnly held out her hand to me, and I shook it gently. Then they clambered into the back seat.

"Thank you for letting me come to your house this weekend," she said softly as Anthony reached forward to fiddle with the car radio dial until he found his favorite station.

Still recovering from my surprise, I replied, "You're very welcome, but I hope your mama won't miss you too much."

In the rearview mirror, I saw Anthony and Brandy exchange glances. "Brandy's brother died in a skiing accident a few years ago," Anthony explained. "That's how we became friends."

"She probably won't notice that I didn't come home," Brandy stated bitterly. "I think she sends me to camp to get rid of me."

"Oh, I'm sorry about your brother." I really didn't know what to say. "Well, you can come to our house with Anthony anytime."

"Thanks, that means a lot to me. I hate going home. It's like walking into a museum. All my brother's photos and football trophies are still on the mantel above the fireplace, and his room is exactly the way he left it on the day he died. My mother gets angry if I go in there. I can't wait until I can get away and go to college."

"I've told her a lot about Callie," Anthony interjected. "She's the only person who understands."

"Well, I'm glad that you're friends," I said, smiling. Maybe they could help each other.

When we got home, Anthony hauled their bags of clothes to the laundry room and deposited them on the floor. "Here, I'll start your laundry," I told him. "Why don't you show Brandy around?"

I watched them from the window as I started sorting clothes and throwing them into the washer. Anthony had cut up some apples and was showing Brandy how to feed the horses. The horses were leaning their heads eagerly over the white picket fence, nickering.

It felt good to have a teenage girl back around the house, laughing, lying out by the pool, eating pizza in the kitchen. So many things that I used to take for granted. She came to visit several more times that summer, and one Saturday she even asked me if she could see some of Callie's photos.

"Oh, she's beautiful," she exclaimed as I showed her Callie's prom pictures. "I bet you miss her a lot."

"Yes, I do." I replied, smiling wistfully at one of my favorites of Callie in her baby-blue prom dress.

When I asked Anthony if he liked Brandy, he stated that they were just friends. That's probably exactly what Anthony needs right now, a good friend, I concluded.

I continued to see Joy that summer. She kept telling me to look for the gift in the experience, which was really beginning to get on my nerves. I wanted to throw something at her. Maybe the gift was to learn never to rely on anyone else for your joy in life. Maybe it was to learn how to have no expectations about what other people will or won't do. Maybe if I only look to myself for my happiness, no one will ever hurt me again, I concluded.

Changing how I felt from the inside out was no easy task. All I could think was *Callie's gone; nothing else really matters. If only she would walk back into my life again, I would be happy forever.*

And I lived for my dreams. In one, I was in my car and it was late at night. Dwayne was driving and Tom was sitting next to me in the back seat. Suddenly, in the headlights I saw a group of teenage girls running barefoot down the road in front of the car, wearing nothing but frilly bras and thong underpants. They were all laughing. They were going shopping for prom gowns and matching roses. Next, I saw a girl I didn't recognize—she had long, curly chestnut hair and sparkling hazel eyes—smiling and looking inside the car as she ran alongside it. Callie appeared behind her in a midnight-blue bra and panties.

"Look, that's Callie!" I exclaimed.

Callie played hide-and-seek, hiding her face behind the girl in front of her and then peering out at me, smiling. Then the scene suddenly dissolved and changed into something very different. There was only light, and Callie was standing right in front of me. Her face appeared more angelic than human. I looked into her eyes and said, "My dear, sweet angel child, thank you for coming to visit me." Then Callie came forward and somehow merged into me, as if she were hugging me from the inside out, before I suddenly awoke.

It was then that I knew this was not a trick of my tortured mind. Callie must be alive in some other dimension. I felt it. And she seemed finally to be happy. *Maybe I am eternal,* I thought. *Maybe this life is not all there is.* Maybe things just happen, and you can't ask yourself why terrible things happen to good people because there may not be any answers on this side. *Maybe this side is the dream, and the answers will come when I cross over and see Callie again.* I guess that's where faith comes in and, maybe, hope that there will be an answer for all the struggles we encounter here on this earth. And maybe the only thing I could do was to just let it be.

Anthony came home from camp and started high school, the same school that Callie had attended. I was concerned about that and suggested he might prefer the private university school downtown.

"But all my friends will be there!" Anthony protested vehemently, glaring at me with his arms folded across his chest. "I don't want to go to a different school!"

Dwayne and I decided to speak to his guidance counselor and several of his teachers a few weeks after school began. I had a strange sense of déjà vu as we climbed the steps to the front door and walked down the corridor past the open classrooms to the counselor's office.

We sat down in plastic chairs at a table in a cluttered conference room. Books, magazines, and newspapers were strewn haphazardly on shelves all over the room. An old microwave oven and a coffeemaker sat on a counter next to a sink. An open cupboard above the sink revealed a multitude of mismatched cups along with stacks of coffee cans and boxes of tea and sugar that looked like they might topple to the floor at any moment.

"How is Anthony doing so far in school?" Dwayne asked anxiously as we sat down.

"He seems to be adjusting to high school quite well," his English teacher replied. "He's very attentive in class, takes lots of notes, keeps up with his homework assignments, and has done well so far on his exams."

"I don't know if you are aware of this, but Anthony's sister, Callie, committed suicide last spring," I stated hesitantly, averting my eyes and twisting my hands in my lap.

The guidance counselor nodded, but the teachers appeared startled and anxiously glanced at one other. "No, we didn't know that," his math teacher finally said. "I'm sorry."

"Will you let us know right away if Anthony seems to develop any emotional problems?" Dwayne asked.

"I'll keep my eye on him, and so will his teachers," the guidance counselor reassured us. "We'll let you know if any issues develop during the school year."

I was still worried, though. The school, like many public schools in the area, was large, overcrowded, and understaffed. The teachers had at least thirty students in each class and were overworked and underpaid. The guidance counselors were overrun with students who acted out or who had disciplinary problems. A quiet child like Anthony would just disappear into the woodwork. No one would notice that he was hurting until it was too late. In those days, I lived in fear that Anthony would follow in his sister's footsteps and I would lose two children. I had suggested counseling, and he said he would rather talk to his friends. I let it go. He was a much more sensible child than Callie. I had to trust that he knew what to do to help himself through this.

In late September, Anthony came to me as I was making dinner and said, "Bobbie would like to stay here with us for a couple of weeks." When Tom moved in with us, Anthony had moved out of his upstairs bedroom and converted his and Callie's childhood playroom into a huge, over-the-garage apartment complete with a desk, bookshelves, dorm refrigerator, big-screen TV, and sofa. He began playing card games with a group of boys every Saturday afternoon at a local used-record, movie, and card shop in town and had met Bobbie there. Bobbie was seventeen and had driven Anthony home several times from the card shop. He was quiet and respectful, and I was glad that Anthony had found such a nice friend.

I talked to the owner of the shop, who told me Bobbie was a really good kid who just didn't get along with his stepfather. Bobbie had a very sweet girlfriend whom I'd met at the shop one day, and her father told me the same thing. I talked briefly to Bobbie's mother; she seemed relieved to have him out of the house for a while.

"Are you sure you won't mind sharing your room with someone else?" I asked Anthony.

"No, Mama, it's not a problem and he has nowhere else to go."

Finally, after some hesitation, I agreed. How strange to be running into these children who needed a substitute mother right now. Maybe Callie was sending them to me.

Bobbie arrived in his old, beat-up red Chevrolet, with an army cot and a laundry basket full of dirty clothes. Actually, I was relieved. I didn't want Anthony brooding alone in his room late at night. A roommate sounded like a good idea to me. Bobbie ended up staying with us his whole senior year of high school. He joined the army after he graduated and was shipped off to Iraq.

After Bobbie moved in, fall arrived abruptly. The evenings grew crisp and the mornings held a quiet chill. I watched as the leaves turned a riot of blazing color before they fell lifeless to the ground—much like Callie had fallen at the height of her luminous and fragile beauty. I imagined Callie living in a cave behind a sparkling silver-blue waterfall that cascaded into a dark pool of gray-green water where dolphins played. Callie would have covered the ceiling and sides of the cave in crystals just like the ones I admired so much in Joy's healing chamber. Large wicker baskets full of seashells—lightning whelks, bay scallops, heart cockles, angel wings—would line the walls. Wind chimes made from jingle shells would hang from the ceiling and tinkle merrily on a slight breeze. She would live there alone, except for her beloved animals that had crossed over before her, so she could reflect on her past life. She would be very peaceful, serene, and happy. There was the Callie I knew in this life, and the Callie who lived in a cave near the ocean in heaven. And yet I was struggling with them both. I struggled with letting go of the one and trying to find the other.

Callie—The Great Escape

I stood there, arms crossed, in complete disbelief of what I was hearing.

"*School?*" I exclaimed to Seraphiel. "Don't tell me there's homework in heaven!"

He laughed, explaining that school in the angelic realm was very different from school on earth. And in fact, I found that there weren't any cliques or social outcasts or girls whispering nasty things about my clothes, my makeup, or my hair behind my back. Or talking trash about me and calling me a ho. Or one of the boys boasting in the locker room about what he did to me last night, and how much I loved it, how I couldn't get enough of him. All the lies. *Thank God there's none of that*, I thought.

Instead, everyone was there to learn more about what truly matters, about how to be loving, selfless, and kind. I was in a group of kids around my age who'd had a difficult time during their last life. We took turns experiencing each other's lives. Someone would start talking and the rest of the class would literally become them and experience everything that they encountered as if we were them. The exercise was called "Passing the Chalice of Heartache." Apparently, when someone has a difficult experience and overcomes it, he or she has that experience for the whole of the universe. The universe becomes brighter because of each person's struggles, strength, and courage.

We also started learning about the seven planes of the angelic realm. Summer Wind was where most humans went when they first crossed over. It's located at the top of the first plane. The lower levels of the first plane are what some humans refer to as the ethers. It's that netherworld between life and death. There's really no place called hell. Hell is internal. It's the absence of light. It's what some people create in their own hearts because of the ways that they think or behave toward others.

After spending a while in Summer Wind, humans have the option to reincarnate, if they have unfinished business on earth, or to move to the second plane. On the second plane, a soul can explore and then choose the path of knowledge, service, or love. Most of the knowledge workers live on the third plane, the servers on the fourth, and the ones who have chosen the path of love on the fifth plane. The sixth and seventh planes are open only to those who have chosen the path of love. Here, they release their own individual identities completely and become one with All That Is. Earth is considered a very difficult environment because of the extreme negativity that resides there. Not much light can penetrate the fog of human uncertainty and confusion.

I decided to study soul rescuing. Somehow, I had managed to escape the ethers when I crossed over but I really didn't know why. Only later did I realize that it was the soul aspect of my mama, that part of her that remained in the angelic realm during her travels to earth, that had saved me. When I was being sucked up into that whirlwind, I saw a trail of little pinpoints of sparkling light leading through the tunnel up to the green meadow. Mama had placed that starlit path in front of me so that I could find my way home. I wanted to help other kids who got hung up in the ethers.

After a few weeks of class, we started our practice rescue missions to earth. We spent some time learning how to rescue lost pets and lead them to a human who could help them or, if they died, to bring them home.

"Animals are much easier to start with than people," Seraphiel explained. "Their hearts are pure, and they recognize love when they see it. They will come right to you. You won't have a problem guiding them home.

"But for many humans, it's a very different story," he continued. "They may not want to leave behind all the material possessions that they acquired in life. Or they may be very angry and bitter about problems they encountered in their lives. They may not believe in an afterlife, or they may be very anxious and afraid that they will be judged unworthy because of something they did."

I loved the animal runs to earth. My only problem was that I brought all of them back to Summer Wind and started hoarding them. Soon, my little Barbie house was overrun with dogs and cats of all shapes, colors, sizes, and descriptions. I brought back two little tan Chihuahuas that were always squabbling with each other over a squeaky toy, along with several black Labrador retriever puppies, a collie, and a German shepherd. They ran amok in a big pack, digging up my newly planted vegetable garden. I chased them around and around in the yard with a rolled-up newspaper but could never catch them. I also had some pet raccoons, squirrels, and rabbits in the backyard and at least three dozen horses and ponies in the pasture, including wild mustangs. I loved the mustangs.

"You can't keep all these animals for yourself," scolded Seraphiel. I really did try his patience sometimes. "Unlike on earth, there are lots of good homes for animals here. You need to share the love of these wondrous creatures with others."

He was right; part of my task was to learn to be selfless, because there's an abundance of love in heaven.

It would be nice to be able to say that I became a perfect angel after I met Jesus and started my animal runs to earth. But I wasn't. I couldn't seem to resist getting into a little trouble even in the angelic realm. It was during one of my animal runs after a hurricane that I discovered the French Quarter of New Orleans. I loved the narrow streets, the quaint town houses, and the gaslights that burned all night, casting creepy shadows in the alleyways. It was my kind of town, where the veil between the living and the dead is paper-thin. I swear there are more dead people in New Orleans than live ones.

On Bourbon Street, bright neon signs in red, yellow, and blue proclaimed the names of strip joints, bars, restaurants, nightclubs, and novelty shops. On almost any night of the week, you could hear music pouring into the street: sultry blues, Dixieland jazz, and country rock. People danced on the sidewalk, writhing and gyrating to the music as if no one was watching them. After I rescued a starving yellow tomcat in an alleyway during a torrential rainstorm, I noticed that some of the bars were still open, playing music, filled with people who were drinking and talking fatalistically about how the only way to deal with a hurricane was to get really drunk. It had been my philosophy when I lived on earth, exactly. I could smell the cigarette smoke, and boy did I miss the buzz that comes from being really drunk, or coked up, or stoned. *Surely*, I thought, *I can find someone on Bourbon Street who is really fucked up and slip into her body for just a few minutes, to get that high one more time.*

When I got back to my Barbie house after my first trip, I cut a hole in the floor of my bedroom closet and dug myself a tunnel through the clouds that went straight down to Bourbon Street. I attached a rope to my four-poster bed that I could use to swing myself down to earth. The hole had a trapdoor that opened and closed, and I covered it carefully with carpet. I thought I had succeeded in escaping from my problems on earth by crossing myself over. Now I wanted to escape the lessons I was learning in the angelic realm by going back to earth. How fucked up is that? But I wasn't thinking logically at the time. I just told myself that I really needed a break! I slipped down a couple of times without anyone noticing when I was supposed to be meditating and walked up and down Bourbon Street, looking longingly at people smoking, drinking, and making out in the alleyways.

One evening, during a group meditation, I decided to sit way in back so I could slink out the door as soon as Seraphiel turned off the lights. Little did I know that Dustin, one of the boys in my class, had decided to follow me. He saw me leave and snuck out the door right after me to see where I was going. I'd had my eye on Dustin for a while. He was really quite enticing. He had a square jaw and chocolate-brown hair with short, straight bangs that hung across his forehead like cute little icicles. His warm hazel eyes were always full of laughter. He had a tall, muscular body, and I had to pinch myself in class to keep from imagining what he might look like naked.

I slipped down my rope with Dustin not far behind me. You know how you can just feel sometimes like someone is following you? I could sense someone behind me and I was a little freaked out. I ran into Saint Louis Cemetery, hoping to lose whoever it was among the old whitewashed crypts with crosses or statues on top of them and the ornately carved tombs. A creepy place, even for a ghost. Inside the crypts, dead bodies are stacked up in coffins on shelves behind the closed doors. When there's no more room, they just dump the rotting bones out of the oldest coffin and leave them on the floor! A lot of the crypts are in various stages of disrepair, with rusty ironwork on the gates surrounding them. I darted among the eerie, twisted paths, stopping briefly at the tomb of Marie Laveau, the old voodoo queen, to leave a shiny new penny next to a bunch of flowers, shells, and votive candles. Even though I knew I was protected by Sera-phiel, I wasn't going to take any chances.

Now this really creeps me out, but in the old days people placed pennies in the mouths of their dead rela-tives or over their closed eyeballs so they wouldn't pop back open again. The penny was also a toll for the fer-ryman who carried people across the river between the living and the dead. Really, it's so much easier just to take the rainbow bridge. Nowadays, people place pennies on graves as a token of their appreciation or for good luck. Not leaving some sort of gift is a sign of disrespect and I really don't want to contemplate what a voodoo queen might do about that!

I hid behind a tombstone, trying to be quiet as a mouse, but Dustin must have hidden on the other side because we both popped our heads up to take a look around at the same time and scared each other half to death.

"Oh, my God, what are you doing here? You followed me!" I exclaimed, pointing at his chest.

"Well, I thought what you were up to was probably a lot more interesting than my homework."

I couldn't help but grin. "Hell, yeah."

"Where are we?"

"This is Saint Louis Cemetery; isn't it cool?" I exclaimed, pointing to the crypts. "The water table in New Orleans is too high, and the coffins just kept popping up out of the ground after a big rainstorm, so they put them all in these little playhouses."

"Well, that's plain weird," Dustin replied. "I'm glad my bones aren't rotting here. I was cremated. How about you?"

"Oh," I laughed. "They turned you into a crispy critter." Then I felt a sudden stab of horror. "I was buried six feet under in a baby-blue coffin. Oh, God, I hope there's not worms coming out of my eye sockets." I shuddered.

"I guess you could take a look."

"There's no way I'm going down there to see my body rotting away. That's disgusting!"

"You know," Dustin whispered conspiratorially, "I've been told that some of the angels will make you go into your coffin and look at your body slowly decomposing if you keep insisting that you aren't dead."

"Seraphiel would never do that." I sniffed. "How'd you die?" I asked, changing the subject.

"I had a very rare disease called scleroderma. It usually doesn't affect teenagers or boys, but it got me good."

"Were you really sick?"

"Well, I convinced myself there really wasn't much wrong with me for the first few years after it was diagnosed. But then it got really bad all of a sudden. My lungs started to fail and I had fits of coughing and throwing up. I could hardly keep anything down and I wasted away until I was just ninety pounds. My doctors put a tube in one of the large veins in my neck to give me food and fluids."

"Why didn't you just stop your treatments and cross over?"

"Well, I didn't want to leave my parents or my girl-friend, Katye, behind with broken hearts. Kids aren't sup-posed to die before their parents. And I'm not a quitter. I felt that if I just kept fighting and praying, somehow, I might get better. I didn't want to just give up."

"Oh," I replied, rapidly becoming very uncomfort-able. But then I asked, "Were you and Katye in love?"

Dustin smiled, remembering. "I met Katye on my first day of high school. Now, I know this is going to sound really corny, but I saw her across the cafeteria at lunch. She was sitting by herself because her family had just moved into town and she didn't know anyone. It was love at first sight. To this day, I don't know how I found the courage to just walk right up to her and ask if I could sit down. You know what she said?"

I shook my head.

"She looked up at me, smiled, and said, 'I was hoping you'd ask.' After that we were inseparable."

"That's so romantic," I sighed. "I wish something like that had happened to me."

"You wouldn't like what happened later. Right after I graduated from high school, I started on a rapid down-hill slide. I had this horrible sense of foreboding. I knew that my time was running out. I could see my life slowly slipping away like an almost-empty hourglass that was once filled with sand. There were so many things I still wanted to do."

"Oh," I said again, feeling an awful sense of guilt welling up inside me.

"My heart couldn't compensate for my shitty lungs anymore. My parents called the hospice nurses to help care for me. They told me they didn't want to see me suffer anymore. I was struggling to breathe, my heart was pounding out of my chest, and I could barely make it from my bed to the bathroom and back. I felt like I had one foot in the grave and the other on a banana peel."

I almost laughed. "Well, now, that's quite a metaphor."

"The day before I died, Katye came to see me. She crawled into my hospital bed and we held onto each other for dear life, just crying. I tried to memorize everything about her, just in case there was a remote possibility that I might survive my physical death. Her hair, the color of ripe chestnuts, was so soft against my cheek, and her eyes were this sparkling color of jade. Her lips were so full, just like ripe raspberries, and when I kissed her I could taste her tears.

"I remember saying, 'I'm so grateful you stayed with me after I got so sick.' She looked me right in the eye and said, 'I couldn't leave. I was in love with you from the moment I first saw you.' People just don't realize how precious life is, just how important it is to make the most of every single moment."

"This makes me feel like a total shit," I sighed miserably.

"Why's that?"

I whispered so softly that he had to lean in close to hear me. "I crossed myself over. I had a perfectly healthy body, except my teeth were full of cavities because I ate too much candy."

"Why did you do that?"

"This is going to sound really lame," I replied. "One of my friends totaled my Mustang. I got my driver's license taken away, and my boyfriend broke up with me. Looking back now, it all seems so silly. My problems weren't really all that bad, especially compared to yours. I was so stupid; I'd do anything to take it all back."

"You can't keep beating yourself up about it. What's done is done. You've got to make the best of your life on this side."

"Yeah, I know now that Mama and I chose this and that she'll understand when we meet up again. But sometimes it's hard to see her so angry and in so much pain. Maybe it wasn't such a good idea after all. You know, I bet Mama's so mad she'd kill me; that's if I weren't already dead."

"I'm sure your mama still loves you, and she'll learn to forgive you in time, maybe even before she crosses over."

"I don't want to talk about this anymore," I mumbled, looking away.

"Well, what was your favorite game when you were growing up?" Dustin asked.

"Uh, hide-and-seek, I guess. Why?"

"OK, let's play hide-and-seek. Close your eyes, count to ten slowly, no cheating, then try to find me," he instructed, taking off down the path ahead of us.

We played among the crypts until we were both too tired to run and then collapsed in a heap on the grass. Before we left I made him swear on Marie Laveau's grave not to tell anyone where we'd been.

"If you break your promise," I warned, "she will come up out of the ground as a huge boa constrictor, hunt you down, and eat you up."

"Oh! I'm so scared," he exclaimed as he shivered dramatically. "But I promise I won't tell a soul about our little adventure."

I smacked him on the butt. He was really very annoying.

If you are sensitive to spirits, you might have seen us as fleeting shadows on the walls out of the corner of your eye or little white globes of light flying through the air. Most people don't notice us at all. Only the black horse that had stopped at a corner with his carriage full of midnight revelers saw us as we raced down Canal Street. He snorted, shook his head, and stamped a hoof anxiously as we passed by.

On another excursion, I went back to my high school in Cassville. The campus was closed for the summer, but I had no trouble getting in, even though the doors were locked. I walked right through the walls. I wandered the halls hearing the echoes of footsteps and laughter. I walked into one of my classrooms and sat at my desk, gazing at the empty seats around me and wondering about my friends and where their lives would take them.

I visited my old house and saw Mama giving away most of my stuff, packing the rest into a cedar chest. That's when I knew that Mama had resigned herself to the fact that I wasn't coming home. Sometimes I would go to Megan's house late at night, look in her closet, and pull out my pants and blouses. Megan would wake up the next morning and find all of my clothes in a heap on the floor. I had to let go, too—of all the dreams that I had for my life and all that had mattered to me. Letting go took a while.

But the thing that bothered me the most was my CDs. I was very possessive about them. I hadn't liked it when my friends borrowed my CDs and didn't give them back. Now they were all scattered among my friends, and I had to find out who had which ones. That's how I ended up in Megan's car one night and practically scared the bejesus out of her! I still can't figure out how I was able to appear to Megan when no one else could see me. We were just that connected, like locks of hair twined into a braid, like twin souls or identical twin sisters; we were that close. And we had the same last name.

"You don't have to cling to what you've left behind," Seraphiel instructed. "Just imagine it and it will be right here with you."

So I imagined myself a huge CD collection and a really awesome stereo system with giant bass speakers. I would turn up the bass as loud as I could until my little Barbie house would start to shake. Finally, Seraphiel threatened to take away my power of imagination if I didn't behave myself. So, then I imagined myself all kinds of frilly underwear and outrageous clothes. Seraphiel never knew how I would show up for class. One day I would dress up as a vampire to be really gothic, the next as a cheerleader or as Barbie herself, and finally as an angel, complete with a halo and gold wings. It was a blast.

I wanted to show Mama how much fun I was having in the angelic realm in one of her dreams, so maybe she wouldn't be so sad. That's why I showed up in my midnight-blue bra and thong, running down the street with a couple of my new girlfriends. And I appeared in another dream that Mama was having about Christmas. I hated seeing her so sad, moping around the house and feeling so lost and alone.

In one particularly difficult class, Seraphiel asked us to think about something that we'd done in our last life that had very deeply hurt someone. Of course, immediately

I thought about how much I'd hurt Mama by crossing myself over.

"For the next class," he told us, "you are going to experience that event as if you were that person."

Oh, no, I wasn't going to do that. I'd get the hell out of there! Far better to sneak down to Bourbon Street to see if I could jump into some poor drunk person's body for just a few minutes. I waited until dusk, then opened the trapdoor to the tunnel and jumped onto my rope, full of excitement and anticipation, this time closing and locking the trapdoor behind me so Dustin couldn't follow. Oh, the thrill of getting away with something that I really wasn't supposed to be doing; it had never left me. But as soon as my feet landed on Bourbon Street, there was Seraphiel standing right in front of me, glaring at me with fire in those piercing blue eyes.

"Callie," he thundered, "how do you think you are going to help someone who is really desperate by becoming one of them again? How many times do I have to tell you that alcohol and drugs solve nothing, absolutely nothing?"

"How'd you know what I was going to do?" I asked sheepishly.

"I know everything about you. There's not one thing that you can think, say, or do that I don't know."

Oh, brother, there really is no escape.

"Yes," Seraphiel agreed, looking me straight in the eye. "There is no escape. Wherever you go, *you* will be there. When you truly understand these words, you can come back to class."

He stopped glaring at me and suddenly pursed his lips, then looked up at the sky and let out a shrill whistle. A huge white eagle with beady black eyes appeared as if from nowhere and started circling in the air above us. Seraphiel gave some sort of hand signal, and the bird immediately plunged down to earth and grabbed me with its claws. I wasn't hurt, but I let out a terrified scream anyway. The eagle swooped me up into the sky, and I watched as the twinkling lights of New Orleans receded into the darkness of a midsummer night. I scrunched my eyes shut. The next thing I knew, I hit the ground with a thud. The eagle had deposited me right in front of a little crystal cave. I quickly crawled inside so it couldn't snatch me up again.

After a while it dawned on me that I was in that damn cave because Seraphiel had banished me there. There was nowhere to go, no one to talk to, and nothing to do. None of my beloved animals were with me. I got up and stomped around for a while, cursing and muttering and throwing rocks down into the pool below and frightening the dolphins. Then a huge rock rolled in front of the entrance, closing it mysteriously. A small light appeared in the ceiling, illuminating the crystals on the walls. I sat down in the center of the cave. I had finally run out of escape options. There was nothing left to do but to quiet my racing mind and attempt to understand the meaning in Seraphiel's words.

As I sat, I saw myself in all my different forms in all my incarnations, who I had been and who I was yet to become. The shapes changed, but the core essence of me remained the same. Then, I looked around at all the crystals on the walls and saw that they too had the exact same core essence as I did. I could see cords of light connecting them to me and to each other. We were all intertwined in a glowing maze of light. There was no sense of separation; we were all one. Then, one by one, all of my animal friends appeared in the cave. I saw that we were all connected in this gridwork of light. That same spark of love and light that was in my heart glowed in theirs as well.

The rock started moving again and rolled away. I looked out and saw that everything everywhere was interconnected in this pulsating gridwork of light. We were all one. It was true—wherever I went, I would be there. I was in everything, in all that was, is, and is yet to be.

I felt such peace. I closed my eyes and felt the love and light surround me as I gently slid into sleep. When I woke up, I was back in my bed in my Barbie house. Great-grandma Ellie was pounding on my door.

"Time to get up, Callie dear, or you'll be late for school!"

Even though I was now transformed, I had to get back at Seraphiel for locking me in that cave. One evening when he was asleep, I snuck up on him with a needle and thread. He was wearing his silver angel wings at the time, and I sewed them together as fast as I could, praying he wouldn't wake up. Then I scampered out of the room. Rachel, one of my girlfriends, and I took turns watching him through a keyhole in the door. When he woke up, stretched, and found he couldn't open his wings, he looked so perplexed that we started to laugh. We rolled on the floor, laughing and laughing until our stomachs hurt. Then we heard the door open. There was Seraphiel staring down at us, glowering. We instantly stopped laughing; we were caught! He wordlessly handed me a pair of scissors. He made me cut the stitches out one by one. I thought he might send me back to that cave. But I could see by the twinkle in his eye that he really wasn't all that mad.

9

Diane—Searching for Callie

I was desperately searching for Callie. I knew she was out there somewhere. I just had to find her, and so I decided to try and contact a medium who might be able to channel her. The famous mediums I had seen on TV were expensive and had long waiting lists. I scoured the Internet, looking at the faces of different mediums on their websites and reading their stories. *Whom would Callie be comfortable connecting with?*

After several hours of searching, I came upon Kira's photo and website and the story of the happy faces. Apparently, Kira began to see cheerful yellow and black smiley faces shortly after her young niece crossed over and felt they were signs given by the child to indicate she was still around. Callie loved smiley faces. She pasted them on the covers of her notebooks and on notes she sent to friends. In fact, she'd always signed her name and added a happy face, I remembered.

Kira had long, light-brown hair pulled up loosely into a bun at the back of her neck, with stray strands framing her heart-shaped face, and the most striking sea-green eyes I had ever seen. She was tall and slender and looked to be in her early thirties. Her expression was enigmatic. I immediately decided to contact her for a telephone reading. I was a little skeptical and apprehensive but decided to try it anyway.

CALLIE

I saw Mama surfing the Internet trying to find a way to contact me through a medium. I went searching for Seraphiel and found him in the library with his shoes off, resting his feet on a table, chilling between counseling sessions with the new kids.

"I wish you'd take your goddamn dirty feet off the table," I grumbled as I stomped into the room.

"My feet are God blessed," he replied with a smile as he removed them from the table and sat up.

"Whatever," I retorted. "I've got a problem."

"What's that?"

"My mama wants to talk to me through a medium and I haven't got a clue about how it's done." I twisted my silver necklace with a half-moon pendant around and around apprehensively.

"That's great!"

I wasn't sure just how great it was going to be.

"Ellie and I will take you to the station. It's like a radio station on earth, but you'll be sending thought waves and images to the medium to answer her questions instead of talking through a microphone."

"Oh."

"The medium may open herself by visualizing a blank screen like a movie screen in her mind, and we'll place the pictures on the screen. It'll be fun!"

I wasn't so sure about that.

"It works best if the medium has a pure heart, if your mama is open to this type of communication, and if the love connection between you two is still strong."

"Mama keeps talking about triangulation," I muttered, "whatever the hell that is."

"It's a research term. It means that the truth of your findings is more believable if you attain it by several different methods."

Oh, brother. I couldn't help but smile. Sometimes I just hated having a scientist for a mother.

10

Diane—The Medium's Message

On a rainy evening in October, just before dusk, I lit a candle, sat down at my desk in my office, and placed my first prearranged phone call to Kira. I hadn't said anything to Tom about contacting a medium. I wasn't sure how he'd respond, so I scheduled the call when I knew he'd be teaching a night class at the university.

"I always start with a prayer, and then I open to spirit," Kira explained. "I'll start describing things to you. I like the loved ones to validate themselves. It might not be who you're expecting. We'll just have to go with the flow."

"OK."

"May we be connected to all things loving, guided by all knowing. Thank you, God, for giving us the perfect outcome for this reading. Amen." Then she added, "I may go silent on you for a minute or two while I'm receiving."

"OK," I said again and waited apprehensively, looking out the window at the rain-washed street, wondering what would happen next.

After a few minutes, Kira said, "Normally, the first thing I get is something indicative of how someone crossed. I'm getting two different things, which means two different spirits. Sometimes they come together. The first thing I'm getting is in the head area, like an aneurysm. Does that have any meaning to you for someone in spirit?"

"Well, my grandmother Eleanor, we called her Ellie, died from a stroke a number of years ago."

"Yes, she appears to be an older female in spirit. I'm also getting half of my symbol for suicide. I'm saying half because it appears to be half accident, half suicide. Does this make sense?"

"Yes, it does."

"It feels male or a very assertive female, a recent passing. Ellie met her when she crossed over."

"Well, it's probably my daughter."

"It feels like she fantasized and planned this but didn't think it would go through; it kind of shocked her that it did. Was there a mental problem, like depression, that she had been dealing with for a long time?"

"Well, we didn't know she was depressed. We thought she was just acting out."

"This feels very internal. She wasn't trying to get back at anybody. There's nothing you could have done to change the outcome. It's the way she perceived things. It's almost like she felt different from everyone else."

"Well, she always wanted to fit in. I took her to some modeling classes so she could learn to do her hair and makeup so she would fit in."

"It feels to me like she went to sleep and woke up there. She says it didn't hurt. She says, 'I'm much better now.' Is there a connection with you two and music? She says she communicates with you through music."

"Our favorite thing to do together was to listen to music."

"People thought more of her than she thought of her-self. She had a problem with self-image. After she passed she understood that she really was loved."

"Yes, almost three hundred people came to her funeral."

"She's OK with it. I mean her suicide. She knows it's hard for you to understand, but she says, 'Tell her I'm not going anywhere.' You two had an affinity, like friends as well as mother and daughter."

"We were really close."

"You know in your heart that she's OK."

"Yes, I do." I glanced at Callie's photo on the book-shelf next to my desk. Her face was in profile, her blonde hair pulled back at the nape of her neck with a blue scrunchie. Large, gold hoop earrings dangled down her neck. She had turned her head slightly toward the cam-era as if she were glancing sideways at an attractive man, smiling, flirting with her eyes, enticing him to follow her.

"You have strong dreams about her."

"I didn't know what it was at first. I thought I was going crazy."

"Well, the dreams are real. She needed to let you know that she's OK. Is there a Sarah or a Raphael con-nected to her?"

"Not that I'm aware of."

"Well, she says she's with them."

"Oh, OK."

"Is there a Sarah or a Raphael connected to Eleanor?"

"Not that I'm aware of."

"Is there one particular stuffed animal of hers that you keep close to you?"

I looked down at the tan puppy that was now sleeping peacefully in my lap. She had wandered into the office while I was talking with Kira, and I knew that if I didn't pick her up, she would start whimpering.

"Well, it's not a stuffed animal; it's her dog Ruffy. It's a tiny Chihuahua. I bought it for her a couple of weeks before she died. In her suicide note, she asked me to take care of Ruffy. So now I sleep with the dog."

"Oh!" Kira laughed. "Now, I wonder why I thought it was a stuffed animal!"

"Does she have any messages for her friends Megan, Ashley, and Jenny?"

"Let them know it's OK for them to go on. It's like they feel guilty that they're still alive and that she's not here. But she is here, if you know what I mean."

"Yes, I think so."

"There's nothing you could have done to stop it. I know that's hard to take as her mom. It's something she needed to experience. But now she's away from that tortured feeling she had, and that's a big relief for her."

"What's happening up there with her now?"

"Has it been less than six months?"

"It's been about five months."

"She's just finishing pulling herself together. She's just getting to where she's healed from it. Now she's deciding what she's going to do. Did she want to work with animals when she got older?"

"Yes, she wanted to be a marine biologist."

"She's going back and forth between helping animals and helping other kids who passed the way she did. She feels very energetic, so I wouldn't be surprised if she does both."

"Yes, she was always very busy, doing a half dozen things at once."

"She says she's bigger than she imagined, her soul is much, much bigger. Now I can feel the energy pulling back. I'm losing my ability to feel her . . . But I want to thank you so much for allowing me to connect with her. She's quite an energy. You have a really strong bond with her. I'm glad I was able to connect with her for you."

I thanked Kira and slowly hung up the phone, pensively patting little Ruffy on the head. Then I put her back on the floor and went into the kitchen to make myself a cup of tea. Had Kira really connected with Callie? It felt that way. I could still sense an energy, a vibration in the air around me that felt like my daughter. But she also seemed so far away. Many of the things Kira told me made complete sense. But a few other things seemed off the mark. None of my relatives were called Raphael, and I didn't think Callie had a boyfriend with that name. Why had Kira been so on target with everything but this?

11

Callie—Hell of a
Good Time in Heaven

"She's doubting what I told her because she doesn't know a Raphael," I complained after the reading was over. "And the stupid medium didn't get that there was an S at the beginning of your name."

"Sometimes the words get a little muddled when they cross the veil. She'll know there's a Seraphiel soon enough," my angel friend implied mysteriously with a twinkle in his eye.

"Now, next, I'm going to let you rescue lost children. We'll see how you do, but if you pull any pranks, it will be back to animal runs for you."

I started with teenagers who had crossed themselves over like me and had gotten lost somewhere in the ethers between the angelic realm and earth. Most teenagers were drawn to the light as soon as they saw it. On some level, they recognized it because they hadn't been on earth very long. But a few resistant ones got really, really lost. Sometimes they were lost for quite a while in earth time.

I guess you could call the ethers a kind of threshold or passageway between the two worlds, the earth and the angelic realm. It's actually a huge garbage dump for negative human thoughts and emotions. The landscape has all the color drained out of it, like a vampire sucks the blood out of the neck of a beautiful young girl. It looks just like the images you old people used to watch on your black-and-white TV sets. The negativity just drains all the color from everything. In the same way cars leave their carbon footprints on the earth, people leave their thought imprints on the universe. If most of their thoughts are negative, they get stuck in whirlpools and end up in this shadowed realm when they cross over.

On rescue missions, the ethers appeared to me as a twisted labyrinth of trails through a forest of barren trees with gnarled branches reaching up to a sky in twilight even during the afternoon. Dark mists often rose from the ground as I walked along the silent, desolate paths. The menacing shadows I saw lurking in the semidarkness always made me nervous. But sometimes I just felt this profound sense of loneliness, isolation, and despair.

It wasn't a place I liked to visit. I always bundled up in several layers of clothes before I went, but I still couldn't seem to escape the bone-chilling cold. I tried to get out of there before darkness fell completely to avoid the midnight freezing rainstorms, the howling of werewolves in the distance, and the rising wind moaning through the trees. Ending up in the ethers wasn't a punishment. No one put you there. People sometimes just became imprisoned by their own negativity and found themselves in a place that matched their spiritual vibration.

I'd find the lost teenagers in some place they'd constructed for themselves in the forest: an abandoned shack, a cave in the ground. Sometimes I even came upon someone in a ruined tavern at a crossroads in the woods. I would sit down on a stool next to them. Usually they wouldn't even look at me. Then I'd pull out a cigarette or a joint. I'd make a lighter appear out of thin air. That usually got their attention, and they'd start watching me.

I'd take a hit, look at them, and say, "You know, this really sucks. I can still light a joint, but I can't get high, because I left my damn body on earth. How fucked up is that?" They would usually nod in agreement. Then I would say, "My name's Callie, what's yours?"

Sometimes they told me, sometimes they didn't. Then I would say that I'd heard that they crossed themselves over. They might nod or look away. I'd tell them that I crossed myself over too, and a little of my story. This got some of them talking, but others were mostly silent.

I'd say, "I know you've probably realized by now that you're not really dead. You know, you don't have to be out here all alone. You can come with me. I know someone who can help you."

Some of them would look at me to see if they could trust me. "Come on. Don't be afraid. You can trust me. Take my hand."

Some would say, "No, I'd rather stay here."

I'd reply, "Suit yourself," and disappear for a while.

But I'd come back. I came back until they finally got the idea that somebody gave a damn. Somebody finally cared about them. The instant they took my hand, I knew that I had them. I flew most of them up to the entrance of the healing chamber, but some were so weak, they'd been lost for so long, that I had to carry them.

Many times, my great-grandma Ellie would be there to greet them, having just baked their favorite treat. Then I would take them to Seraphiel's healing room. The walls of this room were lined with crystals, glowing with all the colors of the rainbow. The ceiling was covered with sparkling white and rose quartz crystals. This usually blew them away. Seraphiel often appeared as young Raphael. The girls really loved him. They thought he was so delicious.

I would tell them, "You can look all you want, but you can't have him; he's mine." This usually made them laugh.

Then I would leave and Seraphiel would talk to them for a while and start their healing with crystals, letters, and colors, much like what I watched Joy do for Mama. Then they would pick a quiet place in the healing chamber to rest. The healing chamber was really a spirit hospital located right next to the library. They could design their healing room inside the chamber however they wanted to. It could be a tropical beach with pure white sand, palm trees, and an azure ocean; a green meadow with purple wildflowers, birds, and butterflies; or a clearing in a deep forest of fir trees. One girl even chose a big, open clamshell in a coral reef in the middle of the ocean. Clearly, she'd seen *The Little Mermaid* too many times!

They would sleep for a while, and I would stop by occasionally to check on them and delight when I could see them getting better—their faces more serene. Some of them even came to my school after they were healed, but they were usually in classes below me. They would see me in the halls and come running up to thank me.

"You sure have a way with these kids," Seraphiel said to me one day. He was smiling. I smiled back at him, but I didn't tell him that I got their attention by smoking a joint!

The boys instantly respected Seraphiel. They learned much faster than I had not to mess with him. Well, actually, a few weeks ago, some boys did mess with Seraphiel, and they got into really big trouble. It all began when I and several of my girlfriends started noticing that some of our bras and thong underwear were missing. At first, we thought maybe one of our friends had borrowed them without asking. But as more and more underwear kept disappearing, we started squabbling and accusing each other of stealing.

Then one morning, as we girls were walking together to class, we looked up and saw that the flags in all the colors of the rainbow at the top of the library had been replaced by brightly colored bras and thongs flapping merrily in the breeze. We all stopped in unison. "Oh, my God!" we exclaimed. "Those are ours! Who did that?" Then we saw a group of boys hiding in the bushes near their classroom and, way behind them, Seraphiel walking up the path to the library with his head buried in a book.

"Oh! This is gonna be good!" we said to each other. We hurried up the stairs to our classroom and peered excitedly out the windows, waiting to see what would happen next. As Seraphiel came closer, he must've heard some of the boys snickering, because he looked up and just stood there staring. Then, glowering, he started looking around for the culprits. The boys, thinking they could get away, sprinted from the bushes toward the back of the library. But he saw them, flew up, and landed right in front of them.

Pointing to the underwear, he said. "Now, how do you think some poor lost soul who has just arrived in Summer Wind is going to feel? He's come to see me for a life review, and he looks up and finds those panties flying in the breeze!"

The boys were trying to look serious, but I could see that several of them were on the verge of laughing. Then Seraphiel saw us girls leaning out of the classroom windows.

"Now, I don't want you girls to get any ideas," he said. "I don't want to see any boys' briefs or banana hammocks up there either."

Then he made the boys climb up to the library roof, take down all the bras and panties, replace them with the flags, and return the underwear to their rightful owners with an apology. We sure did love that! It was one of my best times in Summer Wind.

Sundays were supposed to be our days of rest and relaxation. All the kids went to hear Jesus preach a sermon in the morning. He never preached inside a church; it was always outside in a beautiful setting like a huge, green field or a beach near the turquoise ocean. Souls would come from miles and miles around to hear him. We didn't dress up much. The boys wore clean blue jeans and a nice shirt for a change, and the girls wore dresses or pretty skirts and blouses.

One Sunday, feeling bored, I decided to spend a lot of time, more than an hour, getting ready. I put my hair up, did my makeup and nails, and put on one of my favorite dresses. After the sermon, the boys invited all us girls to see something that they had discovered in the woods. We flew up to the top of a big hill. Going down one side of the hill were several small streams of water, rushing through the trees and ending at a gigantic waterfall that plunged into the ocean. The boys started tossing off their shirts and jeans and then slid down the hill, shouting and laughing and getting covered in brown mud before they plunged into the sea. Then they flew back up to the hilltop. Soon, several of the more adventurous girls joined them.

"Come on, Callie!" Dustin shouted. "This is so much fun!"

"I don't think so," I said. "I'll just watch. I don't want to get all messed up."

He just laughed, picked up some of that awful, squishy mud, and threw it at me. It landed on my chest, and I watched it slide slowly down the front of my favorite white lace dress.

Furious, I glared at him. "You're not gonna get away with this!" I seethed.

Dustin took off running, and I chased him. He jumped into a stream and started sliding down the hill. I jumped in after him with my dress, fancy beaded sandals, even my jewelry still on. I plunged down the waterfall screaming. Dustin got to the ocean and grabbed a dolphin, and the dolphin took off racing through the water. So, I got myself a dolphin to ride, too. I chased him around and around in the water. My hair had come down, my dress was torn, and one of my earrings was gone, but I didn't care.

The other kids stopped what they were doing and started cheering. "Go, Callie! Go get him!"

I caught up with Dustin and leapt off my dolphin onto his back. I was shouting, "Say you're sorry! Say you're sorry!" and beating my fists on his back.

Everyone was laughing. Dustin carried me on his back to the shore and deposited me in the sand.

"Now, Callie," he said. "Wasn't that fun?"

I had to admit that it was. I found out that I could have one hell of a good time in heaven.

12

Diane—Addicted to Pain

I could hardly believe that I, a clinical nurse and budding researcher, was sitting in an Angel Awakening
class, but truth be told, I was actually excited. I walked
into Joy's living room, sat down on a comfortable sofa
under a large picture window, and glanced around at my
classmates. Sitting across from me in a straight-backed
chair was a big, burly man with curly jet-black hair and
turquoise eyes who looked to be in his early thirties. He
was wearing a white T-shirt, jeans, and sandals and was
deeply tanned and muscular. He looked like he spent a
lot of time outside working in the sun.

Next to me on the sofa was a pleasingly plump,
middle-aged woman with short, honey-blonde hair, hazel
eyes, and a warm smile, dressed in navy blue walking
shorts and a tan shirt. But by far the most striking member of the group was a young woman who appeared to be
in her late twenties. She was wearing a red-and-white-
striped sundress trimmed with white lace. Her lips and
nails were painted a bright cherry red, which contrasted
sharply with her porcelain skin and platinum hair. On the
back of her left arm, across her well-defined triceps, was
a tattoo of a large magenta tiger lily with burgundy spots

and a star-shaped yellow center. She had another tattoo as well, a black-and-white angel whose outstretched wings encircled her right arm.

Joy strode into the room carrying four large white loose-leaf notebooks.

"Before we begin, I think you should each introduce yourself to the group. Tell us a little about yourself and what has brought you here. Keep in mind that everyone will hold what you say in the strictest confidence and won't share it with anyone else outside the group. Do you agree?"

Each of us nodded.

"Now, who would like to begin?"

There was complete silence as Joy glanced around at us expectantly. Finally, the beautiful girl with the lily tattoo began.

"Well, I'll start. My name's Angie; that's short for Angelica but I prefer Angie. I make things out of stained glass like wind chimes and suncatchers. Sometimes I even make lampshades and windows. I went to a Tiffany exhibit when I was a little girl and decided right then that this was what I wanted to do when I grew up. I love working with my hands."

"And what made you decide to join this class?"

"Well, I dropped out of college a while ago, and ever since then I've been traveling. I never stay in one place very long. I don't like to be tied down. I do the same thing with men. I'm never in a relationship for more than a few months; I get bored and decide to move on. But I'm almost thirty and I would really like to have a baby, but not by myself. And sometimes I feel really empty and alone. I'd like to understand why I do this."

"You mean, why you're afraid to open your heart to someone, why you're afraid to love?"

Angelica twisted a lock of hair around and around on her finger and chewed her lower lip. "Yes, I guess so."

"Well, the class can help you with this."

The attractive man who looked Italian spoke next. "I'm Ryan. I do construction work around town. I like to work with my hands, too."

He gave Angie what I'm sure he felt was a disarmingly appealing smile but she just knit her eyebrows and glared at him.

He turned his attention back to Joy. "My dad's a partner in a law firm on the East End. I was supposed to take over his law practice. But I couldn't stand the thought of wearing a tie and being caged up in an office all day. I left home and joined the army when I turned twenty-one. I did two tours in Iraq. I drove military supplies to the base. One day, two of my buddies died when an IED exploded right outside their jeep. I was in a truck behind them and managed to pull another guy out before the jeep went up in flames. Now I have flashbacks. I just can't seem to get what happened that day out of my mind. And I can't sleep unless I get really drunk. I feel so guilty that I couldn't save them. Sometimes I wonder why they had to die instead of me."

"I'm sorry." Joy looked at him thoughtfully. "This class will help you let go of your guilt and move on with your life."

"And I'm Jana," said the woman sitting next to me. "I'm a physical therapist, and I used to work for a home health care agency here in town, but now I take care of my mother. She has breast cancer. Last spring, we found out that it had metastasized to her brain. Now she's bedridden and her vision is failing—she's almost completely blind. My mother is cranky and at times she can be downright nasty. Nothing I do is good enough for her. A couple of weeks ago, it all became too much, so now I have an aide who comes to the house several days a week in the morning so I can get out. I love my mother, but sometimes I wonder how I would feel if I woke up one morning and found that she had passed away during the night. At times, I feel really trapped. I have an old back injury and it's starting to get worse because I have to lift her from the bed to the commode and back. At some point, I may have to put her in a nursing home or a hospice. I feel so guilty. After all, she took care of me when I was growing up, and now it's my turn. But I'm so overwhelmed; I just don't think I can do it much longer."

"How to take care of yourself without bringing harm to another is an important lesson that you will learn in this class. And you have taken a big first step by hiring an aide to help you look after your mother. And how about you?"

Joy, Angie, Ryan, and Jana turned toward me. I swallowed and took a sip of water. My throat was completely dry. I looked down and couldn't believe that my hands were shaking. I clasped them tightly in my lap.

"I'm Diane," I began haltingly. "I'm a nurse. I guess I'm here because my daughter died about six months ago. She meant everything to me. I don't feel like I'm coping very well. At first I was numb, but after that wore off I've just been in this incredible pain. I cry every day in the car on my way to work and when I drive back home. I have a son who's fourteen. I've been trying to pull myself together because of him, but sometimes it just seems too hard. I don't know what to do to feel better again."

"Letting go of the bonds that tie us to someone in grief can be challenging," Joy told us. "The first step is to honor the path that each of you has chosen, so let us first talk about honor. What does honor mean to you?"

"To put the needs of your country before your own, to be a courageous soldier," Ryan replied.

"To act according to what you think is right in a challenging situation," Jana chimed in. "I've found it's usually not the easiest choice."

"To do what you think is best for you," Angie suggested.

"This is closest to the truth," Joy told us. "First you must honor yourself before you can honor another in your experience. And to honor yourself is to bring yourself no harm."

Jana frowned and bit her lower lip as if to keep herself from protesting.

"I know some of you may think that putting yourself first is selfish. But being selfish is not necessarily a bad thing," Joy continued. "How can you give to another what you do not have? Here I will give you an example. If you saw someone drowning in the ocean, you wouldn't just jump in to save them—especially if you couldn't swim, or if you felt that they would pull you under the water with them. No, first you would put on a life vest and maybe take one of those surfboards into the water to rescue them. Always put your own needs first.

"Some of you may be so confused that you don't even know what your needs are. So you must become aware of your own thoughts. In this way, you can begin to live your life with clearer focus and intention.

"So here is your homework for the first class. Set aside three hours every day until our meeting next month to work on this assignment: Set a timer, and every fifteen minutes, write down what you are thinking and doing and how your thoughts make you feel. Let's plan on meeting again thirty days from today."

She passed around the white notebooks. "Keep your notes in these," she told us. "Does anyone have any questions?"

"What happens if I can't do this every day for a month?" Ryan frowned.

"Set your intention to work on this assignment every day. We'll discuss what will happen if you don't finish it at the next class."

At first this exercise was beyond irritating. *11:41 a.m.: I'm feeling tired. 11:52 a.m.: I'm feeling very annoyed. What in hell is this going to accomplish?* Then I began to see a connection between my thoughts, feelings, and behavior. It was fascinating. *I wonder how much my thoughts do create what's happening to me?*

At our next class, Joy asked us about our experiences with the fifteen-minute exercise. None of us had completed all thirty days of our homework and we were all feeling some degree of resistance to it.

"It's very important that you do complete this assignment," she urged. "The purpose of this exercise is to help you see more clearly how you can sabotage and harm yourself by your own thoughts. Most of you go through your days unaware, not only of what you are thinking, but of how your thoughts create your life experiences.

"These negative thoughts about yourself and your world prevent you from seeing yourself as the perfection that you are. Honor yourself by bringing these thoughts into the light so you can change them. You cannot change what you refuse to see. Remember that you can choose to experience love or fear. Find out the names of your fears, and this will lead you to their opposite, your joys. For how can you know what something is until you know what it is not? I would urge you to continue working on this assignment until you have completed thirty days."

Joy looked around at us as we fidgeted in our chairs, avoiding her gaze. "Seraphiel would like to come through now. For those of you who don't know, Seraphiel is an angel that I channel. He's always happy to answer your questions, so don't be afraid to ask if you're confused by anything he says. He's not Archangel Seraphiel—some of my students think he is, but they are mistaken." I watched Joy intently, with more than a pinch of skepticism.

She closed her eyes briefly and took a deep breath. Her posture and manner of speaking changed instantly. Joy was very kind and soft-spoken. The voice that now came from her was more forceful, but in a calm, authoritative way.

Seraphiel began by introducing us to the grand dream. "In the beginning, nothing existed except oneness and wholeness, but in your desire to know yourself, you dreamed yourself into existence as separate beings. The only way for you to know yourself is to perceive yourself as separate. You are all love, but often you express yourselves as what love is not—in other words, its opposite—in order to understand love more completely. The opposite of love is fear and judgment. You believe that you are imperfect. You judge yourself and others and this creates pain. Remember, nothing exists that you have not created. You are the architect of your own experience. Let me give you an example."

Then Joy turned toward me in her chair and the voice started speaking directly to me. "You are choosing to experience pain because of this one who has passed. You are giving your pain life, and it is growing inside you. You are becoming addicted to your pain. There are two paths in front of you; only one honors you and the one who has passed. You must let go. The pain comes to show you who you are. Ask yourself why you are choosing to give substance to your pain. The only way to know yourself as whole is to experience separation. Make the decision to see yourself as whole, complete within yourself, and intend to see the joy in your life once again."

Angie, Ryan, and Jana were all watching me intently. I sensed that they cared about me and were concerned about my feelings. I frowned. I didn't like this. I felt that this being, this Seraphiel, was examining me like some kind of insect under a microscope. He, she, it, whatever, saw me too clearly. Seraphiel locked eyes with me for a minute but I couldn't hold his gaze. I felt vulnerable and exposed. It was obvious, right from the start, that Seraphiel brought into the open exactly what he saw, and that his perception was crystal-clear and razor-sharp.

"You cannot live in your history of grief and guilt," the voice continued. "Your daughter chose to leave this side and you decided to remain here. You cannot cling to the way you were together; this will make her move farther away. You have to let go of all attachments to her as she was. Remember, to love someone is to let them be free. Every morning, right after you get out of bed, light a candle, sit and look into that candle, and see yourself as whole. Ask yourself, 'Where do love, peace, and joy exist in my being?'"

The voice continued to focus on me as tears slowly began to slide down my face. "Remember, in all that exists," he said more gently, "you are the dreamer, and the dream is caught up in a web of separation. Your true power is in remembering that you have created your experience. Ask for the sadness to leave. Ask for joy; ask the angelic realm for assistance in bringing joy back into your life. We can't help you unless you ask."

Then Joy hiccupped and suddenly was herself again.

She looked at me sniffling and dabbing my eyes with a tissue.

"Are you OK?"

"Yes, I'm fine."

"Would you like to talk about how you're feeling?"

"No, I'd just like to go home."

My mind was racing as I walked to my car. *I'm in a crazy class. I'm a PhD student, for Christ's sake, attending a class where my teacher claims to channel some supernatural being.* And yet, I couldn't deny the truth of what Joy had said, trance or no.

It wasn't until I was driving home that the totality of the coincidence hit me, and I shook my head in disbelief. Seraphiel. Of course. In my session with Kira, Callie had said she was with Raphael. Could she have meant Seraphiel? I felt a shiver creep up my arms and I broke out in goose bumps. So perhaps there *was* life after death, after all.

❧ 13 ❧

Diane—Two Wolves

The holiday season was fast approaching, and in the first week of November it was already getting dark at five p.m. When I got home, the house was cold and quiet, with Tom working late at the university and Anthony at a friend's house studying for exams. Only the ghosts of what used to be lurked in the corners. The house held so many memories, both good and bad: the sound of high heels on a wood floor, music playing from a now-abandoned room, echoes from a life that was extinguished much too soon. I felt connected to the world by the most tenuous of threads. I wondered whether people have any premonition of their own death. Did Callie know on Monday that she would be dead by Friday? Does something whisper in your ear—don't go there tonight, don't take that drive, don't do that drug—or are we just blind until the semi hits us head-on? And in that one mortal instant, do we realize that the game is up?

Sometimes I had to remind myself that nothing terrible was happening to me right at that moment. I slept in a warm bed with a full belly, Tom and Ruffy curled up beside me. I had good days when I felt lighter and bad days when the weight of the world was on my shoulders and regret hung heavy in the air.

The next week just after class, Joy asked me, "When are you going to decide to let go of your pain?"

"You don't understand," I said, turning on her. "I *am* my pain!" and then stomped out of the room, slamming the door behind me.

I drove home with tears streaming down my face. *Why do I refuse to let go of the pain?* I had done many things in my life, but the most important was being a mother. That was the role I most cherished, but I felt that I had failed miserably. A good mother was supposed to protect her children from harm, and I hadn't been able to save Callie from herself. Callie was my responsibility and I had let my daughter die. I remembered how relieved I had always been when Callie was safely home from work, from school, or from a party with friends. Never in my worst nightmares had I thought Callie would be the instrument of her death when she was supposed to be asleep in her own cherished bedroom. I felt that I must have done something terribly wrong to send Callie over the edge. My guilt was keeping me tied to my grief.

Then I heard a deep voice inside my head say, "It's not your fault. Everyone on earth is on their own individual path of destiny. You can't control another person's destiny. Let it go."

Joy decided to have a potluck dinner before class the Saturday after Thanksgiving. Jana called to let me know that I had been assigned the task of bringing a dessert. "How are you doing?" she then inquired.

I was really grateful that my classmate felt comfortable enough to ask me how I was. It seemed like everyone else tried to pretend that everything was back to normal.

"I'm hanging in there," I replied. That's exactly how I felt. I was barely holding on.

Tom walked into the kitchen Saturday morning as I was spreading some sour cream topping on the pumpkin pie I was bringing. He came up behind me, slipped his arm around my waist, and dipped his finger in the bowl in front of me. I slapped him on the wrist with a spatula and we both burst out laughing. It felt so strange to laugh again.

"It's nice to see you smile," he exclaimed, kissing me on the cheek before he sauntered out of the room.

I felt embarrassed about my outburst after the previous class, but at the potluck dinner no one mentioned it. We gathered around the table and Joy asked us to tell the group what we were thankful for that Thanksgiving. I wasn't feeling grateful for much of anything.

Finally I said, "I'm thankful to each of you for being my friend and for helping me through everything, and I'm sorry I was so rude after the last class."

"There's nothing to be sorry for," Joy replied.

Afterward, Seraphiel spoke again through Joy. "In order to release your pain, you must be honest about how you truly feel. When Diane shouted out, 'I am my pain,' she gave her emotion life so that it could die in its birth. When her soul heart released her pain, then there was room for the truth. The pain was caused by her denial of her need to punish herself. There is a tendency for humans to say to the negative aspects of their life, 'Go away; leave me alone.' They are afraid to acknowledge the truth."

"But how can we accept the truth when it can sometimes seem so unbearable?" asked Ryan. He was always challenging Seraphiel. He didn't seem at all intimidated by talking to an angel.

"Be honest with yourself. You must give life to your pain, so it will die in its birth and no longer torment you. Honesty always carries emotion when it comes from a deep place of pain. The honesty of the pain must be felt from spirit. This will give you freedom. Your pain can become your companion, and without it you may feel that you are truly alone. Remember, every moment you choose to experience pain, you rob yourself of a moment of joy. The intensity of the pain is no greater than the intensity of joy, because they occupy the same space. You are born with two wolves inside you; one is pain and the other joy. Which one are you going to feed?"

"I think I'm afraid to feel intense pain," said Angie as she thoughtfully sipped a cup of chamomile tea she had prepared for herself.

"Your journey is about remembering that you are love, sometimes expressing as what love is not—for example, fear. You have to know yourself in honesty. You are discovering your soul, your truth, your perfection, your wholeness. Ask yourself, what is the gift this experience is bringing me? Remember, you are not controlled in any way by the experience. Do not judge yourself or let others judge you. Do not participate in self-harm."

"I have a problem understanding what self-harm is," Jana interjected, absentmindedly patting Joy's Australian shepherd, Felicia, on the head.

"Once you fall in love with yourself, you will bring yourself no harm," Seraphiel replied. "You also cannot harm another without bringing harm to yourself, for you are me, and I am you. When you are self-love, you will be free. Love yourself consciously; be less critical of yourself. Ask yourself in everything you encounter, how can I love myself in this situation? Learn to seek the gift in your experiences. Ride the ride, receive the gift, and then move on. Live your life with zest, zeal, and excitement."

Then he turned and stared directly at me. "In order to be happy in this world that you have created, you must become your own lover. When you love yourself completely, you won't fear the loss of love. Enjoy the gift of time that others in your world spend with you, but if they're ready to move on, let them go. Let Callie go to dwell inside you as a part of you, not separate from you. Don't hang on to your suffering because you're afraid to know joy. You must learn to create joy when you are in your own presence. When you can feel the joy in your body for no apparent reason, then you are connected to the angelic realm.

"When you say this life is a struggle, you make it more of a struggle. When you suspect that someone else is bringing you less than love, then you have less than love within you. Your relationships create who you are. Always expect the best of yourself and everyone else. Know yourself as love, limitless. Remember always, life is just a ride. Own your power to steer your vehicle, to take your trip where you want to go. We would ask you as homework to apply honesty to all areas of your life, for there are parts of self that all of you still hold in the shadows and refuse to acknowledge."

"Like what?" I challenged. Usually Seraphiel intimidated me, but at that moment I was feeling unusually brave.

"That is for you to discover," Seraphiel replied mysteriously. Then Joy was herself again.

"I just hate it when Seraphiel is so enigmatic. It makes me crazy," I grumbled to Ryan as I stomped down Joy's steps, laden with leftovers for Anthony and Tom.

"I guess that's the price we pay for enlightenment," he laughed as he helped me stuff everything into my car.

~

A few days before Christmas, Anthony called me from Dwayne's house.

"Papa's nephew Scotty has a cat that just had kittens, and he's trying to find homes for them. Can I please have one, Mama?"

"Oh, I don't know about that, Anthony. We already have two cats." They were supposed to be barn cats, and I'd gotten them to keep the mice away from the horse feed. But they had a way of migrating back to the house. They would appear on the back porch as soon as the temperatures slipped below freezing, looking cold, lonely, and pathetic, meowing plaintively, begging to come inside. I, of course, would let them in, and they would happily curl up on the sofa in front of the blazing fireplace and fall blissfully asleep. Then I couldn't get them back outside.

"Please, Mama, I'll take care of the kitten and it can sleep in my room. I already have one picked out. She's got yellow and white tiger stripes and I'm going to name her Cinnamon."

I knew who would probably end up taking care of the kitten, but I relented anyway. "OK, Anthony, we'll give it a try and see how she gets along with the other animals. But if they fight, you'll have to take her back to Scotty."

"Oh, thank you, Mama. You'll really like her, you'll see. She's very sweet."

"So, how's Anthony doing at his dad's house?" Tom asked as we snuggled under several warm quilts in bed that night.

"He seems fine, but he's bringing a kitten home with him tomorrow."

"Oh, another animal for me to take care of."

"I'm afraid so." I smiled and kissed him on the lips.

Tom was an animal lover just like me. He would trudge to the barn bundled up in a down jacket when the weather turned bitingly cold to check on the horses and feed them their hay and grain. The bowls for cat and dog food were always full with a pan of fresh water beside them. Assorted chicken jerky treats were stashed away in the pantry. He really was a wonderful man.

When Anthony brought Cinnamon home, the other cats took one look at her, arched their backs menacingly, hissed, and stalked off. But little Ruffy came up to her and sniffed her nose curiously as Cinnamon stood still, frozen in place. It wasn't long before they were romping through the house playing together.

I managed to put up a tree and bought presents for Anthony, Megan, Ashley, and Jenny. I purchased a little silver bell and hung it halfway up the Christmas tree, thinking of how the bell rang when the angel Clarence finally got his wings in our family's favorite holiday movie, It's a Wonderful Life. We were having Christmas Eve dinner when I started hearing a persistent tinkling. I rushed into the living room. There was little Cinnamon, standing on her hind legs merrily batting that bell around and around.

That night I dreamed I was standing outside on my front porch, watching my neighbor's Christmas lights twinkle on and off. Then I noticed a light coming from behind the oak tree in our front yard. The light moved and I realized that it was shaped like a person but made up of filaments of very bright, beautiful, and radiant light. I gasped. It was Callie. She started walking toward me across the yard. I shouted "Callie" and ran to her, tears streaming down my face, as Callie leapt into my outstretched arms. Somehow we merged, and then I suddenly woke up.

I looked out the bedroom window as a full moon hovered over a glistening landscape of newly fallen snow. White flakes as large as nickels danced in a gust of wind. It was a Christmas miracle; it hardly ever snowed on Christmas Eve in Tennessee. It certainly was magical how Callie always seemed to find her way back to me. I sighed, in that moment peacefully contented at last, rolled over, and gently slid back into sleep.

～

Spring crept in slowly, the winds changing from biting and bitter to soft, warm fingers caressing my face. Callie's room was a mess again. Over the winter, I had taken to compulsively cleaning, and now everything I had decided I no longer needed was piled in that room, along with what remained of her possessions. I hated going into the room. It felt as though everything that had happened was somehow stuck in that space, reverberating like a pulse against the walls, and the air was heavy with desperation.

One Sunday in April, after class, I asked Joy if she knew of anyone who could clear the energy in Callie's room. She laughed. "That's something I can do for you. I've been clearing houses for many years." She agreed to come the following Saturday.

That morning, I got up early to bake some fresh bread to give to Joy to thank her for helping me. I pulled out an old book of recipes written by a Zen Buddhist monk. I hadn't baked bread in years. I opened the curtains in the large bay window in the kitchen so that as I worked,

I could watch the horses graze on the newly green grass that was just beginning to come up in the pastures.

I was stirring the ingredients in a large bowl when Tom strolled into the kitchen looking for coffee. Luckily he was going to be at the university that day to attend a weekend conference. I hadn't told him about Joy's visit.

"What are you making?" he asked as he poured some steaming-hot coffee into a travel cup.

"Oh, I'm just baking some bread," I answered, averting my eyes.

"Sounds good," he said, smiling. "I love homemade bread."

He strode up behind me, wrapped his arms around my waist, and kissed my hair. "See you this evening," he murmured into my ear. Then he was gone.

I turned my attention back to the bread. I rolled the dough into a ball, then placed it on a floured wooden board. As I kneaded, I remembered that the first anniversary of Callie's death was fast approaching. Quickly I became lost in thought.

Why am I holding onto the pain and not letting it go? Maybe I want Callie to see me suffer, so she will know how much pain she caused. Maybe she will feel sorry for what she did. Oh, I must be a little angry. Maybe I want to suffer to punish myself because I feel so guilty that I didn't know how depressed she was. I was so involved in my work and going to school. I didn't see how much pain she was in. Maybe I'm suffering so she will know how much I loved her. If she looks down on me and doesn't see me suffer, she will think that I don't care about her anymore. Maybe I want God to see me suffer. Bad things like this shouldn't happen to people like me. I have always tried to be a good person and do the right thing. If I am happy again, this means Callie's death was OK. Somehow I have to

find a way to let her go in love and wish her well on her journey,
until hopefully we meet again.

When Joy arrived, I took her on a tour of the house. "The energy in here really does feel pretty good, Diane."

"I haven't shown you Callie's room yet. The rest of the house is fine."

"Oh!" she exclaimed as I opened the door. "I see what you mean."

She turned around slowly and gazed at the walls, which were covered in strange wallpaper. Small gray images of all the signs of the zodiac on a white background covered the top half of the walls. The lower portion was papered in tiny white stars scattered across a midnight-blue background. Across the middle was a border made of bright yellow faces of the sun. I had always thought the wallpaper was really weird and wondered why Callie liked it.

"Leave me alone in the room for a while. I'll see what I can do."

She emerged about an hour later. I could smell burned sage, along with the scent from several lit white candles, and I saw that salt lined the doorway and windowsills. Four large, translucent, white crystals were placed on the floor, one in each corner. The energy felt much brighter.

"The crystals will help keep the space balanced," explained Joy as she closed the door. "Now, don't go in there for forty-seven hours to let the room clear. Then air out everything that's been inside. Leave it in sunlight for at least twelve hours. Strip all the wallpaper from the walls and put down some new carpet."

That night I saw Callie in a dream. She was in her bed asleep. Her sheets and bedspread were white and trimmed with lace. White lace curtains fluttered on a soft breeze. Her room was painted lemon yellow.

The next morning, I got to work. I cleaned my garage, emptied out the room, stripped the wallpaper, and started to paint the walls the color of yellow that I had seen in my dream. Tom stopped by on his way to the conference. "That color looks cheerful," he said with a smile. He seemed to be relieved that I was trying to remodel the room.

"Lemon yellow is the color of acceptance," Joy explained when she called the next day.

Right. I smiled. I shouldn't have been surprised.

✐ 14 ✐

Diane—The Wake-up Call

In early May, just before the anniversary of Callie's death, I decided to schedule another reading with Kira. I needed to give Callie another chance to tell me what had happened. Megan decided to join me for the reading. On a Sunday evening, we sat down together in my office with a speakerphone as well as one of Joy's lit white candles between us.

"I try to start with a blank slate," Kira began. "But I'm getting something right off the bat. I'm supposed to mention wings. Callie has wings. She's gotten her angel wings."

"Oh, I get it," I said. "It's like in *A Wonderful Life*, when the angel Clarence gets his wings. I gave each of the girls a bell with an angel on it last Christmas. And the bell on my tree started ringing and ringing on Christmas Eve."

"Is there some kind of braid connection between you, Megan, and Callie?"

Megan leaned toward the speaker and pulled her hair back behind her ears. "We always felt intertwined, like strands of a rope braided together, and we had the same last name."

"It's like there's no guilt here. Someone is still feeling guilty, but it's over and done. And believe me, she's busy. Did she have a counselor-type personality when she was with you?"

"Oh, yes," Megan replied.

"Because that's how she shows herself there, helping other teenagers. Megan, do you feel her around you a lot—like right next to you?"

Megan laughed as she cupped the candle flame briefly between her hands and peered at it intently. "Well, Callie showed up next to me in the car one evening. She was sitting there looking through the CDs, because I have a lot of hers."

"She says, 'Yeah, that was me.' Did someone put something metal like a necklace in her hand?"

"We put her car keys in her hand at the funeral home, and the key chain read: Don't drive faster than your angels can fly."

"She's busy. She's doing ten thousand things. This is a good feeling; she's full of energy and getting a lot done. She says that you should go out and have fun. You shouldn't be afraid to live your lives. She has that go-get-'em kind of energy. She makes me feel like I just drank a pot of coffee."

Kira continued. "She feels healed from her suicide. It was like a growth issue, a lot was learned from it. We may not like the situation or the way it happened. But from that incident, a lot of people learned lessons. She can look at it that way. Her perspective is much different from ours. She feels older than what she was. She was older than her years. She's getting kind of philosophical with you, Diane. She's saying you're both a lot stronger than either of you thought you were. It makes you a deeper person, and more compassionate about what other people are going through. Is there a Seraphiel with her? I know it seems like a strange name, but that's what I'm getting."

"Well, I go to a spiritual healer who channels an angel called Seraphiel," I replied.

"Oh, I see, his name is twisted a little, like it has a French twist."

"That's exactly right," I exclaimed. "He spells his name a little bit differently."

"He's letting you know he's here. Is he like a guide? My cheeks start to burn when it's a guide. It must be because their energy is higher or something. He's big: that's the only way I can describe him to you."

Megan and I exchanged glances. Her eyes were as big as saucers.

"My mom's told me about Seraphiel," she whispered.

"It's like he's everywhere," Kira continued. "He's that kind of energy. Do you meditate with him?"

"My spiritual healer, Joy, gives me meditations that he's channeled for me to do," I replied.

"Is there one that concerns a point of light? Does that have meaning for you? He's pushing the meditation."

"Oh, I know what that is. We're supposed to meditate in complete darkness, except for the light of a candle. I'm supposed to be doing this first thing every morning."

I guiltily eyed the candle we had lit. It was the very same candle I was supposed to be using for my meditation.

"Have you been doing it? Because I feel like he's lecturing you."

"No, actually, I'd completely forgotten about it."

"Don't worry, they're patient. They've got lots of time. He's funny, too. He's with Callie. She's zipping around.

He says, if he can keep up with Callie, he sees her. It's a little bit easier for him to communicate with you, just because that's what he does. His purpose is to foster connections between those on earth and the angelic realm to provide guidance and healing."

"He talks in images, too. He's showing me a mountain. That's the spiritual path, and this whole thing with Callie has ignited this in you. He's showing me that you are at the beginning of the path and going up the mountain. He's backing up on me, because he knows that he's strong. You can tell when they're a higher vibration because they're usually concerned about me. He just feels huge, all-encompassing, with a real strong feeling of comfort."

Megan and I glanced at each other briefly and smiled, then turned our attention back to the speakerphone.

"I'm going to try to get a little more from Callie if I can. She keeps saying over and over again, 'I know it's hard to believe from the physical but trust me, I'm fine.' She says you shouldn't ever feel guilty about going on with your life because that's what she wants you to do. You're not leaving her behind, and when you guys pass, she'll be there."

Megan interjected, "Every morning Callie would call me on my cell phone to wake me up for school, because I drove her to school every day. A couple of months ago, I was in a real deep sleep and my cell phone rang. I had her phone number programmed into my phone and it came up as Callie's cell number. It just happened that one time when I was late for school."

"The wake-up call has a double meaning, not just to wake up for school. It's an encouraging thing, like 'Wake up to the fact that I'm not gone.'

"I'm starting to lose the connection. She knows how you, all of you, feel about her. Just remember it's OK to joke and laugh. You honor her when you do that. It's OK to have fun. I'm supposed to say, 'Love you, guys.' Now my energy is pulling back. I feel like Seraphiel left with her. They were together, but they might not be all the time. And also, Eleanor left with them."

"Well, what did you think?" I asked Megan after we'd said our good-byes and I'd turned off the speakerphone.

"It sounded just like Callie, and Kira was right about her being a counselor person. She was always helping her friends with their problems."

"I can't believe that Seraphiel showed up too," I exclaimed. "And his comment about Callie zipping around, that was just priceless."

"I wonder what happens when they get their angel wings."

"Heck if I know."

"Well I do know one thing, Mama," Megan reminded me as we parted at the front door. "You'd better start doing that candle meditation."

"You're right about that. Love you, Megan."

"I love you too, Mama." She climbed into her car, and in an instant, she was gone.

~ 15 ~

Callie—The Reluctant Angel

Wings are among the few things that souls have to earn in the angelic realm. Most everything else that they want they can imagine, and poof, it's right there. But imagining and manifesting all the shit they thought they ever wanted gets real old, real fast. After I got settled in my Barbie house, I started collecting cars. I got a cobalt-blue Mustang just like the one Mama bought for me, a red Corvette for hanging out in the 'hood, a pink Cadillac just to be funky, a Hummer when I wanted to be a road warrior princess, and a black Chevy Silverado truck for when I wanted to go country. They cluttered up my driveway, and there was no way I was going to have the coolest car because everyone could imagine whatever they wanted, too. So, I got rid of all of them except my Mustang.

Now you may wonder how someone can dispose of an imagined something in heaven. It's really very simple. You just conjure up a bubble like those cute little ones I used to blow with a plastic wand when I was little, only much, much bigger. Then you imagine whatever you don't want inside the bubble and blow on it like you would a birthday candle and it just goes floating up into the clouds until it disappears. The boys like to imagine the things they don't like anymore exploding into a zillion pieces, but this is tidier and much more civilized.

I got my wings on Christmas Eve. Souls do celebrate Christmas in my part of the angelic realm, you know. We turn Summer Wind into winter. It snows big, white flakes and the snow piles up in huge, fluffy mounds everywhere. The fir trees that line the streets all have dark-green needles and are perfectly shaped just like Christmas trees. The snow coats each little pine needle like sugar crystals and piles up on the branches so that they bend down from its weight. We run along the sidewalks, stopping at the trees to shake the branches and let the snow fall all over us. We have huge snowball fights, boys against girls, of course. All the houses are decorated in clear, blue, or multicolored lights that twinkle on and off. Souls light red and bayberry candles and place them in every window. It's so beautiful.

The angel wing ceremony is held in a simple, brown, wooden church deep in the forest—one of my favorite places, with its steep, pitched roof and round turret with a bell tower on top. A winding staircase leads to the tower, and when you pull on a thick, heavy rope, brass church bells ring out in celebration. A large tapestry, depicting a golden cross surrounded by wavy rows of all the colors in the rainbow, hangs in the front of the chapel. The fir trees outside are decorated in strings of silver icicle lights and gold pinecones.

All the new angel's friends, family, and guides come to the angel wing ceremony. Creatures of the forest attend too—deer, raccoons, rabbits, chipmunks, squirrels, and even the occasional bear and her cubs. Jesus preaches a simple sermon on the meaning of Christmas and the role of angels as messengers of hope and teachers of love in God's kingdom. Then each new angel sings a song that he or she has composed for the occasion. Afterward, Jesus places one hand on the new angel's heart and the other in the center of her back, and immediately small angel wings sprout out of her back. New angels are allowed to let anyone in the universe know when they get their wings. That's why the bell on Mama's Christmas tree started to ring the exact moment that I got mine. *It's a Wonderful Life* isn't a fairy tale. It's really true.

After my ceremony, everyone gathered at the nearby frozen lake in the woods to ice-skate, eat s'mores, drink hot chocolate by a big bonfire, and celebrate. But I slipped away early. I went back home, and Mama saw me behind the big oak tree in the front yard. I wanted Mama to see what I looked like now that I had my wings. I knew she would be proud of me.

After I got my wings, I had to start taking classes at a new school. It was kind of like graduating from high school and starting college. A couple of my friends were going there with me. Now that they had their angel wings, some of the girls felt that they needed to become more spiritual. For some stupid reason, they decided that being spiritual meant that they couldn't have any fun! Personally, I thought they were being pretty ridiculous. The girls gave away their thong underwear, high-heeled shoes, and jewelry and took to wearing flowing, long-sleeved, white gowns and no makeup or nail polish. I was still wearing whatever I wanted, partying every Saturday night, listening to music and dancing. There's great music in the angelic realm. All the rock stars who have crossed over have huge concerts in the park, and no one has to worry about rain spoiling all the fun. Anyway, my best friend,

Tamara, pulled me aside the day before we were going to begin classes and said, "Callie, please don't wear anything outrageous to school. You really need to get serious about this. It's a big step for all of us."

"Actually, T, I was thinking I'd wear a gown just like yours."

"That's great!" Tamara said with a smile, relieved.

Well, she hasn't said anything about my not doing something outrageous! I thought.

When my brother was in junior high, he bought a rubber whoopee cushion from a party store that farted when someone sat on it. He delighted in hiding it under my or Mama's seat cushion at the dinner table—but he never did have the nerve to put it on Papa's chair. I decided to imagine myself one of those farting cushions, and I put it on Seraphiel's chair. I wore one of those god-awful white gowns to class, and Tamara smiled at me as I sat down.

We were all assembled when Seraphiel strode in with a bunch of books in his arms. I had taken to pinching myself until it hurt so I wouldn't start to laugh. He put the books down on the table, pulled out his chair, and sat down. Immediately a loud and prolonged fart issued from the depths of the chair. All the kids in class glanced around at each other, trying to maintain a serious expression. Seraphiel looked perplexed. He got partway up and sat back down again, and another loud fart issued from the chair. We all looked down, trying hard not to laugh. Then Seraphiel stood up, pulled the cushion from the chair, and deposited it in the center of the table. Everyone burst out laughing.

"And to whom," he asked, glaring at the class, "do I owe the pleasure of receiving this gift?" We all got very quiet. "Miss Callie," he queried, looking directly at me. "Do you have any idea how this cushion got on my chair?"

"I might."

"You either do or you don't."

"I think I do."

"Please explain."

"I might have put it there," I hedged.

"And can you tell the class why you put this cushion on my chair?"

"Well," I replied obstinately, "I've got my angel wings, but that doesn't mean I can't have a little fun once in a while."

"You are very correct, and so our first lesson will be on the importance of having fun and not taking ourselves too seriously."

I advanced to rescuing kids who had been killed suddenly in an accident or who had been murdered. This was actually more difficult than rescuing suicide kids. The kids who crossed themselves over knew on some level that they had chosen this. They usually suffered from a deep sense of unworthiness and self-hatred. But when they realized just how precious and loved they really were, it was easier for them to heal. The kids who were murdered or killed in accidents were often very angry that their lives had been cut short. The murdered kids became obsessed with trying to get clues to their parents or the authorities about what had happened and who had done it. Kids who had been killed by someone like a drunk driver were absorbed in trying to see that justice was done. They had chosen a difficult lesson, to understand the meaning of forgiveness. They had to forgive everything and move on so they could find the light.

"Being human is like being in a huge amusement park," Seraphiel lectured one day in class, "and you get to choose the rides that you want to go on."

"Well, that's easy for you to say; you've never been human," I interjected. "But a lot of people don't find the rides very amusing at all."

"You have designed your earth experience to learn that you are love. Look for the gift in the experiences you choose. Once you learn to find the gift, the ride gets easier."

As I sat there, tapping my pencil, I knew one thing for sure. My mama must have signed up for one hell of a ride!

☙ 16 ❧

Diane—Struggling to Let Go

I was suffering from an overwhelming feeling of exhaustion right after the first anniversary of Callie's death. I tried the candle meditation for a couple of weeks, then gave it up. I forced myself out of bed every morning to go to work or school, and collapsed back into it at night. I was still having trouble wrapping myself around the experience. *How could Callie leave so abruptly with no warning? She left so impulsively, without thinking of the consequence.* Callie was just gone from my life with no apology for the mess she left behind, and apparently, she had no regrets.

Grief comes in waves; it ebbs and flows like the tides of the ocean. At least, such was the case for me. Sometimes, I felt that as soon as I took one step forward in my healing, I took two steps back.

I knew that I had been profoundly changed by the experience. But the trouble was I really didn't know who I was anymore. I wondered if I would ever feel joy or happiness again. Those feelings were totally gone from my life and had been replaced by a sense of forced resignation.

As I became more and more depressed, I lost interest in my appearance. It was just too much effort to put makeup on or fix my hair. I would throw on whatever wrinkled clothing I had worn the day before and head out the door. I knew that Tom noticed, but he didn't say anything. Tom and I made love less and less frequently. Many times at night, I would curl up into a ball on my side of the bed. I just wanted to be left alone. But I found that I did feel better when we occasionally did make love. The hole inside my heart was somehow filled, if only for a short time. I longed for the sensual part of my nature to return. I wanted to lie in bed with my lover and just enjoy him touching me, the energy between us feeling like a warm breeze or a hot wind. I wanted to spend hours in his arms, feeling the ebb and flow of desire. I wanted to dance naked under the moon and stars on a hot summer night. Maybe then I would feel like I was still alive.

One evening after I brushed my teeth and climbed wearily into bed, Tom touched me gently on the shoulder.

"Diane, you've been so distant lately. What's wrong?"

"Oh, I'm just tired."

"No, it's more than that; you seem so sad. Is there anything I can do? Would you like to talk about it?"

"There's nothing that anyone can do for me. I just want to go to sleep."

I punched my pillow a few times and turned on my side away from him.

"OK," he sighed. He turned off the bedside lamp and we both lay there awake in the dark. We could have been a million miles away from each other; the chasm between us was so deep.

A few weeks later, I decided to start reading the books I'd accumulated over the years about life after death, reincarnation, after-death communication, mediums, channeling, and electronic voice phenomena. Pretty soon, I became consumed by them. Tom would find me in bed late at night wearing faded cotton pajamas and hunched over some book with a yellow highlighter in my hand. Sometimes when my metaphysical studies kept him awake, he would resort to sleeping on the sofa in the family room.

One evening, he walked into our bedroom and eyed the tangled mess of yellow legal pads, research reports, books, and magazines strewn all over the bed. He moved some aside so he could sit down on the edge of the mattress next to me. He took my hand, massaging my palm.

"Do you really think reading all this stuff is going to help you?"

"You have to read some of these articles. Some of the research is actually pretty compelling, especially the work that's been done with mediums in a lab under controlled conditions. There's actually scientific evidence of life after death."

"Well, Diane, I have no interest in reading this stuff. I guess I'll find out if there's an afterlife when I die."

"I can't believe you have no curiosity about all this. After all, scientists are supposed to have inquiring minds." Annoyed, I removed my hand from his.

"I think you're becoming obsessed. You've got to focus on life and stop dwelling on death all the time."

"I'm not obsessed; it's just what I need to do right now."

"Well, I'm concerned about what's happening to us. And what about Anthony? Where does he fit into all this? Anthony needs you—hell, I need you. It's been over a year. You've got to move on."

"I'm sorry, but I have to do this. I have to know if there's any chance that Callie and I will be together again."

He got up abruptly and walked out of the room. "OK, Diane, have it your way."

I knew he was frustrated, but it was only making me retreat further into myself. I had already lost Callie; now I was beginning to think I might lose Tom as well.

≈ 17 ≈

Callie—Graveyard Love

I decided I needed to get my mama a love potion. Dustin told me his parents broke up after he died. His dad, an accountant, went right back to work. But his mama stayed home for six months. Some days she didn't even get out of bed. His dad couldn't understand why she refused to pull herself together and get on with her life. And she felt that he just didn't care. I didn't want this to happen to Mama and Tom.

I made a quick trip to a charm and magic shop in the French Quarter of New Orleans late one night. It was now my favorite city in the whole world. I suppose I could have made up a potion myself, but I loved creeping around New Orleans unnoticed and this was a convenient excuse. I was rummaging through the dusty, old, brown glass jars on the shelves in what looked to be an abandoned storage room in the back recesses of a basement when the overhead fluorescent bulbs suddenly exploded with light.

"Hey, little girl, you get out of my stuff!" a voice thundered.

I jumped, startled, and a jar I was holding tumbled to the floor, shattering into a zillion pieces. God, I just hate it when humans can see me when I'm not expecting them to.

There in the doorway was a thin, wizened old black woman, frizzled hair streaked with gray, leaning heavily on a wooden cane. She was wearing a dark burgundy housedress and black shoes, and her hose were rolled down to just below her knees and peeked out from under the hem of her dress.

"Now look at what you've done," she scolded. She didn't seem afraid of me at all.

"I'm so sorry. I didn't mean to drop your jar."

"No matter." She opened a closet door and pulled out an old broom, dustpan, and wastebasket.

"What are you doing here?" She eyed me curiously as she scooped the glass shards into the dustpan.

"I was looking for a love potion."

"What do you need one of those for? You're dead!"

"You don't need to remind me of that unfortunate fact," I sniffed. "It's not for me, it's for my mama."

"Oh, so your mama's got man troubles."

"Yeah, sort of. Please, can you help me?"

"I've got all kinds of love potions for all the lonely hearts in New Orleans. Potions for enchantment and seduction, to rekindle passion or enhance physical pleasure, to make a man bow to your every wish or make you irresistibly beautiful. What's your mama's trouble?" she asked, running her wrinkled hand across the jars on the shelf.

"Well, she's been depressed ever since I died and her boyfriend, his name is Tom, doesn't know what to do to help her, so they're just drifting apart."

"Oh, that's too bad. Well, I have just the thing for her." She reached up and pulled a purple jar containing a small, pink crystal surrounded by a dark, amber liquid down from a shelf.

"What's that?"

"This is my best potion to mend a broken heart."

"What's it got in it?" I held the jar up to the light, squinting as I attempted to peer inside.

"Well, that's a quartz crystal, and it's got red rose oil, crushed forget-me-nots, spearmint, and aged honey inside. It works real good. Take it back to your mama; put a few drops under her pillow just before she goes to bed—here, take the lid off, it smells so nice—and it will help her open her heart to Tom's compassion as she sleeps."

"Oh, thank you; you don't know what this means to me," I told the old woman.

"You sure do love your mama to be thinking about her like this even from beyond the grave."

"Yes, I do." I grasped the jar tightly in my hands as just one tear slid slowly down my cheek.

She looked at me intently and wiped the tear away with a gnarled finger.

"What's your name, child?"

"Callie."

"Here, Callie, why don't you come upstairs with me and have a cup of chamomile tea?"

I followed her as she slowly and creakily made her way up the steps into the kitchen that she used to mix her ingredients for her magic potions. Soon we were sitting across from each other at an old wooden table, steaming cups of tea in our hands.

"You know, you and your mama had the kind of love that we here in the Quarter call graveyard love."

My eyes widened.

"Graveyard love usually refers to a relationship between a man and a woman that is doomed from the first hello, like Romeo and Juliet. The ties that bind them are conflicted, and one or both of the lovers end up dying young, some people think before their time, sometimes by accident but more often through murder or suicide."

She focused on me with a penetrating stare as I looked down at the tea leaves that were settling into the bottom of my cup.

"But why was my relationship with Mama graveyard love?"

"There were crosscurrents at work and contracts that were made on your side of the veil that couldn't be broken. When was your birthday?"

"September 12."

"Oh, so you're a Virgo. That must be why you're so pretty." She smiled and I blushed. "How about your mama?"

"June 12."

She nodded her head. "Yes, in astrological terms you both were a perfect square. Opposites attract, but squares at some level are always at war with each other."

I sighed.

"On the other hand, your mama and Tom are twin flames."

"What's that?"

"Twin flames are really one, the same soul, but they divide in half, usually into a man and a woman, when they return to earth. But they're destined to be reunited again."

"Wow!" I was amazed.

"Sometimes, though, the weight of the world is so heavy that even twin flames have trouble recognizing each other. You know, life should be all about love, but most of the time it's not. For some stupid reason, we always seem to be fighting with each other. It makes for good business for me, though." She smiled. "Maybe we have to learn what love is by first experiencing its opposite."

"Yes, my guardian angel, Seraphiel, says the same thing."

"Well, he's very wise. It's nice meeting you, Callie. It won't be long now before I join you. These old bones are getting mighty tired. I sure would like to meet your Seraphiel."

"Oh, I think that can easily be arranged. As soon as I see you're a goner, I'll come pick you up."

She cackled. "Well, then, we have a deal. Now this potion may take a while to work, so don't get discouraged if you don't see any results right away." She waved good-bye at the front door.

"OK, I'll remember that," I replied as I took off down Canal Street.

That night, I put the potion under Mama's pillow. I couldn't wait to see what might happen.

DIANE

In early June, I went to West Virginia for my parents' six-tieth wedding anniversary. I stayed at their lakeside cot-tage, deep in the heart of the mountains. Every summer since they were babies, I had taken Callie and Anthony to visit my parents in their cottage in the woods. It felt so strange to be traveling the winding mountain roads with only Anthony by my side. I was dreading going there again; I knew I would feel Callie's presence everywhere. I brought the little cookie Callie had baked for me in cook-ing class the day before she died. I had initially placed it in my jewelry chest but finally decided to dispose of it on this trip. The cookie was hard as a rock but amazingly still intact.

We arrived just before sunset, and my dad greeted us at the back door. He and I were very close. Even though he hadn't spoken of Callie's death since her funeral, I felt he understood my sadness. As is typical of those in his generation, he was a man of few words. But in the days after she died, just his quiet presence was comforting to me.

My dad had been fourteen, the same age as Anthony, when his father drowned in a fishing accident while visiting his parents in Colby, Wisconsin. According to his obituary, my grandfather drove alone to a river where he used to spend his weekend afternoons fly-fishing for trout in his youth. He apparently lost his footing while stepping from one rock to another, fell, and struck the back of his head. Unconscious, he rolled over into the swift-moving current and drowned. A search was initiated when he didn't return to his parents' house that evening, and his body was discovered in the swirling waters the next morning.

My father never spoke about his own dad in all the years I was growing up. There were no photos of him in the house. It was almost as if he'd never existed, except in my imagination, and it wasn't until I visited his sister, my Aunt Peggy, that I found out exactly what had happened.

I suppose because of this early tragedy in his life, my dad was extremely overprotective of me and my sister, terrified of what dangers might be lurking just around the corner. Like Callie, my grandfather died in mid-May, and I wondered as my father sat in the church pew at Callie's funeral if he remembered the funeral for his father so many years earlier.

On the other hand, my relationship with my mother had always been conflicted. She was an only child and had been raised with every advantage. My dad catered to all her whims, and she never had to work outside the home a day in her life.

She had a habit of calling me at the most inconvenient times, especially during dinner, and she could be very critical. During our most recent conversation, when we were discussing why Callie might have been acting out and depressed, she stated, "Well, I never had problems like that with you girls."

"Things were different then, Mom," I tried to explain. "Kids weren't exposed to drugs and violence the way they are now. There wasn't so much social pressure to drink and have sex in high school or even junior high. Life is a lot more complicated for kids these days."

"Well, maybe if you'd been home more she might not have gotten into so much trouble. She would've had someone she could turn to when her life got difficult."

"Maybe I wasn't home all the time like you," I retorted. "But she knew she could talk to me about her problems; she just chose not to. I've got to go and help Tom with dinner." I angrily slammed down the phone. Why did she always make me feel so guilty?

My father's voice summoned me back to the present moment. "Come on inside out of the rain. Your mom's making dinner."

We shed our jackets and umbrellas in the mud room and walked into the den, which was furnished with cushioned wicker chairs and a large rattan sofa. A huge painting of a mallard duck hung above a blazing fireplace. Braided rugs covered the oak floor. Large picture windows overlooking a covered back porch lined one side of the den. Overgrown fir trees immediately outside the porch swayed gently in the evening breeze. I could see the lake shimmering in the late-day sun in the distance.

My mother walked in, wiping her hands on a dish towel and wearing a rumpled blue housedress made out of denim with large brown buttons down the front. She hugged Anthony and glanced my way. "Dinner's ready," was all she said.

The conversation over chicken and dumplings was quite ordinary. We discussed plans for the anniversary party at the country club, my lack of progress on my dissertation, and Anthony's interest in rock climbing. Not a word was spoken about Callie or the fact that this was our first visit to the cottage without her.

After dinner, I took Ruffy and climbed the steps to a path that led through the forest to the ridgeline, where the grass was lit green and gold by the sun setting against the backdrop of the darkening forest. Several red and brown white-tailed deer, startled by my presence, pricked up their ears and then took off, waving their tails from side to side as they bounded into a clearing ahead of me. When I reached the clearing, I almost stumbled across the skeleton of a dead deer lying on its side. Life and death, they really are two sides of the same coin. The other deer had stopped and were watching me curiously from a safe distance through the trees. I decided to bury the cookie there, as if covering it with earth would erase the memory of the day Callie gave it to me and all that happened afterward. I dug a hole with my hands and a stick under a fir tree, deposited the cookie, covered it with soil, and then stamped the ground firmly with my foot.

Darkness was rapidly approaching as I made my way back into the woods, and I almost got lost trying to find my way back to the cottage. I could see the mist rising on the lake and noticed that Anthony was sitting on an Adirondack chair at the end of the dock. I wondered how he was feeling. He had his CD player with him and had listened to music for most of the drive to the cottage. He had just received his learner's permit, and I had let him drive on some quiet roads through Kentucky, but it made me so nervous I couldn't sit still in the passenger seat. I was determined to teach him to drive. I didn't want to lose him in an automobile accident.

I decided to sit with him on the dock for a while, but by the time I got back to the cottage, he had come inside and fallen asleep on the sofa by the fire. I went to sleep that night to the forest sounds—the hoot of an owl, the soft wind in the pine trees—and I imagined that the wind blew the branches of the trees down toward me so they could surround me and comfort me as I slept.

～

That September 12 would have been Callie's eighteenth birthday, and all day I felt her presence. I smelled her perfume in her room and her cigarette smoke in the car. The words to the song from the movie Cinderella, "A Dream Is a Wish Your Heart Makes," played over and over again in my head. I spent the day quietly. Jenny called late in the afternoon asking me if we could meet that evening at Callie's grave.

Jenny and I sat together at Callie's grave in the back of the cemetery in the gathering dusk. A steady stream of cars entered the parking lot of the funeral home. A famous country music star had died that day, and the whole world would mourn his passing. Jenny and I were the only ones there to mourn the passing of a young girl who should have just turned eighteen.

Afterward, I took Jenny to dinner and she pulled out a wallet from her purse.

"This was Callie's rainbow wallet," Jenny explained, pointing to the rainbow on the wallet cover. "I take it everywhere with me. I lost it just one time and tore the house apart trying to find it." Jenny showed me the contents of the wallet. It was full of photos of Callie and also contained the verses of her favorite poem, "Annabel Lee."

"Thank you for calling me today," I said as I dropped Jenny off at her house. "I wasn't planning to do anything for Callie's birthday, but this was really nice."

"I'm glad I was able to spend the evening with you, Mama." Jenny waved good-bye at her front door as I drove away.

~

That night, Callie appeared again in a dream. She joined me while I was at a restaurant waiting for a table. Callie was wearing a blue and gold sari and carrying a baby in her arms. We sat down together at a table, and I was very aware that she was supposed to be dead. Some very harmonic and peaceful music was playing in the background. Several other spirit beings were gathered around our table to witness our reunion. Callie picked up the rainbow wallet from the table and started looking at the photos. She turned to me and said, "I'm glad Jenny has my rainbow wallet."

Then she vanished, and I woke up, gazing at the ceiling in the dark. I was no longer shocked or surprised by

Callie's dream visits. I had come to accept them as part of my reality. I didn't tell anyone except Joy and the members of my angel class about the dreams. I didn't mention them to Tom anymore either. *People will only think I'm crazy.*

Later that week, during an evening meditation, I let my imagination take flight. I went searching for Callie. I traveled in my mind through a gray mist that grew brighter and brighter as I went up a staircase that led to a grassy area in front of a huge castle. The castle was gleaming gold and silver in the afternoon sun and surrounded by a sparkling stream. I stepped onto a bridge over the stream and saw beautiful koi and huge pink and white water lilies below me. Suddenly, Callie appeared before me wearing a very sweet expression on her face. She took me to a multicolored waterfall in front of a huge, dome-shaped building.

"It's a spirit hospital," Callie said. She took me to a crystal healing room, then showed me various places—a forest room, a meadow room, a beach or desert room—where souls could go to rest. "I'm working as a rescuer for injured souls," she told me. "I find them and persuade them to come with me into the light." After a moment, she paused. "I can't take you any farther, Mama; you have to go back. Seraphiel's calling me to class."

The Monday after Thanksgiving, I noticed a light on in my office just after midnight. I made my way downstairs to find Anthony sitting at the computer desk, wads of crumpled paper scattered around him on the floor. His textbooks and assignments were tossed haphazardly on the desk and a chair beside him. An open bag of potato chips and a can of Coke sat precariously at the edge of the desk, ready to topple over at any moment.

I reached over to rescue the Coke can. "Anthony, it's after midnight. Don't you think you should be in bed? You have school tomorrow."

Anthony took off his glasses, tossed them recklessly on top of the heap of textbooks, and glared at me. "No, I can't go to bed. I have to write a report about one of Shakespeare's plays; it's due on Wednesday for my English class. I have a movie critique for sociology due on Thursday and two tests on Friday, one for biology on the Krebs cycle, which I don't understand, and an algebra test on polynomials, which I don't understand either." He scowled at all the scrunched-up papers on the floor.

Anthony was on the college track in high school, and he knew that making good grades was important in his sophomore year.

"I know this semester has been difficult for you, but it's almost over, and you did really well on your midsemester report card," I reminded him.

"Well, my final grades are going to suck if I flunk these two tests and screw up my reports."

"I can probably look over your report and your movie critique tomorrow. I'm pretty good at writing. Would that help?"

He shuffled some papers on the desk. "Yeah, here they are."

"I'm afraid I don't understand the Krebs cycle or polynomials very well. Why don't you ask your teachers tomorrow if they can hold a review session for students sometime this week, maybe over lunch? That's what some of my professors do. I bet there are other kids in your classes who're having the same problems understanding the material."

"I don't know if they'll want to do that."

"Well, it never hurts to ask."

Then I had a light bulb moment. I'd been trying to think of ways to encourage Tom and Anthony to get to know each other better. This seemed like a perfect opportunity. "You know, Tom's a statistician. I bet he understands algebra, too. Would you like me to ask him to help you?"

"Yeah, that would be OK."

"I get overwhelmed sometimes too with work and school," I told him. "I try to read just one chapter from a novel every night before I go to sleep to help me unwind a bit. Right now, I'm reading this story about an adventurer who gets lost on his descent down a huge mountain called K2. It's like Mount Everest."

"I read about Mount Everest in *Outside* magazine."

"It's a very dangerous climb. Anyway, he gets separated from his Sherpa, who has all their food, along with their tent and sleeping bags. Do you know what Sherpas do?"

"They carry all the supplies for the expedition up the mountain."

"Yes, so all this climber has is a candy bar and a canteen of water. Darkness is falling and he knows if he keeps going he might fall into an ice crevice and die."

"I saw pictures of ice crevices on Mount Everest; they looked pretty scary." Anthony pulled the bag of potato chips into his lap and started munching on them. For this once, I decided not to lecture him about his occasional bad eating habits.

"He decides to stop for the night under the shelter of an outcropping of rocks. He's all alone out there on the mountain and doesn't know if he will be able to survive until morning. When I think about that, I realize that things could be a whole lot worse."

"Yeah, I suppose so. I guess we should be happy for what we have."

I smiled. Anthony was at times very mature for his age.

"Let's go to bed; things will look better in the morning after you've had some sleep." We turned off the computer and the lights and made our way back to our warm beds.

The next morning, Tom was up early for an eight o'clock class. "Could you do me a big favor?" I asked as he was dashing out the door.

"What's that?"

"Could you help Anthony study for an algebra exam?"

"Be glad to."

That evening, I found them together on the sofa in Anthony's room, poring over Anthony's algebra text-book. I gently closed the door so I wouldn't disturb them.

Tom's such a nice man and I've been so distant and aloof, I scolded myself. *He's doing the best he can and I've been so withdrawn.* That night I vowed to be more understanding of his situation. *It must be very difficult for him to be with someone who is perpetually in mourning.*

On campus the next day, I saw Tom as I was walking to a lecture at the medical school, his briefcase and a bunch of books in his arms. He was leaving that afternoon for a weekend conference in Los Angeles. He was planning to finish his morning classes and then drive to the airport. We stopped in unison, gazing at each other. Students scurried all around us as they rushed to class, wearing their backpacks and wool jackets, scarves tossed casually around their necks, chattering and laughing.

The last of the autumn leaves mingled with a few flakes of snow swirled around us, but all I saw was Tom.

I walked up to him, wrapped my arms around him, and kissed him on the side of his neck.

"May the angels keep you safe," I whispered.

I backed away and looked at him. He was grinning from ear to ear. Then he turned and walked away.

I felt a surge of happiness and paused because the feeling had become so foreign to me by then. *Never forget that you are loved*, I reminded myself as I made my way slowly toward the lecture hall.

☞ 18 ☜

Diane—Holding You in My Spirit Heart

A few days after the New Year, I was online late on a Friday evening and stumbled on a website called Spirit Light Connections, run by an organization that trained mediums. I noticed that they were holding practice readings for their students that night. On impulse, I decided to enter the chat room. About sixteen people had already logged on for the readings, which were just about to begin.

LAURA: Welcome to Spirit Light Connections. The readers here, Star and Natalie, are graduates of our mediumship classes. They will tell you what they see, feel, and hear. The readers will do their best to reach the loved one you wish to connect with, but please keep in mind that this does not always happen. The spirit that needs to come through will, so please be open to that. Are there any questions before we begin?

The other guests in the chat room and I all typed, "No."

After a few minutes of silence, the medium named Star stated that a spirit had just entered the room.

STAR: I have a tall, slender, young woman. She is in her early twenties, with long blonde hair, very sweet and loving. She is holding up four fingers, which I take is four siblings or four in the family, and she mentions the month of May. May was a very special time for her, spring and the renewal of things. I am seeing apple blossoms on a tree. Does anyone recognize this spirit?

After a few minutes and a series of "no" responses on my computer screen, the typing continued.

STAR: OK, let me recap for those who just came in. I have a tall, young, blonde woman, long hair, very sweet, mentions the month of May, and first name with the initial C. Does anyone recognize this? She is very happy to be here, very loving energy. She likes children.

NATALIE: Please respond only if you think you recognize this spirit, and remember that this may not be a member of your family or the person you are looking to hear from.

STAR: She is humming a song—a lullaby, I think, and rocking a baby in her arms.

NATALIE: I see her playing with a cross around her neck. She is connected to Christ. I also feel she did some writing, possibly a journal.

I sat transfixed, staring at the computer screen. When Natalie mentioned the journal, I suddenly realized they were talking about Callie.

DIANE: I had a daughter who passed named Callie. But she was only sixteen. She wrote lots of poetry.

NATALIE: OK, Diane. Does it sound like her? Does the rest fit, I mean?

STAR: What age would she be now?

DIANE: She'd be eighteen. She passed in May, a year and a half ago. She was very loving, always.

STAR: She is looking at her hands, long fingers. I feel she liked to do things with her hands.

DIANE: Oh, yes. She loved to draw and work on craft projects.

NATALIE: Is there something she kept under lock and key? I see a small key.

DIANE: Yes, that's her diary.

NATALIE: Is there a younger boy? I see her sending hugs to him.

DIANE: Yes, she had a little brother. His name is Anthony.

STAR: She says you were very good to her, and she appreciates it. Even though it may not have seemed so at the time. You were very patient.

DIANE: We were best friends as well as mother and daughter.

STAR: She smiles and says, "We still are!"

NATALIE: She says she's fine, Diane.

STAR: She says you did something special for her recently.

NATALIE: Something you did in memory of her. Does this make sense to you, Diane? She says, think about it.

DIANE: Yes! I sent a "Merry Christmas from Heaven" ornament from her to all of her best friends last month to place on their trees this Christmas.

STAR: She's thanking you for that—for keeping her memory alive. You always did such special things for her.

DIANE: That's because she was so special.

STAR: She's laughing and says, "You were special too." She's still around you and says not to be despondent. She comforts you on bad days. So just remember that. She must have loved flowers, because she keeps showing them to me, apple blossoms.

NATALIE: I am seeing a windowsill in the kitchen, I believe.

DIANE: I have several apple trees and a very large flower garden. She loved my garden and used to pick all my flowers.

STAR: Not your everyday florist flowers, but nature's own.

NATALIE: Do you have something special there?

DIANE: Yes, I made a memorial flower garden for her after she passed.

STAR: She really loves it. She's blowing kisses to you.

NATALIE: I feel a dog around her—an energetic one, a very excited little dog.

DIANE: That's her cocker spaniel, Boo.

STAR: Diane, do you have buttercups in your garden?

DIANE: Yes, lots of buttercups in the spring.

NATALIE: She is thrilled to be here.

DIANE: She always enjoyed being the center of attention!

STAR: Then maybe that's why she just spun around in a little dance.

DIANE: She was a very loving child. She always told me she loved me.

NATALIE: Well, you just took the words right out of her mouth.

STAR: She's showing me a refrigerator. Did you post her artwork on the refrigerator?

DIANE: Well, she had a refrigerator in her room where she stored all of her snacks, and some of her artwork was on the door.

NATALIE: She says the love she has for you has not passed away, and she holds you in her spirit heart. She asks that you give hugs and kisses from her to the rest of the family. And don't forget to tell her goodnight every evening. She likes that. She's waving good-bye, throwing kisses.

Thank you for sharing her with us, Diane. She is so very sweet and loving. It brings me tears of joy.

DIANE: It sounds just like Callie.

LAURA: She pushed her way through all the spirits to get to you. She loves you very much.

I stopped typing and sat at my desk, staring out the window as the flickering lights from several cars meandering down my street briefly lit the rain-washed asphalt.

The readers moved on to connect with another spirit who was able to meet them across the great abyss. The girl they had described to me embodied everything that I loved so much about Callie, her warmth and caring, her creativity, her love of nature and animals.

I picked up a snow globe that I kept on my desk, the one she had purchased on our last trip to the beach. Two dolphins were riding the ocean waves, a large one and a smaller one tucked protectively under the larger dolphin's fin. I tilted the globe up and down a few times, watching the sparkling pieces of blue and silver light swirl and dance around the dolphins. Maybe, although Callie wasn't physically here with me, we were still connected by some magical force of light. The thought was somehow comforting as I made my way quietly to bed.

Diane—The Angel Quest

Angie, Ryan, Jana, and I continued to meet once a month at Joy's house for our angel class. I thought it was amazing how much progress my classmates had made since our first afternoon together almost a year and a half earlier. But I didn't think I'd gotten very far in my recovery.

Angie was in a relationship with a man she met a few months after our classes began. She was learning how to stand up for herself and tell him what she needed instead of just running away when things got difficult. And he was responding to her concerns, which drew them closer together.

Jana's mother had died a few months earlier. She'd been a pack rat, and the large basement in the house where Jana grew up was crammed floor to ceiling with junk. She had never let Jana clean anything out while she was alive. Stuff she hadn't seen in years instantly became her most precious possessions when Jana tried to dispose of them. Now Jana was finally getting the opportunity to empty the house, and this seemed to invigorate her. Her latest find was her grandmother's sterling-silver tea service, which she discovered at the bottom of a large box full of moldy blankets. Jana was thinking about going back to work but wasn't sure about what she wanted to do with the rest of her life.

Ryan still struggled. He would stop drinking for a while. But when life got challenging, he'd fall back into his old habits. The economy was in a recession and he was having trouble finding work. He'd get depressed and resort to alcohol to make himself feel better. I started asking him to come out to my place, which always seemed to need something fixed. Tom, although a whiz with computers, wasn't much of a handyman. He had tried to fix a leaky faucet and ended up breaking the connection to the pipe. Water started spraying out all over the kitchen because he'd neglected to turn it off, and it took him a few minutes to get the geyser under control. I finally called a plumber to get everything fixed.

Ryan happily installed new wood floors in our bedroom, painted the walls, replaced a broken toilet, and hung a new light fixture in the family room. Tom was a little suspicious of him at first.

"He's just a friend," I explained. "He's out of work and I'm only trying to help him out until he gets himself back on his feet."

Tom seemed to accept this explanation and started talking with Ryan, asking him about how things were going with the list of repairs that I'd assigned him. A few weeks later, Ryan started doing the candle meditation religiously every morning and stopped drinking. I was very proud of him.

At the end of our sixteenth class, Joy sat us down in a circle around her and announced, "I think all of you are now ready to go on your Angel Quest."

"What's that?" said Ryan.

"It's very similar to a Native American vision quest. The vision quest was a rite of passage or an initiation into adulthood. It helped the seeker discover his life path. Our Angel Quest is a journey of self-discovery. The purpose of the quest is to heal whatever keeps you from seeing yourself as the love that you truly are." She paused, looking at each of us quietly.

"That sounds very challenging," Angie said.

"It's not meant to be all that serious. You should also come prepared to have fun."

"OK, now it seems a little less intimidating," Jana said.

"We'll spend a weekend in nature in a forest retreat not far from here. On Friday night, you can sleep in a shelter with a roof so you will be protected if it rains, or you can sleep outside on a mattress under the stars."

"Well, I've never gone camping," Jana grumbled, "except in a cabin, and my back hurts when I sleep in a strange bed."

"Don't be such a wuss," Ryan scolded.

"The mattresses are very comfortable," Joy reassured us.

"Well, I don't know," I hesitated, shifting nervously in my chair. "One of my best friends went camping just last week. She got bit on her butt by a brown recluse spider that must have been lurking in her sleeping bag. By the time she got home, her butt had swelled up to about twice its normal size. It was so sore she couldn't sit down. Her doctor gave her tons of antibiotics, but it was still a week before she felt better."

"Oh, I would have liked to see that," Ryan said with a laugh.

"I bet you would," Angie retorted, glaring at him.

"We'll bring lots of DEET," Joy promised.

"What's that?" asked Jana, knitting her eyebrows.

"Bug repellent," Ryan said.

"Let us continue. I'll help each of you build a copper pyramid, and you'll spend Saturday night in your pyramid in deep meditation. You'll be naked inside the pyramid except for a white sheet that you can use if you get cold."

"Ryan might see us naked," Angie said, frowning.

"I promise I won't look."

"The Angel Quest will be held on a weekend that is under the darkness of the new moon. By the time you reach your pyramid it will be completely dark. No one will be able to see you."

"I don't think I'll be able to stay up all night," Jana complained. "I'm always asleep by nine o'clock in the evening because I used to get up so early in the morning to take care of my mother. Now I just can't seem to sleep in."

"You'll be surprised at how alert you will be when you meditate inside a pyramid. The shape of the pyramid magnifies and focuses your energy."

"I think this is going to be an awesome experience," Angie declared.

"You'll need to do several things to prepare yourself the week before the Angel Quest. For three evenings before we leave, you will need to take a bath in beer just before you go to sleep. Pour a twelve-ounce bottle of beer into your bath and soak in it for as long as your intuition guides you."

"That's going to be a new experience for me, soaking in beer instead of drinking it," Ryan said, chuckling.

"The beer bath is an act of purification. It also helps you bring to the surface what you desire to heal during your Angel Quest. In addition, you should eat only raw whole foods from the earth—such as carrots, tomatoes, or squash—during this time. You'll be fasting, except for fruit or vegetable juices, during the quest itself."

"Hey," Ryan protested, flexing his biceps. "I'm a red-blooded American male. I always have meat for dinner. I can't survive on juice."

"Get over yourself," Angie scolded. "You could stand to lose a few pounds."

"Look who's talking," Ryan retorted.

Joy sighed. "I've found that a juice fast is rarely a problem for anyone. You may notice some momentary hunger, but it's usually fleeting. The juice fast will help you expand your consciousness and become more receptive to the messages you'll receive during your pyramid experience." She paused. "Does anyone have any more questions?"

None of us did. The class ended, and we slowly shuffled out the door.

I'd better not tell Tom about this, I thought as I drove home. *He wouldn't like it. He already thinks this class is pretty weird. I'll just tell him I'm going for a weekend camping trip with some of my friends from my angel class.*

The Angel Quest began on a Friday morning in early June. I was the first to arrive at the campsite, which lay in a flat, grassy meadow at the top of a ridge, surrounded by a dark and dense forest. A creek flowed through the property to a small pond; there was a sand beach littered with duck droppings and a square dock with a dilapidated, green, wooden rowboat tied to it. I set my backpack down in the shelter—a ramshackle, weather-beaten structure surrounded by several large maple, oak, and fir trees— wondering what I'd gotten myself into and what would happen next. I looked around. Some cooking utensils hung on hooks on the wall behind a wooden table, and several hummingbird feeders were fastened to the rafters at the edge of the enclosure. I found if I sat very quietly on one of the threadbare mattresses covered in plastic on the floor, the birds would flutter over to the feeders and gaze at me intently as they hovered, drinking the nectar.

Ryan, Angie, and Jana arrived a short time later, and we started exploring. A well-worn path led to an outdoor pit toilet behind some large boulders. Luckily, it possessed a seat and a lid so we wouldn't have to squat over it. Although I'd done some backpacking in my twenties, I'd gotten used to certain creature comforts in my middle age.

"Look out for the chiggers," Ryan warned. "You'd better spray your butts with DEET before you use the facilities. There's probably tons of them lurking in the grass around the toilet waiting to pounce on you."

Chiggers, how could I forget them? Tom and I had gone walking in the woods together a few weeks after we started dating. We sat down for lunch on several large rocks next to some overgrown grass bordering a stream, where the water meandered slowly in the afternoon sun. The next day he showed up in my office, his lower legs and ankles covered in bright-red, fluid-filled pustules. I had coated myself with DEET to keep the flies and mosquitos away and had apparently saved myself from the chiggers. I felt a sudden stab of guilt. There probably weren't any chiggers in Australia.

"Oh, my God, I'm so sorry," I'd exclaimed as I hugged Tom. "I bet it itches like hell."

Then the nurse in me took over. "Here," I said, scooping up my purse, which was hidden in my desk drawer. "You need to go to Employee Health. I know where their offices are. I'll take you."

"Oh, no, I'll be fine. I'm just going to the drugstore to get some calamine lotion."

"You really should get that looked at," I lectured to his retreating back as he made his way down the hall. "It can get infected if you don't take proper care of it."

I'd collapsed back in my chair. I remember thinking that he was the most exasperating man I'd ever met.

"Now I'm his nurse," I'd complained to Callie and Megan that night. "But he's a terrible patient."

"I bet he was looking for some TLC," Megan speculated.

"It's all good, Mama," Callie told me with a wink. "He seems to be getting pretty attached to you."

Now, at the Angel Quest campsite, I pulled my DEET out from my backpack. Better to be safe than sorry.

Joy arrived with tons of groceries and a truck bed full of copper tubing for our pyramids.

"Why don't you help them make their pyramids," she said to Ryan, "while I unload the groceries?"

I gazed with trepidation at the five-foot lengths of copper tubing and the bags of T-connectors and elbows as Ryan unloaded them from the truck.

"I don't have a clue what I'm supposed to be doing here," I told him.

"Well," Ryan instructed, "we'll start by making the top of the pyramid. Get four T-connectors and four elbows out of this bag. When you join them together, they'll make a square."

He tossed the bag to me. Luckily, I managed to catch it.

"Ryan," I scolded, "don't throw things at me."

He laughed. "Next, clean the parts that you're going to connect together with sand cloth."

I sat down on a blanket in the grass and dutifully cleaned each piece.

"OK, now give me a T-connector and an elbow and I'll show you what to do next."

I placed the two pieces into his outstretched hand.

"Coat the pieces with flux on the ends."

He opened a small jar and took a brush to coat the parts with a honey-colored, jellylike material. They he turned on a torch and started heating the bottom of the pipe.

"The joint has to be heated until it glows. Then apply the silver solder around the connection," he demonstrated. "The solder should melt as you apply it."

"I don't know if I can do this," I protested. "Maybe you should put the pyramids together." The torch intimidated me.

"No," Joy interjected, hearing our conversation. "Part of the experience is making your own pyramid."

"OK," I grumbled, "I'll try." The solder came out all lumpy around the pieces I connected, but I finally managed to put the square together.

"The rest is easy," Ryan explained. "Just connect the four five-foot pieces of copper tubing to the bottom of the T-connectors and voilà, you have your pyramid."

"I had no idea you knew French," Angie exclaimed.

"You'd be amazed by what you don't know about me," he whispered in her ear, bending over her as she sat on the ground to help her put the connectors together.

"Now, why can't he be nice like that to me?" I grumbled softly.

Next, Joy had us gather around the table to discuss the tools we needed for our quest.

"Before tonight, you must make a dream catcher to help you remember your dreams. Find some twigs or vines this afternoon on your walk and make a circle with them. Then take this thin, leather twine and string it around the circle to create a grid pattern. Make sure there is a hole in the center. This will allow only good dreams to enter your mind during the quest. The bad dreams will become entangled in the web, where they will perish in the first light of dawn. Hang your dream catcher above you as you sleep tonight."

"Can I decorate my dream catcher with feathers or something?" Angie asked.

"Yes, you can use any feathers you find on your walk, or attach some of these beads to the twine." She set a bag of bright, multicolored beads in front of us.

"During the day tomorrow, make a pendulum to help you find the answers you seek. Unwind about a six-inch length of chain from this spool," she demonstrated, "and use some glue to attach a small amethyst crystal to the bottom."

"How do we use it?" Jana asked.

"Hold the top with your fingertips and let the chain hang. Then ask it a question that has a yes or no answer. If the pendulum swings right to left the answer is no. But if it swings front to back, it means yes. If it goes around in circles, the answer is unclear. The stronger the energy around your question, the faster your pendulum will swing. Use your pendulum to guide you during your quest."

"I would also like you to make a rattle," Joy continued. "The rattle will help you maintain your trance state while you're in the pyramid. Poke a hole at the top of one of these gourds and fill it with small pebbles. Insert a small stick into the bottom of the gourd and secure it with leather twine."

"Where are we going to find pebbles?" I questioned.

"There's a small stream that winds through the property. Look for pebbles along the shoreline this afternoon."

"The last object you will need to collect for your tool kit is a wupie. Your wupie is usually a rock or a stone that calls to you, but it can be anything from nature that holds inside it the message that you seek as part of your quest. Use this chamois cloth and sew the edges together with thread to make a pouch to wear around your neck during your quest. Your wupie stone can be placed inside the pouch."

"I don't know anything about sewing," Ryan protested. "And I certainly can't thread this needle, it's much too small."

"Well, the girls weren't very comfortable using a blowtorch, either, but they did it. You're just going to have to learn how to sew. Ask one of the girls to help you."

Ryan immediately turned to Angie and smiled. "Please help me thread this needle."

Angie frowned but took the needle and thread in her hands. "It's really quite simple. Hold the needle up to the light, find the hole, and poke the thread through it. You must know how to put things in holes."

"Yes, I most certainly do," he replied with a wink.

We sat quietly sewing our pouches together, and then Joy sent us into the woods to collect the objects from nature that we needed for our quest.

That night, Seraphiel spoke to us briefly through Joy before we went to bed.

"Tonight you will have a lucid dream. You'll remember the dream, and it will bring you a gift as part of your quest."

Well, this is going to be a really interesting night.

I decided to sleep in the shelter on one of the mattresses and inspected it carefully on both sides for spiders before I placed my sleeping bag on top of it. Several times during the night, I was awakened by the hoot of an owl or the wind gently stirring in the trees. *I really don't think this is going to work.* Then, just before dawn, my dream began.

I was in a restaurant looking at a menu. Golden letters were engraved on the cover, and it was closed with a gold clasp. I realized I was having a lucid dream because I said, "Open the menu," and the clasp slowly opened by itself and the pages of the menu turned with the direction of my mind. My next thought was, *if I'm having a lucid dream, I'm going to find Callie.*

I started hearing a rhythmic drumming noise in my head and began breathing very rapidly. Suddenly, I shot into the air toward a light that became brighter and brighter as I approached it. Golden filaments of light surrounded me, and I exploded into a place that was pure light. I saw someone in the distance in a golden haze and realized it was Callie. I started shouting her name over and over again and was afraid I would wake everyone else at the campsite. Then, all of a sudden, Callie appeared right in front of me, looking younger than her sixteen years. She was very excited and exclaimed in a loud, clear voice, "Mommy, I know who I am!"

"That's wonderful!" I replied. I touched her cheek with my outstretched hand and was instantly awake.

It was dawn. Birds were singing in the trees, and a fine mist clung to the ground. I lay in my sleeping bag, quite shaken by the experience, staring up at the sky and listening to the chorus of early morning sounds. It turned rose pink and as the sun rose further, a vibrant blue. She was somewhere out there in that vast expanse of blue that stretched off into forever. What had she become, and what did she now know? What was it like to live on the other side of infinity? It was all such a mystery to me.

"Spend some time this morning writing down everything you can remember about your dream experience," Joy instructed as we ate our meager breakfast of ripe bananas, peaches, and fresh strawberries. "Actually, this is a really good habit for all of you to practice every day. Keep a notebook at your bedside so that you can record your dreams as soon as you wake up."

After breakfast, I went wading in a pebble-strewn stream full of dancing minnows, crawfish, and the occasional salamander lurking in the sodden leaves. I was trying to center myself and prepare for whatever was to come next. Later that afternoon, I set up my pyramid, placing it far from the shelter on the grass next to the stream, knowing that the sound of water would help me feel safe. I made my pendulum from the small metal chain and the amethyst crystal, and I made a rattle from the gourd and small pebbles.

We gathered around a roaring campfire at dusk. Seraphiel spoke through Joy again. "Spend the night in introspection. Invite the angels and animal spirits to visit you. If an animal spirit comes to you in your mind, it will come bearing a gift. Listen to the animal, and it will tell you why it has come. Return to the campfire at the time of your choosing, after the first light of dawn. Do not speak to one another until you have written down your experiences and the gifts you've received in your notebooks."

Then he asked us to take a pinch of tobacco out of a ceramic bowl. "Place all your fears into this tobacco and throw it into the fire."

Next, Joy walked up to each of us with a lit stick of sacred sage, directing the smoke toward us with her hands. "Take a deep breath of this sage to protect you during your journey."

Finally, she gave us some long stems cut from the sage plant. "Weave a wreath from these vines and place it on your head. The wreath will shelter you as you travel."

Then Seraphiel sent me and my three fellow travelers to our pyramids to sit and wait for our experiences to unfold. I was apprehensive as I walked down the dirt path toward my pyramid and reminded myself that this was no big deal. All I had to do was sit up all night and meditate and Seraphiel would protect me. I just had to trust that I would be OK.

As I made my way through the gathering darkness, I sensed a presence not of this earth beside me, but it was too dark to tell if anyone was really there. In my mind, that someone appeared as Callie, wearing a brown leather Indian dress and beaded moccasins and dragging a leather bag full of spirit copper tubing behind her. She also had a leather pouch full of string and beads in her hand. I got the impression that Callie was not there to interact with me, just to accompany me on my journey. Apparently, she was even going to build her own pyramid.

I slipped off all of my clothes, covered myself in a white sheet, sat down in the pyramid, and tried to clear my mind, to calm it and make it like water that turns to glass on a clear mountain lake when nothing, not even the slightest breeze, is stirring. But despite my best efforts, images began to flood my mind, fragments of all my previous experiences with animals in the wild: The chipmunks that I fed at my grandparents' mountain cabin when I was a child, which became so tame that if I sat very still they would come right up to me and scoop a peanut gently out of my outstretched hand with their teeth. The possum I discovered on my back porch eating the cat food I had placed in a bowl on the picnic table. The deer I caught eating apples out of the trees in my small orchard, plucking them off the branches with their teeth. The raccoons rummaging around in my garbage cans and scuttling off into the darkness when I shone my flashlight on them. I finally decided to just let go, surrender to the experience, and let the waking dreams begin.

I closed my eyes and an Indian brave approached me in my mind. He was wearing a brown buckskin shirt with thin strips of leather trim and black trousers. He carried a knife in a red-and-tan beaded sheath around his neck. His long, black hair was tied in two braids on either side of his face with strips of red leather. Turquoise and gold stripes were painted on his cheeks and across his forehead. His eyes were very dark and shaded by thick, black eyebrows. He made three copies of himself to stand at each corner of the pyramid to protect me. Then, he turned to me and said, "You will be visited by animal spirits tonight, each bearing a gift. The gifts will help you learn more about who you are as you travel on this journey through what you call life."

I blinked and noticed that a large, brown-and-yellow box turtle had crawled into my tent. "I am the gatekeeper for the animals who will come after me," he told me in my mind. Then he settled himself into a corner, quietly gazing at me with his large, beady, orange-and-black eyes.

I looked up and saw a pure-white rabbit in the grass in front of my pyramid, lit by the barest silver sliver of the new moon. It sat up, looked at me, and then came hopping into my pyramid. It perched on the ground in front of me on its hind legs and began cleaning its face with both front paws. Satisfied, it hopped into my lap and nuzzled the sheet covering me gently with its nose. "I bring you the gifts of beauty and freedom," it said to me in my mind. "Only what is freely given is truly beautiful."

A red cardinal flew into the pyramid and landed on my right shoulder. It started making a trilling whistle but I heard the words, "I am here to bring joy back into your life. Always choose joy and your journey will be much easier."

Next, a great horned owl started its tremulous hoot in a nearby tree, but he appeared to be saying, "I bring you the gift of discernment to see clearly what is truth."

Then, dozens of small pink and white camellias started dropping out of the sky and covering the grass around the pyramid where I sat. A voice in my mind said, "Each flower is for a birth that you attended or from a baby that you helped to breastfeed. Know this: Love births everything into this life here on earth. All that is is contained within you. When you seek to experience it, to know it for what it is, you use love to make it appear real. But this does not make it separate from you. All that is dwells inside your heart forever."

The rabbit in my lap and the cardinal perched on my shoulder asked me to recount all the things that I birthed through love into my life: Callie, Anthony, all my precious animals.

Next, a small tiger-striped cat wandered into my pyramid, gazing at me with its glowing amber eyes. It meowed softly, then started to purr as I reached out to pat its back. But as soon as I touched its fur, it morphed into a huge Bengal tiger. "I represent clarity," the tiger said. "In order to capture my prey, I need to be clear and focused. Whenever you need thought clarity, call on me."

I was starting to feel very tired and overwhelmed by what I had seen and heard. I lay down for a few minutes and drifted into a dreamless sleep. Then, a small pebble hit one of the copper tubes on the pyramid, startling me awake. I sat up and began to hear splashing in the pond by the stream.

I heard Callie's voice say, "They are only dolphins, Mama. I brought some of my dolphin friends with me to keep us company."

Then, I heard a very faint growl that became louder and louder as a black spirit bear started to circle my pyramid menacingly in the dark. I reminded myself, *the bear is not real; it's only my imagination. It represents the sum of all my fears.* And the growling noise stopped as suddenly as it had started.

Then I saw my little, black cocker spaniel, Boo, running around in the grass between my pyramid and Callie's, sniffing the ground intently, then stopping to dig a hole furiously with his front paws to unearth a treasured bone.

Fireflies lit the grass, and several landed at my feet. They became little fairies in my mind with translucent silver wings that fluttered so rapidly I could hardly see them. Their dainty little ankles were circled by silver bracelets with small bells that tinkled merrily as they flew around me. Long, slender fingers were covered in crystal rings that changed colors when the moonlight struck them. There were smiles on their tender, ethereal faces, and their eyes were lit by pure joy.

"We protect the fireflies, guide the bees to the flowers, and spread the dew into the morning air," they said. "We represent the magic in this world, which many humans have long forgotten."

It was getting close to dawn. The sky was brightening, and several small birds began to chirp in the trees nearby. Callie vanished. The white rabbit, cardinal, and owl prepared to leave, and I thanked them for their gifts. The tiger agreed to escort me back to the campfire, as I was still a little worried about encountering the spirit bear. Then he, too, left. I pulled out my diary and wrote everything down exactly as I remembered it, then curled up in my sleeping bag by the fire and was instantly asleep.

Later that morning, after breakfast, Joy asked each of us what we had learned.

"I learned that there is no such thing as separation," I said. "I've been so afraid since Callie died of becoming attached to anything because I might lose it. I'm terrified to lose the things that I birthed into my experience of this life. But I can't really lose anything, because nothing ever really becomes separate from me after all. Everything, all that is, dwells within my heart forever."

"You know, I had a really similar experience," Angie said. "I went flying to all these magical places I've only seen in my dreams. One stands out really vividly in my mind. It was this huge library made of gleaming white marble." She waved her arms emphatically. "The walls were covered in rows and rows of bookshelves. As I was walking down an aisle, one of the books flew, all by itself, onto a table right in front of me. The title, *The Book of Angelique*, was engraved in gold letters on the cover. Then the booked opened and the pages turned as if they were being blown by the wind to the day I met my boyfriend.

"A guy wearing a white T-shirt and baggy blue jeans suddenly appeared right next to me, out of nowhere, and told me that this experience has been saved forever in my book of life and that it can never be taken away from me. Sometimes, I worry about losing my boyfriend, but now I know that I have the times we share together for eternity."

"Wow," I exclaimed, "so everything that happens to us is imprinted in our hearts and recorded forever. That's big. I bet I have a book like that, too."

"Yes," Joy said, beaming. "Once an experience centers itself in your heart, it is yours forever. All the more reason to focus on what brings you joy. And you?" She turned to Jana.

"Well, all I saw were green and gold snakes slithering up a wall in front of me. It was pretty scary. I hate snakes."

"So you connected with your fear," Joy explained. "But snakes are also a symbol for transformation and healing. Look at where you are in your life; you are reinventing yourself now that your mother has passed. The snake sheds its skin when it outgrows its covering; you are shedding your old life but still do not know who you will become. That can be a little scary."

"Now it all makes perfect sense," Jana exclaimed.

Ryan glared at the fire, avoiding our gaze. "Well, I hate to disappoint you all, but nothing happened to me, absolutely nothing."

"That's because you didn't allow it to happen," Joy replied.

"Well, I thought I was pretty open. The one thing I did notice, though, was that all your pyramids were glowing with light the whole night."

"That's something to pay close attention to; go deep inside yourself and discover what that means. Let us know what you find out during our next class."

I was the last person to leave the campsite. It seemed to be an enchanted place. I could see dazzling beams of light bouncing from the treetops in the warm afternoon sun. But as I drove down the ridgeline, ordinary reality descended upon me.

The rest of the summer flew by. I was still writing up my findings for my PhD dissertation. It felt endless. *Forever, for all eternity, I will be writing this dissertation, in this house with all the memories of a life that ended in tragedy on a day in early May, at the height of spring, when all my flowers were gloriously in bloom.* But time marched on, and in the fall, I finally sent my dissertation to my committee.

A few days before what would have been Callie's nineteenth birthday in mid-September, I decided to contact Kira again.

⌒ 20 ⌒

Diane—I'll Always Be with You

"**W**as Callie full of energy when she was in the physical?" Kira asked me over the phone as soon as she finished her opening prayer.

"Yes, she crammed a lot into a very short life."

"Is there a name connected called Joy?"

"Well, Joy is my spiritual healer; she's been helping me through this."

"Does she connect with Callie?"

"Yes, she connects with Callie through her angel guide, Seraphiel."

"Why do I see a lot of colors?"

"Joy uses colors in her healing." Joy's color charts sat near me on my desk, in a folder with a rainbow on the cover. Each color represented a human emotion.

"Callie's jumping up and down," Kira told me. "She's very excitable. Come on, let's settle down here. She's just beaming. To her, it seems like her passing was a long, long time ago, but you are with her in the present. Is there a May connection, around Mother's Day?"

"Yes, May 10, that's the day she died, several days before Mother's Day."

"I don't know if you have dreams of her and then wake up and doubt that you connected with her, but she wants you to know this is her. It's very real. Her friends grew up too fast because of her passing. But there's a lot of wisdom gained, too. They are wise beyond their years. The ties that bind them together are very strong. She's also a real animal lover; it's almost like the animals are drawn to her."

"Yes, she used to collect strays. I've still got them."

"She's telling me, 'We're so much bigger than we realize. This life is just a small experience of us.' You guys have been together before. She says she's still learning, she's going to school, she's got the books, everything. She makes me laugh. She wants you to know she's still wearing her makeup."

"She was a Virgo; she never went out the door unless she was completely made up. You know, I used to feel that all this astrological stuff was a bunch of nonsense, but a lot of it makes total sense to me now. I remember that my best friend in California started studying astrology just after Callie was born. She gave me both our natal charts as a gift before she started doing astrological charts for people as a business venture. I was born on June 12 and Callie was born the twelfth of September. She told me that our birth dates were perfectly squared and that our relationship would be conflicted. At the time I felt she was mistaken, but her prediction sure came true."

"Yes, the square symbolizes that the planets are working at cross purposes. Forces often collide if the connection is a square. Do Callie's friends still come over to hang out with you and ask for advice?"

"Yes."

"You're getting a real thumbs-up for helping her friends. That makes her so proud—a real role reversal; she's proud of you. Did she call you Mama? I'm hearing, 'Love you, Mama.'"

"Yes, she always told me that."

"She's full of advice. She says, 'Try to keep a positive attitude. It's so important to stay positive.' Is there significance to three roses?"

"Yes. My sister, my niece, and I each placed a rose in her coffin before it was closed."

"Her main thing this time is that she's over it, she's healed from it, the whole suicide thing. And she's trying to help you."

I didn't feel completely over it, but I was changed. When I looked at myself in the mirror, I saw a stranger. I didn't know who I was anymore. The person I had been before Callie died had died with her. That person had been naive. That person believed that if she just got up every day, worked hard, and tried to do the right thing, then bad things wouldn't happen. She, unfortunately, had been wrong. But I'd had so many strange and extraordinary experiences since Callie passed that my whole perception of the world had shifted. Nothing was as it seemed before. In years past, I'd read books about spirituality and the afterlife, but it was one thing to read about it and another to experience it.

That night I had another very strange dream. In the dream, I was asleep in my bed with Tom. Someone tweaked me on my big toe, and I asked, "Who's that?" The room was completely dark and I couldn't see anyone. Tom woke up in the dream and said, "I think it's Callie."

Still dreaming, I turned on the lamp on my bedside table and saw a little girl with long blonde hair, about ten years old, standing beside the bed. She was wearing a white nightgown that reached all the way to her ankles. She pulled up her gown to show me a scar on her chest where she'd had open-heart surgery and said, "It's healing well, Mama, and I'm much better now."

Then Anthony walked into the room. In the dream he was taller than she was.

The little girl looked at me sadly. "I'm not sure if I will be beautiful, because of the scar." I reassured her that of course she would be beautiful. Then the little girl walked out of the room to get dressed for school. I wondered, *Why have I been so sad for so long?*

I closed the bedroom door so the little girl wouldn't hear me, turned to Tom in my dream, and said, "I hope you don't think I'm going crazy, but I thought Callie was dead and buried, so who was this little girl in our bedroom?"

The thought shook me awake. Callie had been born with a heart murmur and a small hole between her two ventricles. It had closed up by itself when she was about eight years old. Could this have been a symptom of a much deeper emotional wound that she carried into her very short life?

I defended my dissertation just after Thanksgiving in front of a host of faculty and fellow students. Tom was right there in the front row cheering me on. Thankfully, I passed and it was a relief to have the whole PhD process behind me. The colors of fall faded into the bleakness of another winter as Christmas approached. Some of the old magic came back into that holiday, and I put up two trees and covered the shrubs in the front yard with multicolored lights.

The weekend before Christmas was unseasonably warm. As I was driving home from shopping, I pulled up next to a green sedan. In the passenger seat was a girl who, in profile, looked just like Callie. Her blonde hair was pulled back in a ponytail, and she wore rose lip liner and dark-pink lipstick. I watched her as she languidly put her arm out the window and rested it on the side of the car. Her nails were painted lemon yellow. I stared at the girl but she never turned her head. Another driver honked behind me and I, startled, turned into a parking lot, shaking. Then I quickly decided to get another look and turned back onto the street to try to find the car, which was stopped at a red light. When I pulled along-side, however, no one was in the passenger seat.

A few nights later, I saw Callie again in a dream. I was in a large parking lot looking for my car, and there she was, walking toward me. I reached for her, and we began to walk arm in arm to my car.

"You know, you're supposed to be dead," I reminded her.

"Then why are you always chasing after me?"

"I suppose it's more for me than for you," I told her, meaning that my search for Callie was more for my own healing than for Callie's. "You seem much more mature now than you were when you were with me. I'm really proud of you."

"I'll always be with you." She smiled enigmatically and then vanished.

I finally began to move on. I stopped desperately searching for Callie. My daughter was gone, except in my dreams, and I had to let her go. I tried not to think about what could have been; my dreams for Callie's future were gone as well. But things began to feel simply . . . peaceful. I was beginning to enjoy my time alone, no longer fear-ing that the black hole that had consumed Callie would engulf me as well.

⁓ 21 ⁓

Callie—Mama's Guardian Angel

It's strange watching people in graveyards mourning over what they think is all that's left of you buried in the ground. Because in reality, what's in the ground is like a cocoon after the butterfly has flown away, or a dress that you've grown tired of and left in a heap on the closet floor. We're not there, and what everyone's making such a fuss over is no more than a discarded shell. People on earth are just so clueless.

I was really surprised to find that earth was quickly losing its appeal for me. I had stopped sneaking off to Bourbon Street or visiting my old high school in Cassville. On rare occasions, I still stopped by the cemetery where I was buried to see the flowers Mama placed on my grave or the little notes or trinkets that my friends still left for me. I started to dislike traveling to earth and only went there during my rescue missions. The rest of the time, I went to school and hung out with my friends in the angelic realm, pretty much the same thing I was doing when I was on earth. Now, it might seem that my work in Summer Wind was pretty mundane, a form of social work, certainly an honorable endeavor but not that profound. But life in Summer Wind is very much like life on earth, minus the negativity. There are neighborhoods full of pretty houses, parks, schools, and playgrounds. There are ball games and concerts. It's not until a spirit enters the upper planes that things become more profound. And the experiences there are so awe-inspiring, it's impossible to describe them with mere words.

I'll admit it. I was a little annoyed when Seraphiel said that I had to go on the Angel Quest with Mama. It was probably because I didn't like anyone, especially a guy, telling me what to do—even if he was Seraphiel. And I had other plans for the weekend.

But there's no getting around it when Seraphiel tells you to do something. I sighed loudly several times as I stomped around, gathering up my things. I'd gotten used to the clarity in the air and the higher vibration in the angelic realm. The first six years of my life on earth, my family lived in a small house in the middle of the San Joaquin Valley in California. One winter my family was traveling from Los Angeles, where we'd gone on vacation, back to our hometown. From the top of Interstate 5, more appropriately nicknamed the Grapevine because the road was so twisty, in the clear mountain air at Tejon Pass, you could look down into a disgusting, dirty, pea-green smog that enveloped the San Joaquin Valley. Going back to earth reminds me of that.

"I have placed a higher vibrational force field where they are going for the quest," Seraphiel assured me just before I left. "It will feel almost the same as the angelic realm."

He was right, and Mama could see me in my Indian dress and moccasins dragging the poles for my own copper pyramid behind me and cursing under my breath as I snagged them on a root. Why was I imagining roots to snag my poles on, you ask? I guess sometimes I just like to be irritated. And as long as I was going, I might as well dress the part. I set up my pyramid next to Mama's and amused myself making necklaces from some beads and thin strips of leather I had brought with me. I had one of those Indian bead looms, too, but gave up working on it after about an hour. I didn't have the patience for it or the right size beads, and everything looked lopsided. It was aggravating me and making me crazy.

Seraphiel says that long ago, in the far distant past, humans were much more connected to the spirit world. The Indian shaman was a master of lucid dreaming. He would leave his body late at night and go searching for buffalo herds in his dreams. Then, the next day, he would lead the braves on their hunting expeditions. The very survival of the Indians depended his ability to have lucid dreams.

But I think you people on earth have lost your connection to spirit. You use money to survive, and lucid dreaming has become a lost art. And in the process, you have also misplaced your souls. You focus so completely on the material world—your cars, your big, fancy houses—that you've forgotten who you really are: spirit beings in a human body. Thank God, I've remembered who I am. I had to cross over to do it. All of you stupid people on earth need to wake up now while you're still in human form.

OK, I promise that was the end of my little sermon.

The only time I like to visit earth is Christmas. Mama still picks out a Christmas angel from the tree at the mall. She always chooses a teenage girl around sixteen. When I was little, it used to annoy me when Mama bought toys for kids she didn't even know. But the year I turned thirteen, I changed my attitude about it completely. Megan's mama asked the kids in my class to buy some gifts for children living in a homeless shelter as a school project for Christmas. Mama took me to buy some baby clothes and toys.

"Someone with a new baby will need these," she explained as she picked out some cute little pajama sleepers with brown bears wearing blue bows in their fur, white kittens with heart-shaped pink tags on their collars, and red-and-yellow ladybugs scattered across the fabric.

Megan and I went to the shelter with her mama the weekend before Christmas to deliver the gifts. I saw a young woman, who really didn't look much older than me, sitting in a corner holding a baby girl in her arms. I left my group and walked over to her.

"Here," I said as I handed her my bag of gifts, "these are for you and your baby."

She started to cry. "Thank you," she replied as she wiped away her tears.

I was so touched. After that, I swore that I would always help Mama buy gifts for needy children. And I've kept my promise. Every Christmas I come home to help Mama do that. I whisper in her ear. "You know the girl you chose from the Angel tree would look so pretty in that little, black lace dress or that red, white and gold striped pullover or those bootcut, denim, skinny jeans." Last year, Mama spotted me in that green car as I was going for a ride with a couple of my angel friends. When we come back to earth, we always go cruising through the streets where we once lived. Seraphiel says that whatever gifts we give away when we're on earth come back to us a hundredfold in blessings in the angelic realm.

I have something I want to explain about my last dream visit to Mama. See, she thought I had run off somewhere—hopefully, I suppose, to heaven. And it's true; I was spending most of my time in Summer Wind. But whenever Mama thought about me, I was instantly right there with her. So, there was no reason for her to chase after me. I never really left her. I had become her guardian angel.

The Dreaming Road

∼ 22 ∼

Callie—The Confrontation

When I got back to Summer Wind after my trip to earth, boy, did I get a surprise! My great-grandma Ellie had two sisters, Florence and Beatrice. Flo had been a dressmaker when she was on earth, and Bea had been a schoolteacher. They were vacationing at a desert hot spring on another planet and making plans for their next incarnation on earth when word finally reached them about some of my antics in Summer Wind, especially the incident with the farting cushion. And they were absolutely scandalized by my outrageous behavior.

My great-grandma Ellie had only one child, my grandpa. She had always wanted a daughter and was overjoyed when Seraphiel asked her to finish raising me for Mama. But I guess I was a little more than she had bargained for!

So Flo and Bea postponed their plans to reincarnate for a while, hastily packed their bags, and rushed to Summer Wind. When I got back from earth, they were ensconced in the two guest bedrooms in my Barbie house and were waiting for me in the parlor.

"I'm so happy to meet you," gushed Great-Aunt Bea. "I've heard so much about you." She was short and plump and wore a kindly expression.

"Unfortunately, not all of it has been good," stated Flo, who was tall, thin, and angular. The high collar of her black rayon chemise dress looked uncomfortably tight around her neck, and her wavy, silver hair was pulled tightly into a braided chignon at the nape of her neck. Even to me she looked a little intimidating, especially as she regarded my outfit with a disapproving expression, her carefully plucked eyebrows arched slightly upward and her mouth wearing an unmistakable frown.

I was wearing a tight brown leather miniskirt, high-heeled red leather boots, and a sleeveless, V-necked ivory blouse that I had tied above my waist to show off my new belly button ring.

"We've come to spend some time with you and Ellie," Bea explained, "and I'm looking forward to getting to know you."

"We'll have dinner first," Flo declared. "Then we'll go through your wardrobe, Callie." She paused and looked me right in the eye. "And we'll make some adjustments."

"There's absolutely nothing wrong with my wardrobe," I said.

"Well, we'll see about that," Flo replied as she sat down at my dinner table. "You see, Callie, you are a young angel now, and young angels must not wear skirts with hemlines above the knee or blouses with necklines that are too revealing or go out in public without stockings on. You don't want to give other souls the wrong impression about you," she said as she opened a napkin in her lap.

"I absolutely refuse to wear pantyhose," I exclaimed as I pushed the food around on my plate, mixing the mashed potatoes, peas, and chicken pieces all together into a disgusting lump. "I hate them!"

"Heavens, no, we don't mean pantyhose. They were invented after our time, and they're so bourgeois."

"Well, what do you mean?"

"Why, silk stockings, my dear," Flo responded, handing me a box with silver wrapping paper and a big black bow.

When I opened it, I found a pair of dark-brown silk hose with a sexy-looking seam up the back but no panties on top.

Puzzled, I asked Flo, "Well, how am I supposed to keep them from falling down?"

"You wear a garter belt," she said, handing me a lacy black one.

"Oh."

"Here, put these on with your new silk stockings."

She handed me a gathered black crepe skirt with a tailored waistband, a white satin blouse with pearl buttons, and black high-heeled shoes. *Well, you never know, great-aunt Flo may not be so bad after all,* I thought as I scampered upstairs to try on my new clothes.

Every morning after that, I had to stop by the parlor for Aunt Flo to inspect my outfit before I rushed off to school. I quickly learned that she'd have a fit if my bra strap was showing or if she could see my panty line under my clothes. Or if I forgot to wear a slip under my dress, or if the slip was too long and showed beneath my skirt.

"You don't want to look tacky," Flo would say. "We want you to be a respectable young angel."

So I would put on something I knew Flo would approve of before I left for school and change it as soon as I got out the door. I'd unbutton my blouse a little or tie it above my waist and adjust the length of my skirt. Occasionally I would hide another outfit in my purse and change into it when I got to school. I guess I could have imagined myself into another outfit, but this never really occurred to me. It's hard to let go of old earth habits sometimes.

Things were going along pretty smoothly until my so-called best friend, Tamara, decided to snitch on me. I saw her in the parlor as I tiptoed up the stairs to my bedroom after school to change outfits before Flo caught me.

"I really don't mean to tell on Callie," she explained to Flo as she sat nervously on the sofa crossing and uncrossing her legs and twisting a ring around on her finger. "But I think you should know what she's doing."

"Well, what's she done now?" asked Flo.

"Sometimes she changes into other clothes when she gets to school. And I don't think you would approve of what she's wearing."

That little shit, I thought as I reached the top of the stairs and quietly opened the door to my room.

The next morning, Flo called me over as I was preparing to rush out the door.

"That's an awfully big purse you're taking to school," she observed.

"Well, I have all my makeup and my gym clothes in it."

"Let me see," Flo ordered, holding out her hand.

"Why do you want to inspect my purse? You're becoming just like my mama."

"If you have nothing to hide, you won't mind my taking a look," Flo replied, as she took the purse from me.

She pulled out the skin-tight, hip-hugging, leopard-print bell-bottom pants and the gold blouse that I was planning to change into when I got to school. "Are these your gym clothes?" Flo asked as she held them up.

"No, of course not," I said belligerently.

"Well, then, what are they doing in your purse?"

"I was planning to change into them when I got to school."

"At least you're telling the truth," Flo observed.

"You know, you should be more concerned about what I do than what I wear," I retorted.

"I am concerned about what you do. I'm concerned about your leaving the house wearing one outfit and changing into another when you get to school. I'll tell you what," she said, pausing for emphasis. "You can wear whatever you wish."

She must have seen my jaw drop in amazement, because then she started to laugh. "You're not shitting me?" I asked.

"No, go ahead and wear whatever your heart desires."

So, I started to wear the most outrageous outfits. I even wore a black leather dog collar with silver spikes around my neck. But no one said anything—not Flo, or Bea, or Ellie, not even Seraphiel, or my so-called best friend Tamara, or any of my other friends, although once I caught one of the boys looking straight down my black V-necked blouse, which plunged almost all the way to my belly button. It was a vast conspiracy against me. One day, I wore a neon-orange, canary-yellow, fire-engine-red, and black psychedelic paisley dress with a very high hemline that just barely covered my booty, along with tall, bright-pink, vinyl go-go boots with three-inch heels. I actually thought about not wearing any underwear and sitting in a chair across from the boys and crossing my legs so they could see up my dress. But believe it or not, even I didn't have quite enough nerve to do that. I finally realized it was hopeless. I wasn't going to get a rise out of anyone no matter what I did, even if I came to class completely naked except for my belly button ring. And I finally gave it up.

The whole thing had begun to remind me of an incident that occurred when I was really little. I'd started to have temper tantrums when things weren't going my way, like when I wanted gum or candy at the grocery store and Mama wouldn't buy them because she said it would rot my teeth. I would work myself into a real fit, lying down in the aisle of the store, kicking, screaming, and crying, my face beet red. Papa would say that I was having a case of the Little Princess's Attackies. Mama was so embarrassed that she was tempted to buy me the gum or candy so I would shut up. But then she got this idea.

The next time I had an attack, Mama stood over me and instructed, "OK, Callie, let's see how loud you can scream. I want you to scream so loud that everyone in the store will hear you. And let's see how hard you can kick those little legs of yours."

I immediately stopped crying and glared at her. I was furious. I picked myself up off the floor and stomped away. I refused to speak to Mama for the rest of the afternoon, but I never did have another case of the Attackies at the grocery store.

Of course, there *was* the time I had an attack in my room when I found out that my boyfriend Rusty had been cheating on me. I got so mad that I slammed my fist into the closet door, and it went straight through the wood paneling. If you were to walk into my room today, you'd still see the hole in the door created by my fist.

⪧ 23 ⪦

Diane—The Eye of the Storm

The August after I received my PhD, I attended a final retreat with my angel class. Once we completed this class, we had all agreed, we'd attend Joy's version of graduate school: her spiritual alchemy course. Jana and I rode down to Dolphin Island together in her beat-up blue Cadillac convertible. She drove most of the way and I rode shotgun. We traveled the winding roads to the Gulf Coast, passing through countless hot, dusty, somnolent Southern towns where time appeared to be standing still. Finally, we arrived in the late afternoon at a pretty, wooden beach house, painted yellow and resting on stilts. A long, white porch stretched across the front, and several comfortable-looking rocking chairs faced the ocean. Ryan and Angie were already there. Always playful, Ryan immediately took us down to the white-sand beach.

"Here," he exclaimed. "I'll show you how to make sand angels."

He lay down on his back in the warm sand and moved his legs out and back and his arms up and down. Then he carefully stood up. He was covered from head to foot in sand.

"Now," he said, turning to Angie, "you make one right next to mine."

"Oh, no, I don't think so. I don't want to get sand in my hair. I just washed it."

"I'll help you with that," he said, scooping up some wet sand in his hands and dripping it on her hair as she started to walk back to the beach house.

"You little shit!" she screamed. She shook her head and started to chase him as he laughed and took off running through the surf.

"Well, it looks like they're having a good time," I said wryly to Jana as we sat down on the rocking chairs to watch.

Joy arrived with bags full of groceries. After a delicious dinner, we gathered on the beach, just before dusk, to write down what made us feel the most melancholy and to talk about it with the group.

When it was my turn, I said, "The last time I felt truly melancholy was when I packed up the last of Callie's things and put them into a big cedar chest in the back of my bedroom closet. I packed some of her favorite blouses and dresses that now she would never wear again, several locks of her hair that I cut at the funeral home as I dressed her for the last time, some of my favorite photos of her smiling and laughing. One would never know that underneath it all she was so sad. I packed old letters from boyfriends, pictures of little mermaids she drew when she was in grade school, all of her poetry, several of her favorite CDs—Brandy, TLC, Destiny's Child—and an audiotape of her funeral. I have never been able to listen to it. I put in a CD with her voice recorded on it from her cell phone message, and a CD of "I Can Only Imagine," the song they played at her funeral. And I knew she would never grow up, or get married, or have children of her own. She had been frozen forever in time at the age of sixteen. Then I closed the chest, hopefully forever."

My hands were trembling, and my words on the paper became blurry from my tears as I tried to read them. I choked back a sob. I wouldn't give in to my desolation. When it welled up in me like that, I was afraid I might drown.

"Oh, Diane," Joy said softly. "Is there anything the class can do for you?"

"No." I shook my head but gave the group a wan smile. "I have to learn to carry this burden by myself."

All of us felt drained as we made our way to bed that night. Jana and I shared a tiny room with two twin beds, a bureau, and a small closet. I opened the windows so I could hear the roar of the surf tumbling against the sand. A full moon was rising over the ocean, creating a sparkling path of silver light on the water. *The ebb and flow of the tides will be strong tomorrow,* I thought. I lay my head on the soft feather pillow and let the pounding waves lull me to sleep.

The next morning after a breakfast of bacon, eggs, and toast, made by Ryan no less, I went alone to the beach to work on my next assignment for the retreat. I said to Jana as I hopped down the front steps, "I bet Ryan made those eggs just to impress Angie."

"Wouldn't surprise me one bit," she replied with a wink.

I waded into the ocean and lay on my back in the water. Closing my eyes, I listened to my heart beating and heard the rattle of shells and rocks on the ocean floor as the waves gently lapped the shore. I concentrated, and then I heard a deeper, vaster, all-encompassing sound. It was the heart of the ocean beating very slowly and rhythmically, and I knew in an instant that the hearts of everything that existed were contained in it. And I knew that every emotion in the universe was held within this vast heart, and that the ocean could encompass and hold all of my sorrow, pain, and loss. I wouldn't have to carry it all alone anymore.

Titanic was the last movie I saw with my daughter. She'd seen it already but loved it so much she'd begged me to go see it with her at the local theater. I wasn't sure I wanted to see some silly teenage romance, but I finally relented. Much to my surprise, I really enjoyed the movie and was captivated by the Heart of the Ocean necklace. I bought a replica of the necklace for Callie, gave it to her, and then promptly forgot about it. Just last spring, I decided to give Callie's jewelry armoire to Jenny. I cleaned it out and put it in the dining room for Jenny to pick up. Several days later, I was walking through the room and noticed that one of the drawers was open and a dark blue velvet box sat inside. *That's strange*, I told myself; *I thought I took everything out of that armoire*. I picked up the box and opened it. Inside was the necklace.

Joy asked us to take a beach walk and write down our discoveries of becoming one with the sand in our diaries. I sat on the steps of an abandoned beach house and tried to imagine myself as a grain of sand. Not a word came to me, so I got up and started to wander aimlessly along the beach.

The shore was littered with debris: flotsam and jetsam, the sailors call it. A pile of feathers amid a carcass of bones marked the resting place of a seagull. I imagined it soaring in the updrafts above the ocean. A little farther down the beach, I found a skeleton shaped like a crucifix, and in my mind, I saw a fish swimming merrily among the coral reefs. But these creatures weren't really a gull or a fish. They were pieces of light vibrating very slowly, so that that they appeared solid and real. They were eternal. The bones were now remnants of lives once lived, and as I observed them, their light flickered, was almost extinguished. In an instant, I realized that the source of light that animated them had begun to vibrate faster and faster, finally becoming so bright that this dense planet could no longer hold the eternal part of them. And this was all that was left of what they had become.

Hurricane Ivan had ravaged the island just a year before. The houses closest to the ocean had been swept away, and all that remained were pylons jutting out of the water. About half of the remaining homes were boarded up or in various states of disrepair. In one, a large air-conditioner unit still hung forlornly from a broken window, swaying back and forth in the breeze. Sand had been scraped from the roadways and was piled up in large mounds against the remaining houses like huge white snowbanks. The ocean was extremely warm, the sky an almost cloudless blue. The gentle breeze gave absolutely no warning of the furious storm that would become Katrina, then off the coast of Africa, gaining strength, and moving slowly and steadily westward. That storm would descend upon the island in just one short week, destroying almost everything that was still standing.

As I wandered alone along the beach, I began to wonder why I'd had so many difficult experiences leading to the cataclysmic death of Callie. When I got back to the house we were renting for the retreat, Joy asked me to go find another quiet spot on the beach and ponder that very question. "Don't come back until you have discovered the answer," she instructed.

I sat on the steps of an abandoned house that was about to be swallowed up by the ocean. I closed my eyes, asked the question, and waited. After several minutes, a distinct male voice came into my consciousness from somewhere deep inside my head.

"You are here to collect experiences. Each experience is like a swatch of fabric on a quilt that is woven together so at the end of your life on this side it will tell a story which can only be understood when the last piece of fabric is sewn. Then will you understand the significance of each piece to the whole. And when you cross over, each life on earth becomes a swatch of fabric that is woven together to form the totality of you as your angel self. Then, all the angels in the universe together weave a fabric that becomes the sum total of all they have experienced. All things and all experiences are interconnected with beams of light like threads on a quilt. Through this process, the universe expands. This evolution of being through love is the purpose of the soul group of which you and Callie are members: the Covenant of the Red Rose. All of you have traveled through many incarnations together with this calling.

Later I asked Joy, "Does this mean that the life I'm living now is not the only life I've lived on earth?"

"Oh, you've lived many lives. You're an old soul. After this life, you can choose whether you want to come back here again."

"If I've lived so many lives, why can't I remember them?"

"So you won't be influenced by them. You start each life with a clean slate. But there is a way to access previous lives. I can take you on a regression journey back through time to any life you choose to remember that has significance for you."

☙ 24 ☙

Diane—Going Back in Time

Several weeks after the graduation retreat, Joy took me on a past-life regression.

"The experience will be similar to what we do during a healing session," Joy explained as I lay down on her massage table and she placed a pillow underneath my head. "First, I'll guide you into a state of deep relaxation; next, I'll take you back in time." She then asked me to close my eyes and tighten and relax all my muscles, starting with my toes and moving up to my forehead, while she slowly counted down from ten to one.

Finally, she said, "Open your mind's eye and look around you. Directly in front of you is a large, two-story Tudor-style manor house with red-brick walls, ornate casement windows, and a gray, stone roof. You walk up the steps in front of the house and find yourself facing a heavy oak door that opens slowly as you approach it. In front of you is a long hallway carpeted with red-and-gold oriental rugs. The walls are covered with tall mirrors and as you walk down the hall, intricately shaped mandalas start to swirl in each mirror. Choose the mandala that will take you to the lifetime that you would like to remember now."

I stopped in front of a spinning star that threw off sparks in all directions from each of its seven points. I touched the center of the star and it dissolved and I found myself gazing at a little American Indian girl about six years old. She walked out of the mirror into me, and everything around me melted to the ground. I looked down and saw I was wearing moccasins and a brown calf-skin dress. I spun around in a circle and saw that I was in a canyon surrounded by massive, thousand-foot, pink and orange sandstone cliffs, the vertical rock meeting the canyon floor at right angles. A red-tailed hawk swooped overhead, high in the sky, carried on the updrafts from the canyon floor. The wind smelled sharply of sage as it gently caressed my face.

Standing next to me was my grandmother Catori. She had a cleft in her chin that was identical to Callie's, and I instantly recognized her as a much older version of my daughter. Her thick, gray hair was held in one long braid that reached almost to her waist. Deep lines crisscrossed her tanned face. She wore ornately beaded blue, gold, and white moccasins and a white beaded necklace with a deep-blue star in the center. Her gnarled hands grasped a wooden walking stick with an eagle's head carved at the top. When she turned and smiled at me, her dark-brown eyes sparkled knowingly behind heavy eyelids.

Then the scene shifted and I, as the Indian girl, was climbing up a high cliff over some large, red rocks. I looked down and saw several muddy streams winding their way through the valley floor like undulating snakes. Ragged piñon and juniper trees clung to the rock ledges below me, bent over sideways by the wind. Some ominous black clouds started to descend suddenly as a fierce summer rainstorm approached. I watched jagged bolts of lightning strike the valley floor and heard claps of thunder echo throughout the canyons. The heavens let loose sheets of rain that turned the little streams into raging torrents. As the storm receded, I saw a colorful rainbow materialize, arching above the rain-drenched ground. I began descending and stumbled upon an eagle's nest in a tree high above the desert floor. I brought an eagle feather back to Catori as a present. My grandmother gasped and clutched her chest when she saw the feather, because it signaled that I was to follow in her footsteps as a medicine woman.

The scene dissolved and another appeared. I was a tall, slender girl of sixteen with long, flowing black hair, standing naked, waist-deep, in a lake in the woods. It was dark except for the full moon hovering overhead. Catori handed me a brown earthen bowl filled with honey. I took the bowl and slowly raised it high above my head to the sky, then tipped it to pour the contents over my head.

In the last scene, I was a young mother in my twenties sitting beside my grandmother's bed, weeping softly because Catori was dying. She raised herself up on her forearm, pulled a peace pipe from underneath her bed, and handed it to me. The pipe was intricately beaded and covered with brown rabbit fur and doeskin leather fringe. The bowl of the pipe was cut from a large deer antler. I reached out my hands and accepted it reverently. Then she patted my hand and said, "Do not weep, my little one. I will always be with you." Then she lay back, closed her eyes, took one last deep, ragged breath, and died.

I lay there on the massage table literally between two worlds, tears streaming silently down my face.

"Do you know anything about American Indian culture or traditions?" Joy asked after I described my experience to her.

"No," I replied.

"Well, then you did connect with a previous life. The honey pot is part of an Indian coming-of-age ceremony and celebrates the passage of a young girl into womanhood."

"It was a wonderful experience," I said. "I felt connected to all things. It was very different from how I feel now in the modern world, where everyone seems so isolated and alone."

"More pieces of this life may come back to you in the next few weeks. Take some time to sit quietly and ask for the memories to come to you," Joy suggested.

A few weeks later, I was in my garden picking the last of the tomatoes, squash, and beans. The humidity that descended upon Cassville every summer like an oppressively hot, wet, and moldy blanket had lifted, replaced by cooler Canadian air, and I stretched myself out blissfully in the grass to take a catnap.

In that netherworld between wakefulness and sleep, I saw my mother from my previous life. She appeared to be about eighteen and heavily pregnant. She was walking slowly through the desert wearing a long, tan calfskin dress, soaking up the warmth of the sun, her ebony hair flowing to her waist. The desert was alive with wildflowers. She stopped to touch a fluorescent orange bloom that had burst open at the top of a plump, round, barrel cactus. Small, white butterflies circled around her head before they alighted on the stamens of the sleek tubes of scarlet honeysuckle vines scattered at her feet.

The vision swirled and I saw her sitting cross-legged inside a tepee, mending clothes. Every few minutes, she put down her mending and grimaced, bending over and clutching her stomach tightly with her hands. My grandmother Catori sat quietly in a corner, watching her intently. Toward dusk, Catori gestured to her to stand up and follow her.

"Come with me, my child," she said. "It's almost your time."

Several other elderly women joined them as they made their way laboriously toward the birthing hut, stopping for each contraction. They started a small fire with sticks of cedar outside the hut and encouraged my mother to walk around it until she began to grunt with each powerful contraction. Then she entered the hut and grabbed hold of a wide sash belt hanging from the ceiling while the other women placed fragrant sweet-grass mats under her. I saw her squat, holding onto the sash and pushing, until I slithered out between her legs, screaming indignantly.

"Oh, she is a strong one!" Catori exclaimed as she bent down to cut the umbilical cord with a sharp knife. Then she picked me up, bathed me gently in warm water, and massaged my skin with oil while my mother bore down again to deliver the placenta. Another old crone helped bathe my mother, and then they all sat down silently by the cedar fire while my mother nursed me to sleep. The vision fast-forwarded and I found myself strapped to her back on a cradleboard, looking up at the huge red-rock formations as she walked through the desert gathering medicinal roots, herbs, and bark for Catori.

Next, I saw myself in my parents' tepee, pulling myself to my feet and clutching the fur on my little dog's back with my fists to keep myself from toppling over. The dog turned toward me and started to lick my cheek, and I woke up feeling my Labrador retriever Beau's hot dog breath on my face as he nuzzled me with slurpy, sloppy dog kisses.

That night, I had one final dream about my earlier life. I was curled up in the tepee next to my mother, somewhere near a place that looked like Sedona. It was almost midnight, and she was asleep. I heard the faint sound of pounding drums in the distance. My father had gone to a ceremony. I slipped outside the tepee. There was a full moon sparkling on the canyon floor. As if in a trance, I headed up a small winding path, walking toward the sound of the drums. As I got closer, I could see my father and a group of men sitting on blankets in a circle around a blazing fire by an outcropping of rock. They were all naked except for loincloths, and black and red stripes were painted all over their bodies. Colorful round, beaded medicine bags hung from brown seeded chains around their necks. The shaman walked behind them fanning smoke from small sticks of cedar held in an abalone shell around them with eagle feathers. Then he sat down and started to shake a rattle made from a turtle shell in rhythm with the thrumming drums. A huge, painted seven-point star adorned the deerskin on top of each drum. I watched the men, mesmerized, as they all began chanting hypnotically.

Near the fire was a small bowl filled with a yellow-green liquid. I sneaked over to it, picked it up, and took a gulp because I was very thirsty. It was quite bitter, so I put it down. After a while, I started to feel queasy and dizzy. I lay down behind a rock and fell into another world. I saw a white-and-tan Appaloosa pony coming toward me at a fast trot, its white mane and tail waving like a flag. The pony stopped in front of me and I grabbed hold of his mane and climbed on. Much to my amazement, we started to fly. We flew over jagged mountains, turquoise lakes, lush, green meadows, and dense, dark forests to the ocean, where frothy waves shot up toward the sky as they broke against vertical cliffs. As we traveled back to the camp, I saw a herd of bison to the north, next to a stream on one side and surrounded on the other by large, red-rock outcroppings in distinctive shapes.

I woke up suddenly just after dawn, startled by the swoop and cry of an eagle as it glided right above my head on the updrafts of the wind. The Indian warriors were asleep around the campfire. I sneaked back to my fur in the tepee. My mother, luckily, was still asleep. Only my black dog, which had followed me to the campfire, knew what I had done.

A few hours later, I saw my father stride into the tepee. He embraced my mother and stated, "The shaman has located some bison two days' travel from camp, and we're leaving on a hunting trip in a few hours."

I exclaimed, "I know where the bison are!"

And he replied, "Oh, you do? So tell me, where are they?"

I described the location I saw in my dream. He looked at me and his expression got very serious. "How did you know that?"

"I just guessed."

He gave me a strange look and then said, "Well, that was a very good guess."

⚍ 25 ⚏

Diane—Understanding the Gift

I t was time to start letting go of Callie. I finally canceled her cell phone service, thinking, *she obviously doesn't need her cell phone anymore, wherever she is.*

Pausing by Callie's memorial flower garden, I saw the woman I had been—brokenhearted, pulling up weeds, moving rocks, planting dozens of flowers and shrubs—when I created it a little more than three years earlier. I realized that it was time for the garden to go. Not wanting to destroy all the flowers, I decided to move them. Ryan came over and helped me remove all the shrubs from the front of my house and till the soil. One by one, I dug up all the flowers in Callie's garden and moved them to their new location in the front yard, seeding the old area with grass.

I bought a book about how to have lucid dreams and started practicing the techniques. My favorite was just lying down on my back, relaxing completely, putting my awareness in the center of my chest, and visualizing my heart beating. Sometimes, I would feel the pulse inside my wrist to get started. Then I would drift off to sleep. I had another bizarre dream the night after I finished moving Callie's garden. I was learning to fly, and at first I shot up into the air like a rocket, then fell back down to earth, hitting the ground with a thud. A blackboard appeared in front of me. Scribbled in white chalk were the words 'You have too much power. Try taking off more gently.' The next thing I knew, I was rising slowly into the night sky, looking around in wonder as the dark clouds, lit by a shaft of moonlight and twinkling stars, surrounding me. I decided as I was flying to go looking for Callie. I flew through cities and over deserts, mountains, and oceans but couldn't find her anywhere. I was getting worn out from flying, but I wouldn't give up. Then I called out to Jesus in despair. "Please," I begged, "help me find my daughter."

He appeared in front of me wearing a crown of thorns. He held up a small, gold cross and I followed it, knowing that surely he could help me find Callie. I landed in a small nursery. In a corner of the room was a wooden crib and inside it was a baby about six months old. I walked over to the crib and very tentatively said, "Callie?"

The baby immediately recognized me and began to crawl toward me, chortling and smiling. I reached my fingers through the slats of the crib to touch the baby and exclaimed, "Callie, what have you done?"

The baby looked at me and answered me in my mind. "I wanted a body again, because I wanted a drink of water." Callie had always loved to drink water and had a refrigerator full of bottled water in her room.

"But you were supposed to grow up with me!" I protested. I plopped myself down on the wood floor, massaging my forehead, which had begun to ache, and sighing loudly in despair. The next thing I knew, I was awake in my bed. *Did Callie decide to reincarnate already?* I wondered. *Does she exist somewhere else on this earth in another person's body?*

The next week, in my new class on spiritual alchemy, I stated wistfully to Seraphiel during the time that Joy was channeling him, "If only I could sit down next to Callie and talk to her one more time. If only she could tell me what happened to her." I guess I wanted the answers to come directly from her.

I got the sense that a shuffling was going on inside Joy's body, as if one entity was leaving and another was taking its place. Then a very soft, but distinct voice said, "I wanted to know what it was like to die in that way."

What could Callie possibly mean by that? Speechless and shocked, I stared at Joy. After a moment, Joy hiccupped and was herself again.

~

Fall faded again into winter, and another Christmas loomed. It was the fourth Christmas since Callie had died. I sometimes couldn't believe that I had survived as long as I had. Surely some cancer or heart problem should have caught up with me, caused by all the sorrow and the stress. But many days I felt much better.

Anthony had taken an accelerated academic program and was now a senior in high school, caught up in his own life and getting ready to leave home. But there was always evidence of his continued presence at the house: dirty dishes in the sink, laundry left in the washer or dryer, towels scattered about by the pool. I guessed that I was as ready as I ever would be to let him go. All fall, he had been studying for the SATs and completing myriad college applications. He couldn't seem to decide what direction to go in and was causing me endless aggravation.

"I think I'd like to try music business," he stated one evening as he strolled into my office, an application for a local college with an excellent program in hand.

"That's a great idea, and you wouldn't have to move so far away."

Then the next night he ruminated, "You know, I've been thinking, the music industry is much too cutthroat. I don't think I'd like the music business program. I'd rather design websites for bands."

"OK," I replied cautiously, "but you'd need to apply to a college with a good computer-science program."

He shuffled out the door to think about that and returned a few hours later.

"I don't think I want to be cooped up in an office working on a computer all day. I like being around people and I love to cook. Maybe I should become a chef."

I sighed. "Well, Anthony, if you want to become a chef you'll need to send in an application to a culinary institute. And chefs have terrible hours, just like nurses. You'd have to work every evening and on weekends and holidays."

I really didn't think becoming a chef was a very good idea. Exasperated, I exclaimed to Tom, "He's making me crazy. Every time I talk to him, he changes his mind about where he wants to go to college and what he wants to do with his life."

"Well, he's just trying to find himself, Diane. He's only seventeen. It's a big decision that he'll have to live with for the rest of his life. It's good that he's thinking about all this and weighing his options."

"Yes, I suppose so," I said. "I just hope he makes an initial decision sometime soon."

The next morning over breakfast, Anthony announced, "I think you're right, Mama. I'd hate working every weekend, and if I have a family, I'll want to spend time in the evenings with them. Maybe I should go into the agricultural end of the food industry. I could learn about organic farming or soil and crop science. Then when I graduate," he declared, warming to his subject, "we could turn some of the horse pastures into an organic farm or a grape orchard. I could sell our produce at the farmers' market downtown, or maybe I could start an exotic-plant nursery."

"We've got lots of time to think about that later, Anthony," I replied, rolling my eyes and glancing quickly at Tom, who was covering his mouth with a napkin and trying hard not to laugh. "Right now, we just need to decide where you should go to college."

After several weeks of ongoing debate, he finally decided on a large university a little less than an hour east of Cassville. The school had computer-science and agricultural business programs as well as a culinary institute. Relieved, I said to Tom as we snuggled in bed, "It's a good choice. This way, my little Renaissance man can sample a bit of everything."

Other than his indecision about college, Anthony was a great kid. Sometimes, I wondered how Callie could have made such poor choices in life when Anthony seemed to be doing everything right. I'd raised them both the same way, save the unintentional neglect Anthony suffered because of Callie's problems and then after she died, of course, when I retreated from the world for a time.

I still struggled with understanding what I had to learn from all of this. At times, I thought that perhaps I needed to learn that I have all I need inside of me, and that I should stop looking outside myself for people or possessions to make me happy. Or maybe it was to learn that it's not all about me. If I weren't so focused on myself or my own pain, maybe the pain would finally go away. Maybe I had this experience to become more compassionate, or to help other parents who'd lost children. But I hadn't been able to get over it myself, so how was I going to be able to help someone else? Maybe the gift was learning that there is no beginning and no end and that love will never die.

The one thing that I was beginning to understand very clearly, though, was that healing from loss wasn't a linear process. Sometimes, I just seemed to be going around in circles. I became frustrated about my apparent lack of progress when I felt myself slipping back into that all-consuming sadness yet again. But then I would talk myself out of it. *No more pity parties,* I'd tell myself. *Pull yourself back up on your feet, no excuses, and get on with it.*

On New Year's Eve, I had another lucid dream and, realizing I could take it in any direction I wanted, decided instantly to search for Seraphiel. I started to fly and ended up in a beautiful red-and-gold room in the tower of an enormous castle. I looked into a large, ornate oval mirror and saw that I was dressed in black boots, a Grand Prix top hat (similar in shape to a magician's hat), jodhpurs, and a black riding coat with a long whip across my thigh. I was astride a huge, prancing, black Arabian stallion. His wavy ebony mane reached almost to the floor, and his tail looked like a long, black sheet of rain. Then I heard a deep voice that reverberated throughout the room, saying, "I am a part of everything." And I realized that Seraphiel was everywhere.

I woke briefly from sleep and then plunged into another lucid dream. I went searching for Callie. I found myself in a warm, pitch-black place, floating on my back somewhere in space with my hair flowing out behind me. I felt very peaceful. Then I heard flutelike music. It was light and jazzy, sophisticated and happy with an upbeat rhythm. I suddenly realized that Callie was in the music; the energy of the music felt just like her. Instantly, I understood that the music was love, and that everything that existed was composed of this element of love. All that is has a song to sing, if we would but listen. Then I woke up. It was six in the morning, just before dawn. I lay in bed, this time knowing that everything Seraphiel said was really true.

Diane—Climbing the Glass Mountain

On a cold winter morning in early January, Ryan, Angie, Jana, and I trudged up the steps to Joy's house, shaking the new-fallen snow from our hats and stomping it off our boots on the front porch. Cassville was in the grip of one of its rare winter snowstorms. The day before had been warm, but during the night the temperature had dropped precipitously, and I woke to find huge, white snowflakes falling gently outside my bedroom window and the ground already covered in about two inches. Just this much was cause for alarm in the South, and Tom had insisted that I take his jeep to class for better traction on the roads. Joy made us hot chocolate as we scrounged some extra blankets from the healing room and bundled ourselves up on the sofas, waiting for class to begin. All except Ryan. He sat across from us in a short-sleeved T-shirt and jeans.

"I'm hot-blooded," he said to Angie with a wink.

"I bet you are," she replied.

"We have a new exercise for this class," Joy began, "and I'm going to let Seraphiel introduce it to you."

Her posture changed almost imperceptibly as Sera-phiel started to speak.

"Your task is to create a map of your present life. Start with your earliest memory. Using that memory as an anchor, go into a space of deep meditation with the intention of remembering. Will yourself to travel back even further in time to before you were born, when you made the choice to travel here to this lifetime. Why did you choose to return? What was like to be inside your mother's womb? How did it feel to be born into this earth experience? If you encounter anything that displeases you, write what you experienced. Then write what you wish had happened. Believe the rewriting of your experi-ence to be your reality.

"Then identify the major events, the crossroads or turning points where your life might have evolved very differently, depending on your choices or the choices of your fellow travelers. Did you make this choice out of love or fear? What were the gifts that you received from your choice? Look to see if there is a theme flowing through your experiences. This will help identify your life path and the purpose you sought to fulfill on your journey to planet Earth. Go into your silent space, and then write down your understanding of your life path based on your discoveries. Are there any questions?"

Overwhelmed, we looked at one another, but no one dared say anything.

"All right, then, we will leave you now."

Joy took a deep breath and hiccupped. "You have your instructions, but if you don't mind my saying so, you look a little shell-shocked."

"That's because we are shell-shocked," Jana replied.

"Well let's try a meditation here in class. Let's all go back to when you made the choice to return to earth in this lifetime and see what gifts we can discover there."

We closed our eyes and let Joy lead us back in time.

"Find yourself a comfortable position and relax completely. Imagine a beautiful, golden light just above your head. The light starts to move and you find yourself lifting off the ground and taking flight, following the light into a cornflower-blue sky. The light leads you to a bright, green meadow and you feel your feet gently touch the soft, lush grass. As you stand there in the center of the meadow, a large, beautiful, midnight-blue seven-point star appears underneath your bare feet. There is a door at each point of the star. Spin around in a slow circle and ask to be guided to the door that leads you to your decision point to return to planet Earth. Walk toward that door, grasp the handle, open it, and step inside. A scene materializes in front of you and you let yourself become a part of the experience."

When we were done, Joy turned to me. "Tell us what you discovered during your meditation."

"Well, first I saw myself in a tall, dim room," I began. "The walls and arched ceiling were made with large, round rocks held in place by something that looked like cement, and there were some candles in sconces on the walls that shed some light in the darkness." I took a deep breath.

"Continue," Joy urged.

"I was sitting at the end of a large, wooden table. Believe it or not, I was wearing a one-piece, white lace swimsuit, but it was covered by a purple robe that I wrapped around myself. Callie was sitting at the opposite end of the table watching me, and Anthony was next to me on my right. Seraphiel came into the room from a doorway on my left, looking exactly like the wizard in one of Joy's paintings and carrying a large book covered in gold leaf. I saw something like *The Book of Diana* engraved in red letters on the front."

Angie sat up and leaned forward on the sofa, locking eyes with me. "Well, what did he say?"

"Well, he looked at me and then at Callie and told us that we chose each other because we were opposites, two sides of the same coin. He said that I would be a giver but would feel that no matter how much love I gave, it would never be enough. And he told Callie that she would be the receiver but would find that no matter how much love she received, it would not fill her up, and that our challenge would be to heal these beliefs in our next life together. He said that when we learn to love ourselves unconditionally, we would let go of the need to find it in others."

"Wow!" Jana said. "That's profound."

I continued. "Then he said I would never fully understand Callie. She would be the mysterious one, but Anthony would be my anchor, my faithful son during our travails here on earth. He also told me that Callie would choose to return home before me, but she would prepare my path and light my way on my journey home. So, I guess I knew before I was born into this life that she would die before me."

"Does that surprise you?" asked Joy.

"No, I think I knew it all along, maybe even when she was little. I just didn't want to believe it."

"Do you remember anything else?"

"Well, next I was standing in front of a dark, deep-blue pool of water. I think it was supposed to take me to my mother's womb. Just before I discarded my robe and dived in, Seraphiel said to me—I remember his words exactly—'You will encounter many hardships and sorrows in your life, but never forget that you are love.'

"I think I got a little aggravated with him and asked him why I would have to experience hardship and sorrow."

"OK, what did he say this time?" Ryan smiled.

"He held up a mirror, like one of those antique, silver hand mirrors. In it, I saw myself standing at a podium in the church at Callie's funeral. She was lying there in an open casket in front of me. I was saying, 'Only love is real.' He put the mirror down on the table and said, 'For others to know that you can be the light in the midst of darkness, they must first know that you too have suffered.' I looked into his eyes and knew that this was true. Then I turned away and dove in."

"Oh, my God, I can't remember anything!" Jana said. "I know I went there, but it all disappeared in a puff of smoke when I came back to this reality."

"Diane had a past-life regression with me a while ago," Joy explained. "And she's able to bring all the memories back with her. What about being inside the womb? Do you recall what that was like?"

"It felt very peaceful and calm," I answered. "I heard lots of noises, a piano playing, my mother singing, an orchestra getting ready for a concert. But my space was a bit confined. Then, I felt a force pushing me out but I didn't feel afraid, because I knew I'd been here many times before and I remembered. Then I burst into the world. It felt cold and very bright. I filled my lungs with air and stretched my body. I was filled with exhilaration. I had made it back to earth again."

"That was magnificent, Diane." Joy exclaimed. "Does anyone else want to recount their experiences?"

Angie and Ryan shook their heads.

"Well, work on this assignment for the next class as Diane has done."

I sat down that night pondering my encounter with Callie just before I returned to earth. It seemed we had planned this all along, and as I pondered, I finally realized that my life path was to metaphorically climb the glass mountain. That when I got to the top of the mountain on a crystal-clear day, I would be able to perceive my entire life as it stretched out before me as far as my eyes could see, even beyond this life. My understanding would be limitless. If it was night, I would be so close to the stars that I could almost touch them; if it was winter, I would see dazzling white; in fall, a riot of colors; and in spring, a verdant green. I would feel whole and complete and I would understand it was all perfect, my experiences were all necessary to reach my final destination—the jumping-off point into infinity.

⇒ 27 ⇐

Diane—Free Will and Destiny

Winter passed slowly, but finally the ides of March had arrived. I could feel the season changing into spring, always my favorite time of year. Everything still looked like winter, but underneath it all, I could feel the potential and energy of warmer times, and it was all before me. Soon the darkness and cold of winter would be gone. I spread more grass seed on Callie's dismantled garden. I planted spring vegetables.

One day, I made a huge bonfire behind the barn from wood that had been stripped from the trees during a winter storm. As nightfall settled in, I dragged an old mattress behind the barn and stirred the dying embers from the fire with a stick until they glowed orange-red in the darkness. Then I lay on my back and gazed at the sky, which was a beautiful midnight blue and sparkling with stars. I closed my eyes and began to dream. I felt myself lifting off the ground and starting to fly over snow-covered mountains. Then, suddenly, I dove into the snow and ended up in front of a little frost-coated window. I rubbed with my fingers to clear the glass panes and peered inside. Two children were playing in a room, a young boy about three and a little girl with wavy, blonde hair that encircled her angelic face like a halo. She looked to be not much older than a baby.

A sweet little pixie came to the window, saw me, and smiled. She looked just like a Christmas elf right out of a children's fairy tale. She had short, curly lavender hair covered by a brown cap shaped like an acorn top, tall, pointed ears, and slender fingers with dainty nails coated with cherry-red polish. She wore a green dress with a flared hemline and a gold belt covered with large bells, along with green tights and brown boots.

"That little girl must be Callie in her next life," I exclaimed to the elf, "and you must be one of her imaginary friends."

"Oh, I'm very real," the elf said, curtseying and smiling again. "But only little children can see me."

"Well, then, can you give the little girl a kiss for me?" And in an instant, I woke up.

Anthony went to senior prom with his best friend, a beautiful Hispanic girl named Serena. He'd arranged for a limousine to take him and his friends there. I watched them all posing for photos on the steps of a large, tan-and-white brick house where one of them lived, the boys in their tuxedos with ties to match the color of their dates' dresses, the girls in formal gowns that were long and form-fitting or short with flared skirts or ruffled hems. Serena looked like a film star in her knee-length, strapless, red satin dress. And it was so gratifying to see my son looking dapper in his rented black formal wear and valentine-red tie. Wistfully, I thought back to the days of my youth as I watched them so innocent, carefree, and happy, life an exciting new adventure. They all climbed into the limousine, chattering and laughing, after their proud parents snapped their photos. Serena caught my eye and waved as they drove away.

Oh, what I would have given to feel that exuberance for life once again. I brushed away a tear. Afterward, several parents came up to me to thank me for arranging for the limo service to take their children safely to and from prom.

"It was Anthony who made all the arrangements," I replied proudly.

Anthony kept getting stronger, surer of himself, more independent. A few short weeks after prom, Tom and I went to the high school football stadium to see him receive his diploma. Again, I wondered, was Callie somewhere up there watching him as well?

That summer flew by. Anthony was working at a local restaurant and packing for college. During his spare time, he developed an interest in my new little filly, Jazz, and spent countless hours down at the barn grooming her. I'd found her on the Internet and brought her home early in the spring. I'd instantly fallen in love with the photo of a gangly, dark bay with a crescent moon on her forehead and a jet-black mane and tail. Tom caught me gazing at her photo one evening, debating whether I should buy another horse. I think he must have been anticipating my soon-to-be-empty nest, because he insisted that we drive to Kentucky the next weekend to have a look at her.

The day Anthony left for college came much too quickly. I helped him pile all his stuff into his truck and arranged for movers to take the heavy furniture to his apartment near the university. He really wasn't supposed to be living off-campus, but the freshman dorms were old, dilapidated, and unappealing. I finally relented and suggested that he indicate that he was commuting from home. A few weeks after Anthony moved out, around what would have been Callie's twentieth birthday, I phoned Kira again. She now felt like an old friend.

After a few minutes of catching up on how my life was going, Kira contacted Callie. She paused for a moment and then stated, "She's letting me know she's with you. Is there a connection with education, like reaching higher?"

"I finished my PhD a little over a year ago."

"She went back to school, too. She's telling me that she connects with you directly a lot, in your dreams and things like that."

"This is something I wanted to ask her about. The last really vivid experience I had with her was when I was doing some lucid dreaming and getting out of my body and going to look for her. She came to me in a parking lot and asked me why I was always chasing after her. I said, 'I think it's more for me than for you.' She didn't look very happy about it, and she said, 'Well, I'm always with you,' and then she vanished. After that, she hasn't come to me again in a dream."

"There's always an ebb and flow to it. But they're always there. There are some times when I can't read. I don't know why. The way I would interpret it is that it's your subconscious fear that you're holding her back. She says it's almost like she's so much a part of you that you can't feel her. She says, when you think you're holding her back, it's a human thing; it's not something you're capable of. You can't hold her back. She's got that sense of humor, too. Did she roll her eyes a lot? Like 'Come on, why would she even think that?' It's that kind of message."

"Yes, she had a great sense of humor and liked to play pranks on people."

"But as humans, we can't become too wrapped up in the afterlife. You have to live your life here. You can't get obsessed about trying to contact them because they're not in the physical anymore. And if you let go of trying so hard to connect, it will happen. Does somebody have her computer?"

"I gave it to her best friend."

"Was she big into school?"

"She was planning on going to college."

"This sounds like a contradiction. Is there a tattoo connected to her? She doesn't feel like the type who would have a tattoo."

"Several of her guy friends got tattoos with her initials and her birth and death dates on their arms. They all came to my house and showed me their tattoos a couple of months after she died. Did she and I contract for this experience before we came over here? Was it prearranged that I would be her mother and she would be my daughter and she would pass from suicide?"

"They're funny when we ask them questions like this. I get yes and no. They never give straight answers. It's hard to understand, because there's both free will and destiny involved."

As Kira and I talked, I was sitting outside on the back porch, sipping a cup of tea and watching the orange monarch butterflies fluttering between the lantana bushes and honeysuckle vines in my garden. A ruby-throated hummingbird darted into a red trumpet flower and then rose to my eye level, gazing straight at me as it rapidly fluttered its wings.

"If we contracted for it, why did we choose to have this experience together?"

"She keeps bringing up that there's more going on here than meets the eye. She feels very lofty to me, which makes me think she's an older spirit. Did you get the impression, when she was in the physical, that she intuitively knew things?"

"Oh, yeah." I watched the hummingbird, mesmerized. "She seemed much older than her years. She was a total contradiction. She made all the wrong choices, but she was so smart in terms of understanding things."

"It's almost like she got it without even knowing that she got it," Kira told me. "She could read people and understand where they were coming from. You guys have been together a lot. I believe we travel with the same group a lot of times. She may have been the older one in a previous life. If you look back on your relationship, she may have been the one guiding you at some point. The lesson is that, as she says, there's more here than meets the eye. It opens up the spiritual side, not just for you. There are other people whom this made a big impact on, who started seeing things more spiritually. We'll never get the full answer because we just can't comprehend it. That's where faith comes in; that's what she's saying."

"It seems that she chose a life that was very difficult for her," I reflected, twisting a lock of hair around in my fingers as the bird finally flew off. "It was so difficult that she must have concluded, at some point, that suicide was the only way out. And I wonder, from her perspective now, why she chose such a difficult life."

"I get the roll-of-your-eyes type of thing; she must think we're clueless. She says when you're planning your next life, you feel you can get all these things done. Once you get into it and you add feelings to it, it becomes much more difficult, and you forget that you chose all of it. She doesn't consider it a failure. It's all a learning experience. She got what she needed."

"But she was healthy, she was beautiful, she was intelligent, she had everything going for her. How could she cross herself over, when she had so much going for her?

I just don't understand." Even though I'd had so many healing experiences, my heart still protested that she wasn't here in the physical with me.

"It's hard for us humans to wrap ourselves around it. It's almost as if everything is a contradiction. There are two sides, and there are extremes in everything that we as humans do. Because of that, it's even more meaningful. Because everything looked so perfect on the outside, and then she passed, it makes the passing even more meaningful for those who were left behind. Things are never what they appear to be. Callie says, 'I'm OK, Mama knows I'm OK.' It's easy for them to say, because they know what's on the other side. But as humans, sometimes no matter how much proof we get, we're always questioning."

"What did she feel she learned from her experience as Callie?"

"Her sense of humor comes beaming through," Kira told me. "She says, 'It's not always about me, even though sometimes I acted that way when I was on earth.' There's something about being vulnerable—she felt it was bad to be vulnerable, to ask for help."

"Yes, she was so good at helping other people. But no one—not me, her best friends, anybody—knew she was seriously depressed. She never told anyone. She had three really close girlfriends, and they were as shocked as I was."

"Maybe that's where the vulnerability comes in; she didn't let her guard down. That could be part of her lesson."

"She was acting out, she was having some problems with drugs and alcohol, but no one suspected that underneath all that was depression."

"She says she is still working on that, too. It almost feels to me like it was ingrained in her. It was just how she was. She didn't know she could ask for help. It was beyond the scope of what she could understand at the time. She's working through it. Again, that's why I get the half-accident, half-suicide. It was her way of saying, 'Hey, I need help here.' Is there something about two hearts together?"

"That would be the necklaces I purchased on a shopping trip after a conference—I got one for myself and one for her and let her pick the one she wanted. She took the purple heart, and I have the rose heart. They're together in my jewelry chest."

"She's letting you know that the closeness is still there. She also says thanks for the balloons."

"Yes, I put balloons on her grave on each of her birthdays since she died. What's she doing now, what's she learning now?"

"She's funny. I get a sarcastic edge with her. It's almost like 'What? I'm doing the same thing I would do there.' But it feels like counseling. She's helping other teenagers who have crossed to understand what happened and why. She can relate to these kids who are crossing, because she was the same age. She's still a student. She wants to learn a lot. She's showing me big books."

"Is she going to reincarnate and come back to earth again? Or is she going to stay over there for a while?"

"She makes me laugh, because again, there's that bigger feeling that we as humans just can't understand. It's like, 'I already did, but that doesn't stop me being here too.' She's not limited in terms of time and space. When they talk like that, I think, right, whatever you say. She can still connect with you. It's going to end here. Know that her love is unconditional."

After I thanked Kira for the reading, I put down the phone and sipped the last drops of tea as I gazed thoughtfully at my garden. The hummingbird reappeared, hovering directly in front of me for a split second and then rapidly flying in circles to create a perfect figure eight. It paused, again locking eyes with me for a moment, then took off, darting across the horse pasture to the distant trees.

Maybe the hummingbird was trying to send me some sort of message. The figure eight is the symbol for infinity. *Maybe Callie's trying to let me know that nothing ever ends and love never dies.* I picked up my cup, went inside, and carted it to the sink. *I wonder what Tom would think if I told him about all this?* I mused.

That night, in a lucid dream, I found myself flying rapidly through the pitch-black sky, and as all the silver stars shot past me, I decided to search for Seraphiel again. I landed in what looked like a shopping mall or an amusement park. Brightly lit shops surrounded a courtyard with a huge merry-go-round in the center. The ponies were alive, snorting and prancing, and when the music played, they galloped merrily in a circle with children holding onto their waving manes, shouting and laughing.

I saw a very handsome young man in a white T-shirt and jeans next to the carousel gazing at me intently. He wore a baseball cap turned around backward, and he had piercing blue eyes. The eyes gave him away.

"Oh, my God," I exclaimed. "You must be Seraphiel!"

"Yes," he laughed. "I think you might be right."

"Where am I?" I wondered, looking around, awestruck. He smiled. "Why, you're in the angelic realm."

"But this looks just like earth."

"Well, you create your heaven from projections of your earth experiences."

"But I never encountered live horses on a merry-go-round."

"I bet you imagined them."

"Touché." I laughed. "I sure have."

"Here, let me show you around."

We stopped at a little pen filled with chortling babies who were crawling all over the floor. Seraphiel picked up a smiling, happy baby and handed him to me.

"Oh," I exclaimed, cradling the naked baby in my arms. "I just love babies."

But then the baby started to spit up on me. "Oh, dear," I said. "I didn't know angel babies spit up."

I put the baby back in the pen, where it merrily crawled away to play. When I stood up and looked around, Seraphiel was gone.

So I decided to search for Callie. I stopped a young woman with shoulder-length brown hair who was wearing a stylish little black dress and waiting on an elegantly dressed customer inside a fashionable shoe store. "I'm looking for Callie Murray. She's about sixteen, tall, slender, with long, blonde hair."

"I saw her just a few minutes ago over there." She pointed to the line at the cash register.

Callie was at the end of the line, a pair of navy-blue, platform high-heel pumps in her hand. Delighted, I ran to her. "Where else would I find you but in a fancy shoe store?" I exclaimed.

She laughed. "I'm happy to see you Mama, but you have to go back."

Callie vanished into thin air and a broom instantly materialized in her place. I gazed at it in total disbelief. Then I woke up.

At my next appointment for a healing a few weeks later, I told Joy, "I had another lucid dream. I think I found Seraphiel, but he didn't look at all like the painting you have of him here in the healing room." In the picture, Seraphiel was dressed as an old wizard, with long, white hair and a flowing white beard. "This guy looked like he was in his early twenties."

"Oh, that's young Raphael."

I described the journey that I had taken in my dream. "What does it mean?" I asked her.

"Well, the baby symbolizes your new life. But it won't be without challenges. And the broom? Well, it means that Callie is still cleaning up her house."

It was mid-October, the peak of the fall colors in Cassville. On a brilliant, blue, Indian summer morning, I made my way to Joy's house for class. Her garden was ablaze with red, purple, and yellow chrysanthemums, pansies, violas, and the last of the season's roses. The weather report was predicting the arrival of a strong cold front that night with rain and thunderstorms, and a brisk breeze blew the scarlet and orange maple leaves in circles around me as I made my way to her porch. Angie, Jana, and Ryan tromped in a few minutes later. Joy had made us some hot mulled apple cider and spice cake, and we sat around her kitchen table, steaming cups in our hands.

Joy pulled some small, unpainted wooden boxes out of a paper bag along with tubes of acrylic paint and brushes. Then she placed some smooth, round rocks on the table.

"Today you will be making a creation box," she announced, "and placing inside it what you would like to manifest in your life. While you are painting your boxes, Seraphiel will talk to you about creation." She took a deep breath and he began to speak.

"First, you must acknowledge your fear and pain. We have spoken to you of this before. You must surrender in full acceptance of yourself and all that exists in your world before you can move out of your pain and create your life in a new way. Remember, creation comes from a place of calm acceptance. Otherwise, your ego will not be able to let go of what it has been creating. Then, set the pain aside or imagine pushing a pause button on the pain, get quiet, centered within yourself, and create a new choice—a new situation you want—and put your focus on that. Soon, your reality will start to change. You have a tendency to change your focus from being an awesome creator of your reality to fear of what you're going to create."

"I think that's what I'm doing," Angie replied pensively as she painted a large, red heart on the top of her box.

"So in each instant I tell myself I am awesome; I am all that is; I create my reality," Jana ventured.

"Yes, you did not create your experience here on earth to be painful or harmful. This started when you forgot that you are spirit residing in a human body. Break your bondage to the pain. Learn what love is in your experience of separation by experiencing love, not what love is not. Do not choose to make pain part of your experience."

"So it doesn't exist unless we choose to experience it?" Jana interjected as she inspected the tubes of paint scattered on the table.

"Correct. You are not at the mercy of life. Life is your design. You can create your world exactly as you desire it to be."

"Is this the dichotomy of living in this dimension?" Angie asked, puzzled.

"Yes, you are creating love through what it is not; you can learn to create love through love. The instant you are in now is all that exists. Because you create in each instant of your life, you can change your creation. Maintain yourself in the instant you are in right now. Yesterday is gone; the future is not yet here. All you have is your present. The present is your gift, and each moment you are choosing to open the gift of the moment."

"That's an interesting play on words," Angie said, laughing, as she took a paintbrush to the sink to wash it.

"Your past is your story. Your future is your expectation. Your present is your gift to yourself."

"I like that," Jana said with a sigh.

"But if you choose not to open your gift of the moment, it becomes part of your story that has never been read, and you are left with nothing," Seraphiel added.

"What do you do if you have battle fatigue?" Jana wondered as she applied a rainbow of colors to one side of her box.

"You love yourself and let go of the pain that is causing it and give yourself some respite. You can learn to draw to yourself what you want with ease and grace. Create your reality with your imagination, thought, words, expectation, and belief. Imagine what you want first, know it intimately, and use all your senses. Imagine what it looks like, feels like, sounds like, tastes like, and smells like. Create what you want with intention and clarity.

Remember never to use judgment and fear as creation tools, or you will create what you don't want."

"I can't get a grasp of how to do that," Angie grumbled, putting down her paintbrush and inspecting the rocks on the table.

"Surrender to your omnipotence. Do all of you understand the meaning of the word *omnipotent?*"

"All-knowing? All-powerful?" asked Ryan.

"Infinite? Unending?" I guessed.

"Being omnipotent means you are all-powerful to create in your existence everything you require to successfully awaken to the love that you are through separation," Seraphiel replied.

"It's so hard when you are used to making things happen and controlling things," Angie protested.

"You must let go of ego control and use spirit control."

"What can I do in the moment to create what I want?" asked Jana.

"Create a picture in your mind of exactly how it will appear. Then, put what it is into words. Believe in yourself; have faith in your ability to draw it to you. Gather it into your soul heart and blow it out through your divine breath into the angelic realm. Then, act as if it's already done, that what you desire has already happened.

"Here's an excellent example. Your desire to remember who you truly are gives me, Seraphiel, existence. You created me in your world. I am pure essence of love vibrating as required for those who seek to know themselves as love through my teachings."

"I think we're awesome for creating you," Angie exclaimed.

"If there are no more questions," Seraphiel said, looking solemnly around the room, "we will leave you now."

It was always disconcerting when Seraphiel used the term "we." Evidently, according to Joy, he was the leader of a host of angels and was the spokesperson for the group.

Joy hiccupped. "I trust you have learned all about creation, so let's try it out. Pick up one of these stones." She gestured toward the rocks at the center of the table.

"Let's start small," she said. "Create something that seems possible—not world peace, for example," she added, laughing. "Place the energy of your creation into your stone, and when you're done, hold it in your hands in front of you and blow your desires out forcefully to the angels. Then place the rock inside your box."

I picked up a golden-yellow stone with flecks of white in it and held it between my hands and closed my eyes.

What do I want to create? I saw an image of me and Tom holding hands and lying on sun-kissed white sand near dazzling, turquoise-blue water. I felt a warm sea breeze caress my cheek and tasted salt in the air. I heard the roar of surf breaking against the shoreline. I sent the energy of all I'd created into my stone and blew it out into the universe. Then I placed my stone into my box.

After we were done, Joy asked, "Who would like to share what you've created?"

"I'll start." Angie picked up her box. "My boyfriend and I are moving in together. I've conjured up a log cabin in the woods with a redwood deck that's enclosed so I can paint and work on my stained-glass projects. This will be the start of my peaceful life."

"And I've imagined the perfect job," Jana chimed in. "You know, I think I'd like to be a personal trainer. I could use my skills as a physical therapist and work at a place like the YMCA to help people become healthier and more physically fit."

"That's a great idea!" Angie said enthusiastically.

"I've decided to try my hand at woodworking," Ryan offered. "So, I've created lots of buyers for the hand-carved furniture I'm going to design."

"I'm bringing a tropical vacation with Tom into my life," I told the group. "I can't wait."

"Very good," Joy said. "You know that one of the best ways to let go of the past is to have something beautiful that you're walking toward. Now, take your boxes home and place them in your sacred space."

∽ 28 ∽

Diane—Living in Two Worlds

I felt that I was nearing the end of my search for Callie but decided to have one final reading with Kira on the Sunday after Thanksgiving. But first, I invited Megan, Jenny, and Ashley and their boyfriends over for a belated Thanksgiving dinner on Saturday night. The holidays were always so different without Callie, but this one was boisterous and merry. Everyone seemed to have a good time. I collapsed in a chair afterward as Tom cleaned up the kitchen.

"Here, Anthony," I said, gesturing toward a pile of leftover-filled Tupperware containers. "Take these downstairs to the refrigerator in the basement."

When Anthony returned, he announced, "There's a strange cat in the garage."

"Are you sure it's not one of our barn cats?"

"I've never seen this one before."

"OK, I'll check it out." I wearily hauled myself to my feet.

Evidently lured by the smell of fresh turkey cooking in the oven, a scrawny, half-grown, snow-white kitten with aquamarine eyes huddled on the stairs leading from the garage to the kitchen. I carefully sat down on the step next to her and held out my hand. She froze briefly, then stretched out her neck and cautiously sniffed me. I reached back and stroked her ears as she began to purr. I picked her up and carted her to the kitchen.

"Well, what have we here?" asked Tom with a smile.

"I'm afraid it's a stray kitten." I sat her down in front of a bowl of turkey scraps. We watched as she hungrily scarfed down all the food.

"Well, it looks like a new member of the family to me." Tom sighed.

"Yes, I'm afraid so."

"What's her name?"

I looked outside. In the light of the back porch, I could see dainty little pellets of snow falling gently to the ground.

"I think I'll call her Snowflake," I replied as she perched on my lap, licking her paws and then rubbing her little face vigorously with them.

On Sunday morning, Kira started the reading by saying, "It feels like Callie was very artistic. Is there a picture hanging somewhere that she drew?"

"Yes, there's a color-by-number picture that she gave me on Valentine's Day when she was ten years old. It says LOVE in capital letters. It's hanging in the room where I am right now."

I was sitting in Anthony's bedroom on a sofa that had been too big to cart to his apartment. I had placed some of Callie's artwork in the room along with several green-and-black dragons that Anthony had built as a child from Lego blocks.

"That makes sense to me. It's to let you know she's here. Is there an animal whose name starts with a P there with her?"

"That's Piddles, a cocker spaniel we had a long time ago."

"He would be with her, right?"

"Yes, he probably would be with her now."

"Was that dog a little bit nippy?" Kira asked.

"Yes, Piddles bit Callie on the nose when she was about six years old."

"Are you going through some work transitions right now?"

"I'm teaching at the school of nursing and I work at the hospital," I told Kira. "The transitions aren't really at work, they're more in my head. I'm still having these out-of-body experiences. I go back and forth between two worlds; it's kind of schizophrenic. I don't talk about it at all at work. But I do go to a class where the teacher channels Seraphiel. So, we talk about a lot of that stuff there. My boyfriend is starting to open up a little to it. He used to be really closed, but I'm careful about what I say to him or to anyone else, for that matter."

I was continually in conflict about my experiences. I had endless debates with myself about sharing them, even with Tom.

"Yes, when you bring it up to people who aren't open, it hurts you more than them. But you can't explain everything. You can't prove everything scientifically. Not that our rational brain doesn't want to. You've got the science and the metaphysical; it's hard to mesh the two. I have a degree in chemistry. What I do makes no sense to the other side of me. So, I know what you mean. Your life purpose is to try to bring the two closer together. You're walking that line for a reason. Do you connect rainbows with Callie at all?"

"Oh, yes, she had a wallet with a rainbow on it that I gave to her best friend, Jenny, on what would have been her eighteenth birthday."

"You're further away now from her passing; the grief is a little bit dissipated. So, you can analyze things a little better without feeling it so deeply. Your daughter is very flighty. Was she flighty, jumping from one thing to another? She's telling me, 'Now, don't forget to tell Mama this and this and this.'"

"Oh, yes."

"She also has a clever twist to her in a creative, quirky way. She was very pretty, too, right?"

"Yes, she was beautiful."

"She wants you to know that everything is working out perfectly. Don't get stressed out when it feels like it's not. It's like you get into a negative mood, and she wants you to stop and step back and remind yourself that this is not where you want to be. She's trying to say, 'Take a deep breath; it's not the end of the world.' The main message here is uplift. Keep walking that line. Right now, you're walking that line between both worlds. It can be hard, but she's always there. I also feel like you're socializing more than you were. You're probably more healed."

"Yes, that's definitely true. After she died, except for my son, boyfriend, Megan, Jenny, and Ashley, I really didn't want to communicate with anyone. I talked to my sister occasionally. But I pretty much withdrew as much as I could from the world."

"Callie is definitely a positive energy, and you feel this when you connect with her. It's like a relief to you and an escape from the physical. Some people drink, some smoke cigarettes, some meditate. Your thing is connecting with Seraphiel and Callie. That's a good thing, because in a way you're just connecting with your own source. That's how it manifests itself, but it's really your connection to source. We are all much larger than we think we are. Do you have any questions you'd like to ask?"

I got up and started to pace around the room. I had written down some questions I wanted to ask Callie on a yellow legal pad earlier in the day. I thumbed through my notes and then said, "I've been wondering about the whole suicide issue. If someone gets overwhelmed by their life, and they commit suicide, will they encounter the same or a similar situation when they are reincarnated or come back? Will they have to do this over and over again until they learn to walk through it instead of trying to escape every time?"

"To me, we put certain things in our lives as a challenge, but if we decide it's too much, we don't have to go through with them. It's not like you're going to have to do this until you get it right. It's more like, 'I think I'd like to try again and see if I can do better this time.' There's never any pressure to get it right, because we're eternal and we never get it all done, because we're never done. It's more playful. As humans, we think of it as right or wrong, and then we're punished if we're wrong. She may voluntarily want to try again, but it's nothing she feels pressured about. When we put on the physical body, we do feel pressured because we forget, but that's more the illusion than the reality."

"That makes complete sense to me," I said. "I have another question, though. Knowing what she knows now, if she had a friend who was thinking about suicide, what would she tell them? It creates so much pain for those who are left behind. And I wonder, how do they feel about it over there?"

"It's a very individual thing, our free will. We can't tell each other how to feel, or really even explain how we feel sometimes. It's an individual decision, but each person needs to understand the ramifications of the whole thing and how it will affect other people. But it's still a decision you make."

I plopped back down on the sofa, thoroughly exasperated.

"Even at sixteen, it was still her decision?"

"Sixteen is an arbitrary number that we apply. It's still her life, her choice, and her decision to make, no matter how much it hurts someone else. It's hard to accept the fact that we may not understand everything completely until we ourselves cross over."

"She said in another reading with you that she'd gotten her angel wings. Can she tell me what that means?"

"My soul interprets the angel wings as flight. You know here on earth when we imagine things we want, they don't appear right here, right away, because we're in this time-space reality. When she thinks things now, they appear right away; that's how I interpret the wings. They fly right to her. She's getting good at manifesting. She's learned how to use energy. When she puts her mind to it, it's there. She's very uplifting. She has a very positive flow to her. She's always around you." Kira paused. "I feel like it's going to end here."

29

Diane—Finding the Joy in Me

The Saturday morning before Christmas, Ryan, Jana, Angie, and I trudged up the steps to Joy's house laden with brightly colored bags full of gifts. Joy had a tradition of exchanging presents during the last class before Christmas, and I looked forward to my Christmas class as much as the holiday I spent with Anthony and Tom at my house.

We scarfed down a breakfast of orange juice, scrambled eggs, bacon, and Belgian waffles before making our way to Joy's living room for class. She had set up a tree right in front of her large picture window and decorated it with tiny, blinking, frosted white lights and multicolored heirloom glass ornaments that sparkled in the morning sun.

Ryan gave me a clear, white, glass paperweight with an angel etched inside, wings outstretched, hands folded in prayer. I received a blue, green, and white cloisonné dolphin from Jana and a beautiful painting of Callie from Angie. In the painting, she was wearing her baby-blue prom dress and a deep-purple teardrop necklace. Her hair was loosely wrapped in a bun, tendrils framing her delicate face. Her smile could just light up a room. Angie had captured the essence of Callie at her best. Joy gave me a turquoise and silver angel necklace. I was overwhelmed by their kindness and generosity.

After we had stuffed all our presents back in their bags for the journey home, Joy announced, "Seraphiel would like to speak with you now."

She took a deep breath, looked at each of us warmly, and closed her eyes briefly to allow Seraphiel to enter her body. "I want to tell you something important this morning because I think you're ready for it. The number seven is sacred in all major religions on your planet. There are seven stars of the great bear, seven rays of the sun, seven pillars of wisdom, seven branches to the tree of life, and seven versions of you happening right now. Remember the critical choice points in your life that you identified during our class a few months ago? Often, these choice points are times in your spiritual growth when you find yourself at a crossroads and either take a leap of faith or ignore the call to change direction. Go back to your life map and identify your seven most important choices, where you took a different road through life because of your decision, and label them from one to seven."

I opened my notebook and pulled out the lined loose-leaf papers containing my map. My choices came to me one by one. I remembered my first choice: the time my father slapped me until I fell and almost fainted when we were out on a family picnic at a state park in New York. I was just fifteen. I picked myself up and ran blindly into the woods, crying. I came back several hours later because I felt I had nowhere else to go.

Next on the map was the time I decided to drop out of college and join the Rochester Zen Center. I sat cross-legged, terrified, in front of the roshi while he decided whether to admit me into the Zen training program. He asked me, "Now tell me, Diane, are you coming here to learn zazen or to be with your boyfriend?" I was honest and said, "I'm really not sure why I'm here." Looking back, I realized it was a little of both.

And my third choice: betraying my first love while he was at a meditation retreat with the man who would become my first husband. Having that husband tell me as I made my fourth choice—to walk out the door ten years later—"I'm giving you enough rope so you can go and hang yourself with it."

Looking Dwayne straight in the eye as I walked out on him as well when he asked me, "So, Diane, is it over?"

"Yes." I slammed the door behind me, making choice number five. "It's over!"

I remembered my sixth choice with Tom in the dead of winter on that beautiful night when I first heard him sing. I took his hand and led him to my bedroom as he asked me, "Are you sure?"

"Yes," I whispered. "Let's do this."

Then, finally, finding Callie dead on her bedroom floor, where the only choice was to try to survive and carry on, or to follow her into the abyss.

"Now," Seraphiel said, bringing me back from my reverie. "What if you had made other choices at these decision points? How might your life have evolved differently?"

I picked up the cup with a yellow smiley face wearing a red Santa hat, which I had pulled out of Joy's kitchen cabinet and filled with my favorite orange spice tea. I took a sip. The tea was still hot, its taste comforting and tender, like mother's milk.

Yes, what if I had decided to run away from home when I was fifteen? Or to stay in college and not join the Zen Center?

Or to marry my first love? What if I hadn't decided to become involved with Tom? Would I have been able to bear the loss of Callie with only Anthony and Ruffy to comfort me? What would have happened if I had committed suicide as well?

"Well, there are six other parallels of you living in other dimensions and having these alternative experiences."

"Are parallels like simultaneous lifetimes?" Jana asked, frowning, as she scribbled notes furiously across her map.

"Yes."

"Are you still in the same body?"

"No, you are in the body that you create there."

"Is it the exact replica of the body you create here?" asked Angie, as she wrapped herself up like a little Eskimo in a plush blanket from the healing room.

"Yes, at the age that it enters the parallel experience."

"Can we go to these different parallels to help out the other aspects of our self?" I asked. I was puzzled. I didn't understand how all this worked.

"Yes, you do this in dream time and they come here, for you are still one having seven different experiences."

"Do all seven appear at the same time?" asked Ryan, twisting himself up like a pretzel in his chair. He could never sit still.

"No, they appear as you encounter each choice point. But they are all set in motion before you cross over to this time-space reality on earth. It is best if you make your decisions from the love that you are, but unfortunately many forget and make their choices from fear."

"Why do we forget?" asked Angie.

"Sometimes the experience feels too difficult or too painful. Sometimes we run into things that are so heavy that we feel we cannot carry them. This almost happened with Diane."

"So basically you're saying that each time we move into a different parallel, we start fresh," Angie said, smiling.

"Yes, at the age that you choose each fork in your path. This belief that you have that you cannot overcome the obstacles you face in life—well, there is another one in another parallel that already knows that you can. You are the oldest of the parallels, however, for each is traveling at its own pace. It's awesome as you have designed it. You are never alone. And when you cross the veil, all seven of you will merge on the other side.

"Where does karma play into all this?" I asked. My logical mind seemed to want to cling to the belief that whatever someone does, good or harmful, comes back to them.

"There is no karma. There's always healing. For you see, beloved ones, it's only about remembering that you are pure spirit, having an experience of separation from spirit. God is you—not out there, not some cloudy, nebulous being, and not some power that controls you, for you are in control. You're the creator of all. You design your experience to remember the love that you are. No matter what choices you make, no matter what you decide to experience, you always have the opportunity to remember."

"Is this what we consider the small voice within?" Angie asked as she buried herself deeper in her blankets.

"It is the truth of you. Recognize yourself as you truly are, not through the web of ego and excuse-ridden judgment of yourself, but through the clear perception and knowing of your perfection as designer, creator, and fulfiller of your divine plan. *You* happen to the experience. The experience does not happen to you. Claim your power. Acknowledge that this is your creation. Understand what it is you choose to know about yourself through it. Say, 'Thank you for participating with me in this experience.' Move on to another opportunity to know your wholeness as love."

Angie nervously chewed the tip of her pencil. "I've found that for me change is very scary, and it's easier to go back to your old habits when you get stressed or when you get upset," she said.

"Here's how we would ask you to see this," Seraphiel replied. "Say to an experience that you wish to release, 'You have served me well. I thank you for being my teacher, for helping me on my way as I learn to create consciously. You've done your job, and I thank you for that, and I release you now, for I am choosing to create without your assistance through the love that I am, not through the fear that you represent.' This is your freedom. Before you can become master of the knowledge of the ages, you must know yourself as all of it, not possessing it, not knowing it, but being it, fully and completely. In each instant, fully be the love that you are. Remember your tools of creation. You create your own reality by belief and by knowing."

"How do you go from belief to knowing?" Jana looked up from her papers and fixed her gaze on Joy's body.

"You create it, not as an expectation but as a reality in the moment. Then know it. Knowing happens when the spirit feels it. It's a feeling. Change the feeling and you change the experience. Change the experience, and you change the feeling. It works either way."

"After all the struggle I've been through, it almost seems too easy," Angie said with a groan.

"Well, I feel like at least now I have a road map," Jana interjected.

"So, what is your response to what I've spoken? What will change for you because of this knowledge?"

"I'm in the process of letting go of being the victim," I replied, "and letting go of wondering why these awful things have happened to me. I've realized that I can choose my response to any situation I encounter. I'm completely free. Whatever comes my way, I can find the joy in it, the gift in it, or choose to be miserable in it. It's all up to me. I'm looking to find the joy inside me. I'm not looking outside of me anymore. I can't blame Callie for being unhappy. I have to let go. I have to look for the joy in me."

"Is there freedom for you in that?"

"Yes, total freedom."

"So, the bondage that you have lived in is gone. Are you fully aware in this moment that you are creator of all that is in your world?"

"Yes."

"There's no room for struggle, for resistance, for self-recrimination, no room for judgment. It is what it is. And it has served its purpose well. It takes all control from the experience and brings it directly into the self. And then you are free!"

Joy looked around at each one of us to measure just how much had sunk in. Then Seraphiel said, "We will leave you now." And Joy was herself again.

"Well, tell me what happened," she exclaimed. I always wondered where she went when Seraphiel took over.

"I'm very proud of all of you," she said, after we had filled her in on the morning's events.

We then picked up our notebooks and our bags of presents, hugged her and each other good-bye, skipped down the steps joking and laughing, our arms wrapped around each other, and bounded into the afternoon sunshine.

30

Callie—The Attitude Adjustment

I hate to admit it, but Aunt Flo led me to a change of heart. It was because of her that I finally underwent a (probably) much-needed attitude adjustment. I realized that Flo wasn't judging me; she was trying to help me. Flo cared about me and had my best interests at heart.

Flo decided that I should sit with her, Bea, and Ellie in the parlor every evening for a while after dinner. Bea would bring her embroidery and Ellie her knitting. Flo would just sit there sipping a glass of sherry. I would sit in a floral-print high-backed chair, fidgeting and sighing. Flo, Bea, and Ellie would sometimes have quiet conversations about this and that, but often they were silent. After about an hour, Great-Aunt Flo would tell me that I was excused and could go upstairs to finish my homework. I would just shoot out of that chair and into my bedroom.

I finally got fed up with the silence while I was imprisoned in the parlor and began to speak. Once I started talking, I found I couldn't shut up. I talked about my childhood, how I always felt different, how I didn't fit in, how lonely I felt. How I only felt loved and accepted by my animals. How I always tried to please everyone—my parents, my teachers, my friends—but I could never seem to get anything right. They always seemed disappointed in me, like I didn't measure up to their standards of perfection. So, I decided to rebel. I sought out kids who were troublemakers, but then I found that I was trying to please them by doing drugs and partying all night long. In the end, I didn't know who I was anymore. I felt like I didn't exist. I had become invisible. That was the hell of it all.

One night, after I'd gone on like this for a while, Flo put her glass of sherry down on the coffee table and eyed me pensively. "Well, you must remember these words: First, to thine own self be true."

"Yeah, I guess I learned that lesson the hard way."

They would make suggestions about things I should remember when I decided to reincarnate again. "You must realize that you have everything you need inside of you," counseled Ellie.

"You must love yourself above all others," Bea instructed. "Then you will never do anything to cause yourself harm."

"Don't get caught up in all the drama on earth," warned Flo sternly. "Remember, you're not a victim. You create your own reality. Learn to seek the gift in your experiences."

This time I finally listened, and I got it. And I learned to trust myself and express my feelings and not to run and hide from them. Flo reported my remarkable progress to Seraphiel, who was very proud of me.

"Callie, I'm looking for an assistant counselor," he told me one day. "There are so many kids coming to me with so many problems."

He gave me my own office in the library, looking out over that beautiful courtyard where I met Jesus right after I crossed myself over. At that moment, our relationship began to change. I was so in awe of him when we first met, but now we were becoming colleagues and friends. He would sometimes pop into my office unannounced to discuss a particularly difficult case. I realized that I'd had the answers inside me all along, but now I was actually able to give him some advice. And—no shit—he really valued my opinion.

After a few weeks of helping Seraphiel in the library, I noticed that he always retired alone to his rooms after work. And I started to worry that he might get lonely in the evening. So I decided to ask him to my Barbie house for dinner.

"I've asked one of my friends to come to dinner on Saturday night," I mentioned casually to my companions at breakfast one morning.

"That's very nice, dear," Bea replied.

"Is it one of your girlfriends or a new boyfriend?" asked Ellie, with a twinkle in her eye.

"Well, it's none of them," I stated mysteriously, pausing for dramatic effect. "I've asked Seraphiel."

."You've done what?" Flo exclaimed, nearly dropping the coffee she was drinking, spilling some of it into her saucer.

"Well, what did he say?" asked Ellie excitedly.

"He said he'd be delighted to come," I told her, smiling mischievously.

The commotion that Seraphiel's imminent arrival at my Barbie house caused was epic. Everything had to be perfect. Bea and Ellie pored over recipes while Flo recruited several of her friends to help her clean the house from top to bottom. They scurried around in a fever of anticipation, scrubbing, polishing, dusting, and ordering me not to step on the floor because they'd just waxed it, not to sit on the sofa because they just finished fluffing the cushions. Now I suppose you're wondering why they couldn't just imagine a sparkling-clean house. Well, creation comes from a calm and centered space of belief. And they had all worked themselves into such a state of agitation that it was easier to just do it than to imagine it.

Go figure. I flopped on a chair, watching them in amazement. People aren't perfect, even here in heaven.

Flo worked herself into a frenzy over the details of the dinner. How formal should it be? Should the meal be served outside on the patio or inside in the dining room? Which china should she use? Should there be music? What about flowers and candles?

Late Saturday afternoon, as I was dressing for the party, I snagged a black silk stocking on a jagged fingernail as I was pulling it up my leg. Damn, I cursed as I watched the run in my hose travel all the way down to my foot. I pulled it off, disgusted, and tossed it into the trash. I was so mad that I forgot I could imagine my stockings mended in an instant.

I stomped into Flo's bedroom, pulled open one of her bureau drawers, and started rummaging through it, looking for another pair of stockings. I felt something soft and furry underneath a pile of scarves. I jerked my hand away. *What the hell is that?* I wondered. I carefully removed the scarves. Staring accusingly up at me with their pathetic beady black eyes were several dead mink carcasses with their disgusting tails and dirty little feet still attached to their bodies. The heads of two poor minks were sewn to the hind legs of a third, and I shuddered in revulsion as I gazed down at them, horrified.

After I recovered, I opened another drawer and carefully removed a pair of long white gloves. I slipped them over my fingers and pulled them up to my elbows. Then I gingerly retrieved the minks from the drawer, holding onto them by their tails. Completely forgetting that I wasn't supposed to be rifling through Flo's bureau drawers without permission, I indignantly carried the minks down the stairs. I held them accusingly over the elegantly set dining table with the thumb and forefinger of my left hand and pinched my nose closed with the fingers of my right.

"What the hell is this?" I asked angrily. "These poor, pitiful creatures, what have you done to them?"

Flo glared back at me. "And just where did you find my mink scarf?"

"In one of your bureau drawers."

"And who gave you permission to sort through my drawers?"

"No one," I answered, glowering at her obstinately. "I snagged my hose. I was just looking for a new pair."

"Would you like it if I went looking for God-knows-what in your drawers?"

"No, I don't suppose I would."

She carefully took the minks out of my hand and started stroking their fur with her fingers. "In my time on earth, women of fashion wore these scarves."

"That's detestable!"

"Yes, I'm inclined to agree. It's amazing what people will do in the name of fashion. Now," she continued, handing the minks to me. "You go put these poor creatures back exactly where you found them."

Despite all the fuss, the dinner was a rousing success. Seraphiel was his most charming self, and I even managed to behave myself and not get into any more trouble. Afterward, Flo was delighted to be able to say to all her friends in a hushed tone, "You'll never guess who came over for dinner last Saturday night!"

⤝ 31 ⤟

Callie—Our Thoughts Create Our Reality

Here's another little secret everybody learns in the angelic realm, but it also applies to our lives on earth. Ready?

Our thoughts create our reality.

This is really one of the most important things I learned in heaven. As usual, I learned this lesson the hard way fairly soon after I arrived in Summer Wind. After the incident with the hill and the waterslide, when I chased that boy, Dustin, around and around in the water while I was riding a dolphin, I decided I liked waterslides but not muddy ones. I said to my new girlfriends in heaven, "You know, we're much more civilized than those nasty boys. Let's imagine ourselves a huge water park with some great, big waterslides in it."

My friends thought this was a great idea. So, we began holding secret meetings in the basement of the library late at night to design the park. Only girls were invited. Of course, all the boys and the adults got really curious about why we were disappearing every evening. But we swore one another to secrecy. We met until we had the park perfectly planned out, then together we imagined it into being on a midsummer night after midnight. The grand opening ceremony would be the next day.

It was our first experience of collectively imagining something into life together, and we gazed at our creation in awe. There were five waterslides spiraling down a huge glass mountain with pools filled with multicolored fountains at the bottom. Inspired, we had also built a pretty little miniature golf course, several tennis courts, a picnic area, and a huge pool with a big-screen TV at the back of the deep end so we could all watch movies while we lay on floats in the pool after dark.

The night before the big opening, I lay in bed waiting for morning to come. I had just this one nagging worry: What if, after all this work, it rained on opening day? I couldn't get this thought out of my mind. *Out! damn thought*, I kept saying to myself, but it didn't work. It reminded me of the night before prom, when I stewed about what I would do if it rained and my dress or my hair got all wet.

The next day dawned bright and sunny, but as the morning wore on, dark clouds began scuttling across the horizon, and when I arrived at the water park in my Mustang, huge raindrops were beginning to fall from the sky. Tamara was in a foul mood as we girls all assembled at the entrance to the park.

"OK," she exclaimed, glaring at us. "Who imagined that it was going to rain on our opening day?"

We looked at one another but no one said anything. Finally, I raised my hand timidly. "Well, I worried all night last night that it might rain, but I certainly didn't *want* it to rain."

Tamara was thoroughly exasperated with me. "Well, Callie," she explained, "that's the same thing as imagining it would rain."

Then she made all of us imagine bright, blue sky and sunshine, and just like that, the rain stopped, a rainbow appeared over the water park, and the sun began to peek out from behind the clouds.

"What the hell did she mean by that?" I grumbled to Seraphiel later when I cornered him after the opening ceremony. "Tamara thinks I made it rain because I was worrying so much about it."

"You probably did."

"What? That's totally fucked up."

"Well, Callie, whatever you focus your attention on is going to happen, and it will happen pretty fast here in heaven. So you must put your attention on the positive—on what you want—and not on what you don't want. Worrying about something you don't want to happen will bring it right to you."

"Well, I've been worrying all morning about one of those nasty boys stealing my beautiful Mustang, but I bet you it's still in the parking lot where I left it," I retorted as I stomped off to find my car.

But it was gone. I looked everywhere for it and it was totally gone. But then something clicked in my head. I stood there, quieted my mind, and imagined myself another Mustang, and like magic, it appeared right in front of me. I remember thinking. *This is just too damn cool! Now, how am I going to remind myself to always think positively?*

Counseling the new kids was very hard work. People bring so much drama from earth to sort through in the afterlife. It was my job to help them find the gifts in their experiences.

Sometimes, after a particularly difficult day, I'd head over to the animal hospital where pets that were old or sick when they crossed over have a chance to recover. It's in the middle of a huge forest and it's always fall there. The leaves sparkle in multicolored hues of orange, red, and gold, and the air is crisp and refreshing. There are a number of trails scattered throughout the woods. I would pick up a couple of the dogs who had been restored to the energy and vigor of their puppy days and were waiting for their owners to cross over. I'd take them for a walk in the woods. Now, this might sound strange, but animals can talk in heaven. Not the way humans talk, but they can imprint what they want to say in your mind.

They'd start jumping and barking, and in my mind I would hear, "I want to go to the lake."

But then I would hear, "No, not the lake. I want to go to the top of the hill and run through the wildflowers."

And yet another, "No, let's go climb the rocks to the big waterfall."

They would start pushing and shoving and squabbling like a bunch of kids. And I would say, "If you won't behave and get along, we won't go anywhere."

Then they'd all roll over on their backs with their paws in the air, and I would hear, "I'm sorry, I'm sorry, I'm sorry. We'll go anywhere you want to go."

So we'd start off. The dogs would run in front of me, barking and wagging their tails. Unfortunately, some of their earth impulses were still with them. They'd see a squirrel hunting for acorns or nuts and take off chasing it.

And I would yell, "Stop that! Don't chase the poor squirrel!" They'd slink back to me with their tails between their legs.

Once, a very irate squirrel turned around and started chasing them back to me, chattering angrily. Squirrels have the most awful language. "You goddamn m-f pieces of mangy shit, stay away from me!"

"Mr. Squirrel, there's no need to talk like that," I reminded him.

He sputtered, glaring at me, "Don't tell me what I can and can't say, you puny little girl!"

I tried to keep myself from laughing, not wanting to anger him any further. "Come on, dogs; let's go. That squirrel's not worth chasing." The dogs followed me, sniffing and wagging their tails, having a wonderful time.

One of my greatest successes was Jordan. He was the son of a real-estate executive and one of Cassville's socialites. He'd been the golden boy in high school, captain of both the football and debate teams, president of the senior class, accepted at Cornell during early admission. But he led a secret life. He was gay. His father caught him in bed late one night with the son of one of his business partners and threatened to disown Jordan if he didn't straighten himself out. A couple of weeks later, just before his high school graduation, he disappeared. It wasn't until the next fall that some hunters found him. He had driven his red Firebird deep into the forest, down an old logging road, and shot himself.

Jordan had then stayed put, refusing the help of all the angels who came to assist him. I discovered his car in the woods when I was on one of my walks with the dogs. I wasn't on a rescue mission at the time but had become curious about a small clearing that appeared to be in perpetual twilight, shrouded in clouds and mist that weighed heavily on me as I approached. I noticed a boy in a red car holding a handgun in his lap with a gaping hole in the side of his head. I walked over and banged on the side of the driver's window with my fist.

"Why do you still have that fucking hole in your head? You look a goddamn mess."

"What's it to you?" he spat.

"I don't like your messing up my scenery."

"Then don't look."

"Well, I just don't understand. Why don't you imagine yourself healed?"

"What if I like the way I am right now?" he retorted.

"Are you fucking crazy? Take a look at yourself," I exclaimed, pulling a mirror out of my purse and holding it up to his face.

He stared into the mirror, shocked. "I guess I do look pretty horrific," he admitted.

"No shit. Do you mind if I join you? I think it's going to rain." I walked over to the passenger side of the car, opened the door, climbed in, lit a cigarette, and rolled down the window. "I don't suppose you have a fucking ashtray in here."

"No."

"So tell me, why'd you blow your brains out?"

"None of your goddamn business."

"Well, my suicide was a lot tidier. I overdosed myself on my antidepressants."

Startled, he looked at me. "Why'd you do that?"

"I was being stupid; I thought nobody loved me, and I wanted to get everyone's attention. I didn't know the pills were that dangerous. Man, was I pissed off when I found out I was dead!"

"No shit. Well, my dad threatened to disown me when he found out I was gay. So I decided if he didn't want me around the way I was, I'd just blow myself off the face of the goddamn earth."

"Sounds like you were pretty angry." I flicked the ashes from my cigarette out the window.

"No shit."

"So . . . why are you still hanging out here in your car?"

"Uh, I guess I don't know where else to go. None of the angels who showed up, that is until you," he corrected, "seemed to understand how I felt."

"Well, I know someone who can help you."

"Yeah? Who's that?" he challenged.

"His name is Seraphiel. He's really hot. He looks just like those sculptures of the Greek god Adonis."

"Oh, yeah?"

"He's not available. He's mine. But it won't hurt for you to look."

"Well, I just might do that," Jordan said, cracking a smile.

"But first we have to fix up your head."

Callie—The Cavern of Creation

About this time, Seraphiel, Flo, Bea, and Ellie started the great debate. Should I stay in Summer Wind and continue helping lost children? Or should I reincarnate and go back to earth?

"Callie needs to return to earth as soon as possible," Flo stated emphatically during a heated argument. "If you fall off a horse, you've got to get right back on."

"Oh, no," Ellie replied. "Callie needs to spend more time here with us. We don't want her making the same mistakes all over again."

"The house will be awfully quiet without Callie," Bea reminded them. "And think of all those poor children; what'll they do?"

They started talking all at once until finally I jumped up on the table in my high-heeled, pink go-go boots. "Everybody stop!" I shouted, pounding my foot on the table and waving my arms in the air. "This is *my* next life! Funny that no one has asked me what *I* want to do."

"Well?" Seraphiel asked. He had been observing the proceedings from a chair in the corner of the room with a glint of amusement in his eyes. "Miss Callie, what would you like to do?"

"I want to do both."

"That's not possible," Flo replied.

"Oh, yes it is." Seraphiel rose slowly from his chair. "And I think it's an excellent idea. When souls reincarnate, a piece of their soul essence remains here in the angelic realm. Sometimes that piece almost goes to sleep, if the soul puts most of its energy into life on earth. Some souls can continue their activities in the angelic realm on a limited basis. And believe it or not, some energetic souls who are very ambitious and in a hurry may reincarnate into several bodies at the same time. They'll live parallel lives. Callie can reincarnate but also leave a piece of her energy here to continue helping lost children."

After the decision was made for (one of) me to return to earth, I traveled to the Cavern of Creation to pick out my color bubbles for my next life. The Cavern of Creation is a huge, black room buried deep in the ground next to the library. The entrance is in the side of a small hill and is obscured by trees and rocks. A long, narrow path goes underground between the rocks, and a stream winds its way beside the path. The path is dimly lit by small candles along the rock walls. The room itself is totally black. Seraphiel says it's completely empty and yet full of all that is, at the same time.

The ceiling of the room holds a multitude of bubbles, like those clear soap bubbles I made with bubble wands when I was a child, but they are glowing in all the colors of the rainbow. Each color represents an emotion, such as joy or sorrow, that we may want to experience, or a character trait, such as courage, that we may want to develop in our next life. The bubbles are carefully chosen to aid our soul growth and, as a result, the never-ending expansion of the universe. That's the purpose of life. As I sat in the room, lily white, Navajo red, blush rose, and golden chrysanthemum bubbles floated down from the ceiling into my outstretched hands, and I placed them inside a glass bell jar where they glowed in the dark.

With my jar in hand, I left the room and raced up a brightly lit, gleaming-white staircase, taking two steps at a time, to the back of the library. I grabbed a ladder from the deep recesses of a storage room. It's for angels to use when they're too agitated to fly and it was coated with dust and cobwebs. *Damn*, I thought as I brushed them off with my hands, *I guess no one else gets agitated like me*. I pulled the color-bubble dictionary down from a top shelf and started thumbing through it. Lily white was the color of forbearance in love and was defined as a love that endures all things. *Wow, that's powerful*. Next I looked up Navajo red. It symbolized endurance, the ability to soldier forward no matter what obstacles life throws in your path. *I guess I could use some of that*. Blush rose was deep, abiding self-love, understanding your inherent worthiness in just being. *Well, I must still need to work on that*. And golden chrysanthemum was defined as conscious choice, the ability to make decisions from a state of awakened awareness. *If I manage to achieve this in my next life, I'll be doing all right*. I clapped my hands together and almost fell off the ladder after I put the book back on the shelf. I ran to Seraphiel's office and barged in, forgetting to politely knock first.

"I think these are Mama's bubbles, too," I exclaimed as I waved the jar under his nose.

"Yes." He smiled mysteriously. "In your next life, it will be your turn to claim them."

Next, I attended numerous planning meetings regarding the situations I would encounter that would help me experience the emotions I had chosen and nurture the character traits I wanted to develop.

"Both free will and destiny are involved," Seraphiel explained. "You'll plan the major events of your life and decide whom you'll meet. But there are several critical choice points built into your new life. This life can evolve in several different ways, depending on your decisions. You may choose one of several possible paths, but they all lead to the same place in the end. It's like writing a script for a play or movie. Everyone has his or her own role. You've met several souls here in Summer Wind who will be major supporting actors in your next life. But of course, Callie, you'll always be the star of *your* show."

"So this means that once I get back to earth, my script can be edited depending on my responses to my experiences?"

"Yes, you can learn that you're love the easy way or the hard way."

"Well," I said later to Jordan, as we were sitting in my Mustang in the parking lot smoking cigarettes after I left Seraphiel. "I wish I could tell some of my girlfriends back on earth what I know now."

"No shit." Jordan laughed.

"You know, one of my old friends, Melissa, is still with her jerk of a boyfriend. He always disrespects her. He likes to control her and tell her what to do. When she doesn't do what he wants, he threatens her and slaps her around. I guess she must have caught the bubble of honor in that cave and carried it into her life on earth. She needs to learn to honor herself and not let her boyfriend push her around."

"Have you tried telling her this?"

"Yeah! I've tried to talk to her several times in dreams but she just ignores me. She thinks I'm a figment of her overwrought imagination. You know, if she doesn't learn honor, guess what will happen when she finds a new boyfriend? Pretty soon, he'll start acting the same way as the old one. And it'll go on like this until she learns to honor herself and not put up with that shit from anyone ever again."

"People on earth are so fucked up."

"I think most of those idiots down there are really clueless; they have absolutely no idea what life is all about," I told Jordan. "They think their purpose in life is to acquire shit. They spend all their time making money to accumulate all this shit that they don't need. And then they spend all this time arranging their shit and trying to impress other people with all the shit they have."

"Yeah, my parents were sure like that," he said, sighing. "And they wanted to have pretty children who excelled at swimming or soccer or gymnastics, went to Junior Cotillion to learn all the social graces, graduated with honors from high school, and went to an Ivy League university or an exclusive college. Then I'm sure they hoped we'd meet someone from a nice family with money, get married, have pretty children, and start the whole damn thing all over again."

"You know what I think? They use all these things to entertain themselves in order to hide from the pain of knowing that they haven't got a clue who they are, or what the hell they're doing on earth. I can tell you right now, it's not about money or possessions; it's about the expansion of your soul. OK, enough lectures. It's been really nice knowing you. I've arranged for us to meet up again on the other side. Now I have to go."

"So you get to take a mulligan," Jordan joked.

"What's that?"

"It's a term people use when they play golf. I used to caddy for my dad and his business partners. It's a freebie, a do-over. It means if you screw up the first time, you get to try the shot all over again."

"Whatever," I replied.

"What have you got planned for us the next time around? I hope it's something romantic."

"That's for me to know, and you to find out."

I reached across him, opened the passenger door, kissed him right on the lips and shoved him out of the car. I stomped on the accelerator and my Mustang peeled out of the parking lot in a cloud of smoke.

After all the arrangements had been made, I readied myself to go back to earth. I felt like a soldier preparing for battle. I was apprehensive, but I knew what I wanted to accomplish. Still, I wondered if I would be able to see it through this time.

Suitcase in hand, I said good-bye to Flo and Bea and to my great-grandma Ellie in the parlor. The part of me that remained in Summer Wind was going to reside with Seraphiel in the library. Bea held a white lace handkerchief and kept dabbing her eyes with it. "Now, remember, don't look for your joy in others," she said. "People on the other side of the veil make too many mistakes. Look for your joy inside you." She touched my heart with her outstretched hand. "Here's where you will find it."

"You're much wiser and a whole lot stronger now," Flo added as she inspected my outfit for the last time and tucked a stray wisp of hair under my hat. "Your recovery has been truly miraculous. You're such a shining star. Now go back there and act like one."

"Callie," Ellie counseled, "never forget that God is inside you. Remember you are your own true north. Always live fearlessly and with great love."

"Thank you so much!" I said to the three. Then I made my way down the front steps, holding onto my hat to keep it from blowing away. "I couldn't be where I am right now without all your help."

Flo opened the driver's door to my Mustang and I slid inside. "Never lose hope. You're not alone. Call on the angels to assist you in your times of trouble. Trust in their gifts of grace and understanding. Now go and create your next life exactly as you want it to be."

She closed the door as I turned on the ignition and the radio. My favorite song, "Hope Has Wings," exploded from the speakers. I hit the accelerator and took off down the road. I could see the three of them on the steps in my rearview mirror, waving good-bye.

The part of me that was returning to earth had a final meeting with Seraphiel. He carefully reviewed all the signs that I should look for in my next life.

"These signs will help guide you along your chosen path," he said, handing me a cup. "This is the Cup of Forgetfulness."

I sipped at the concoction. "Ugh! This stinks, and it tastes so bitter." I pinched my nose closed with one hand and held the cup with the other.

"It will cause you to forget everything I've told you, except what's imprinted in your unconscious mind, so that you can start your new life with a clean slate."

I drank the rest of the potion and lay down. The next thing I knew, I was plunging through another dark tunnel into my new mother's womb. It was dark, warm, and comforting. I could hear the rhythm of my mother's heartbeat. A few short weeks later, I exploded back into the world.

Somehow, Mama found me in my new baby body in a lucid dream. She defied all the laws of nature when she showed up next to my crib. She reached her hand through the slats of that crib to hold my tiny fingers one more time. Finding me was all about perseverance; Mama just wouldn't give up.

❧ 33 ❧

Diane—The Dolphin's Journey

Callie always was a lover of dolphins. She had a huge poster in her room of smiling dolphins wearing red, purple, and blue sunglasses on their long noses, and she had assorted dolphin figurines, necklaces, and earrings. One of her dreams was to become a marine biologist so she could study dolphin behavior. The fifth anniversary of her passing was fast approaching. I had been mulling over the idea of swimming with dolphins in her honor when Tom received an invitation to speak at a medical biostatistics conference on the Big Island of Hawaii in late February.

"Why don't you fly out and join me when the conference is over?" he suggested. "I would be happy to take you to the dolphins."

And so it was that I found myself on a cold and blustery February morning sipping a cup of steaming cappuccino and waiting in the airport lounge to board my first flight to Kona. The trip was a marathon: Cassville to Houston, Houston to Los Angeles, and L.A. to Kona. It all passed in a blur of airport concourses, boarding passes, and fatigue. Finally, I slept on the flight from L.A. to Kona, waking up just in time to see the sun setting outside the airplane window. It was the color of molten lava, fiery red to burnt orange, and as it set, the sky faded to black, lit only by the silver sliver of a crescent moon. The plane touched down at eight p.m. in a rustic airport open on all sides to palm trees, bougainvillea, hibiscus, and poinsettias that swayed gently in a warm breeze.

Tom met me at baggage claim wearing shorts and a multicolored T-shirt with a peace sign on the front. It always amazed me how he could transform himself from a college professor into a tie-dyed hippie in the blink of an eye. As soon as I saw him, I dropped my bags, ran to him, and threw my arms around his neck with abandon. I was so happy to see him. He was my shelter from the storms of life, and with him I always felt cared for and safe. He had booked us a room at a resort hotel on Kamakahonu Bay, and it was spacious and elegantly appointed with Polynesian decor. I collapsed in the luxurious king-size bed while Tom burned the midnight oil, working on a grant proposal that was due as soon as he returned to the university.

The next morning, Tom and I met several other couples from the conference at the harbor for our first excursion out to sea. I had loaded myself up with Dramamine to keep from getting seasick. Waiting for us was a large, blue-and-white power catamaran captained by Janet, a short but powerfully built, deeply tanned woman with salt-tinged blonde hair, who was accompanied by a scruffy little brindle cairn terrier, Sailor. I and several others on the trip hadn't been snorkeling for a number of years, so Janet decided to take us to a nearby coral reef for snorkel practice before we ventured out in search of dolphins the next day.

I sat on the diving platform of the boat, apprehensively rinsing my mask and placing it on my face, carefully pulling back my hair so the mask would seal properly, and then snapped my fins over my feet. But after I jumped in, I found that snorkeling was like horseback riding. It all came back to me in an instant, and I happily followed Tom as he led me from the boat to the coral reef below.

Tom never ceased to amaze me. Awkward and shy on land, in the ocean he was truly in his element. He would glide through the water, arch his hips, give a swift kick, and dive effortlessly to the reef to catch a closer view of an angelfish or sea urchin. I was almost as fascinated watching him as I was by the schools of tropical fish that glided past me. If ever there was poetry in motion, this was Tom. From the boat, the water was a breathtaking color of blue, just like a baby's eyes, and I was lost in the beauty of it all and in Tom.

As we rode back to the hotel, I watched the gray clouds scuttling across the horizon, obscuring the sun setting over the distant hills. "Looks like rainbow weather," I observed.

Tom turned to me and smiled. "You know, that sounds like an excellent beginning for a song."

That evening, a group of us gathered around the swimming pool at the hotel as Tom pulled out his guitar. He had become much less self-conscious about playing, having recently released his first CD. He was also scheduled to perform in the spring at Nightingales, a café in a small strip mall in downtown Cassville where up-and-coming songwriters could play their own music. Watching him sing mesmerized me as I sat at his feet, gazing up at him like a starstruck teenager.

The next day we went swimming with the dolphins. I will never forget that day. Tom dove into the water and held out his hand to me as I jumped off the ladder of the boat. He smiled, and our eyes locked as I took his hand in mine. "Come with me, Diane," he declared as he grasped my hand firmly, "and I'll take you to the dolphins." We swam a short distance away from the boat, and he motioned for me to look down into the water. I peered through my mask and saw black lava rock and sea grass undulating in the ocean currents. They were lit by beams of sunlight that created a circular pattern below. Tiny bubbles of air floated slowly to the surface.

Then I saw the dolphins, gliding effortlessly above the sea grass with such grace and beauty that I was instantly entranced. They captured my heart in that magical moment of time. A baby dolphin nestled close to its mother's side as she swam along. Then, as if at an unseen signal, they began to rise to the surface of the water in unison, five or six dolphins together. I watched them, enchanted, as they broke the surface just in front of us before slowly moving away. I finally understood Callie's love for these gentle sea creatures.

We followed them, hand in hand, as other groups of dolphins rose up around us. Finally, Tom motioned for us to return to the boat. We'd been in the water for more than an hour, but time had ceased for me, and I didn't realize how chilled I was until we started back toward the boat. As we waited our turn to climb back up the ladder, I threw my arms around Tom's neck and kissed him.

"Thank you for bringing me to the dolphins."

"You don't need to thank me," he said and smiled. "Thank the dolphins."

As we were motoring back to the harbor, I noticed a solitary dolphin swimming out to sea a short distance from us. Across her back, just behind her dorsal fin, she carried another, much smaller dolphin with a deep gash across its abdomen. The baby appeared to be dead. The captain cut the motor of the boat to let her pass by. The idle chatter ceased as we watched her struggle against the white-capped waves to keep the baby on her back.

"It looks like the dolphin was injured by a boat propeller," Janet observed. "Unfortunately, this happens sometimes. I think she's going to take the baby out to deeper water to lay it to rest. Sometimes the mothers carry their dead babies on their backs for days. It's so sad."

I felt tears brimming silently in my eyes as I watched this dolphin mother. I wondered if she grieved her loss, just like me, and how she would survive.

I was quiet and withdrawn that night, insisting that I just wanted to order room service for dinner and watch TV. Tom finally left me and joined his friends for a few drinks at the bar. I knew he felt lost, not knowing how to help me, but all I wanted was to be alone.

The next day, to cheer me up, Tom rented a Jet Ski to take us to a deserted beach not far from the hotel that was difficult to access by land. As we swam in shallow water, I saw the image of the mother dolphin struggling against the sea like a mirage in the distance. I stood and a dam inside me broke. Shaking my fists at the cloudless blue sky, I screamed, "NO!" Instantly I felt Tom's arms gently encircle my waist. My feet buckled underneath me and he cradled me in his arms, my face pressed against his chest. I clung to him as if I would hold on forever, racked with sobs and wailing like a lost child, tears streaming down my face as the ocean gently rocked us both.

"Let her go, Diane," he whispered gently in my ear. "Let her go."

In that magical moment of time, I cut the cords that still bound me to Callie and, like the dolphin mother, surrendered her to the sea. And because the universe abhors a vacuum, I instantly filled that space in my heart with the most profound gratitude, reverence, and love for the source of all things beautiful—and for Tom, the man who had helped me set her free.

The most amazing thing happened next. I snapped a few photos of the beach from the Jet Ski before we headed back to the dock. When I looked at one of the photos later that evening, the shoreline was obscured by a wide shaft of golden and white light that reached down from the heavens to the sea.

"That's the energy of Callie as she was released into the vortex," I exclaimed.

Ordinarily, Tom would have tried to explain it away by stating that my finger had probably gotten in front of the camera lens, but this time he replied, "Yes, that's exactly what it is."

He kissed me on the top of my head then as I wrapped my arms around his waist.

☙ 34 ☙

Diane—My Mount Everest

My flash of insight came to me one cold March morning somewhere between emptying the dishwasher and folding the laundry. As I looked out my kitchen window, I could see the wind-driven snow still licking the windowpanes after a late-night squall and the cardinals, blue jays, and little sparrows flocking to my feeder in the backyard. A quiet calm hung in the air like a soft, woolen blanket. After the furious, raging storm, the peace I sought had finally come.

I remembered Callie saying through Joy that she'd wanted to know what it was like to die by her own choice. I had often thought about this comment in the years after Callie's death. *If Callie wanted to know how it felt to die like that*, I thought as I watched the birds outside hungrily eating the sunflower seeds I had left for them, *then maybe my soul wanted to learn how to survive the suicide of my beloved daughter.*

Since childhood, I'd had a fantasy about climbing Mount Everest. I heard a story about a famous climber, George Mallory, who, when asked why he risked his life just to get to the top of a mountain, replied, "Because it's there." I was sure there was more to it than that. These climbers were seeking their own boundaries and, in the process, found that they were much more resilient than they ever thought possible. Maybe this experience was my Mount Everest. It came to show me who I truly was. Looking back, I could see that I possessed more strength and raw courage than I'd believed. I had more perseverance, determination, and outright will to carry on no matter what life threw my way. My experience of losing Callie had brought me these gifts. They made my spirit stretch, finally making the light in my soul seem like a beacon in the darkness of a cold winter night.

I had striven long and hard to accumulate my big brick house overlooking the lake, the Jet Skis, the cars, and the bank accounts. But when my time finally came to cross over and see Callie again, I wouldn't be taking any material possessions with me. Instead, I would be taking these simple gifts of the soul.

I had it all planned out. I was going to have one hell of a party when I finally made it to the other side. It would be held outside on a warm summer evening somewhere in heaven. All the flowers would be in bloom, scattering their scent into the night air. Fireflies would flicker in the grass. Hundreds of round tables would be set around a huge stage and dance floor. There would be a full moon. A giant silver globe would circle above the floor, scattering the starlight in all directions. All my friends and soul mates from every life would be there. I would arrive at the party with Callie. She would be dressed in silver, and I would wear a plum rose gown. Luther Vandross would sing "Shine."

Tom and I would dance, and maybe even get a little drunk on the sweet nectar the angels poured into fluted glasses—that is, if spirits are allowed to get drunk in heaven. People would sing along with the music, dance on tables, and celebrate that I had outlasted the storm and made it home again. They would see that I had grown by leaps and bounds in my long and arduous time on earth. Yes, indeed, *I truly have survived*.

Callie—Death Is
an Urban Legend

Now, I have a message for all you kids out there who are doing drugs and thinking about suicide:

I've got news for you. There's no such thing as death, at least not in the way you're looking at it. It's not the ultimate escape. It must be some kind of urban legend perpetuated by our parents, because I'm more alive now in heaven than I ever was on earth. I learned the hard way that wherever you go, you'll be there. I'm telling you this because I don't want to have to fetch your sorry ass and haul you to Seraphiel if you cross yourself over. And when you open your spirit eyes and realize you're not dead, I'll try really hard not to say I told you so. I know I can be a bit of a smart-ass sometimes.

Looking back now, I can honestly say that I wish I'd told my mama or one of my best friends about how depressed I was. Although I've been able to help a lot of kids because I've had the experience myself, I wish I had told someone that I was thinking about suicide. But that wasn't my journey in my last life. I had planned to die young.

As Seraphiel says, "If you acknowledge your own feelings of pain and despair and give them life, they will die in their birth." It would have taken a lot of courage for me to do that. But guess what? I've come back. I get to start all over in another life. I get to be a baby again, and wear diapers, and pee and poop on myself. How disgusting! I get to come back until I face my problems and stop trying to run from them.

Drugs won't help you; in fact, they're worthless. You don't have to get high to feel better. I know you'll probably think this is really stupid, but you could try meditation. My mama did, and it made her feel better. Don't you just hate it when your parents are right?

I know I took everyone on one hell of a ride, but I bet all of you learned something from it. Like, when you're on earth, you never know what's going to happen next. So don't take anything for granted. Life changes in an instant; my mama learned that. You're not imprisoned by your history. You can own it and then let all of it go and move forward with faith and courage. You have the power to forgive everything and everyone, even yourself, and this will truly set you free. Believe me, things on earth are not what they appear to be. There are no accidents. Everything happens for a reason—to help you know you're love.

Now, I have this to say to all you people still on earth. This is my story, the story of Callie Murray, and I'm sticking to it. I'm telling it to you exactly as it happened to me. I know a lot of you people out there who are reading these words are going to think, what a terrible tragedy. A beautiful (I admit I was beautiful) sixteen-year-old girl with her whole life in front of her goes and kills herself for no apparent good reason. But in Summer Wind, we don't look at it that way at all. You see, Mama and I were the perfect match, and we both got what we were looking for when we went to earth. I learned what it was like to die by my own hand, so I could help other kids who crossed themselves over. And Mama, well, she got to climb her version of Mount Everest. So from the perspective of our side, it was perfect. Everything in my life as Callie unfolded exactly as it was meant to.

To all my friends: I know you've moved on with your lives. But sometimes I'll catch you unaware as you go about your day, and you'll remember me. Maybe it will be the lyrics from an old song we used to play. The scent of the perfume I used to wear. A photo of dolphins playing in the ocean. A smiley face on a greeting card that catches your eye. A cobalt-blue Mustang that passes you on the highway at midnight with a blonde-haired girl in the driver's seat. You'll stop for a moment and remember me, and guess what? In that instant, I'll be there! You may think I'm really far away or gone forever, but I'm not. And we will be together again. When you cross over that rainbow bridge, I'll be there to greet you, and it will be just like I was never gone. The time we were apart will seem like the blink of an eye. This truly is your friend Callie speaking to you from the other side of eternity. Peace out! Now and forever!

Epilogue: Diane—Moving On

"My quest is over but the dream lives on."
—"The Dream Lives On" by Shawn Gallaway

The world moved on, taking me with it, even if at times against my will. The world didn't stop because of Callie's death, although I once wished it had. In the years after, I remained in the home where we had lived and where Callie died. Megan gave birth to two baby boys. I was with Megan for the birth of her first child, and I remember her mama, Ruth, turning to me as Megan was pushing, saying, "I think I'm gonna faint." Getting her to a chair and putting her head between her knees, I took over and helped Megan push her baby—my godson—into the world.

Jenny moved to Switzerland in search of her long-lost father. I often thought of her, bundled up in fur and walking down a quaint little street gazing in shop windows in the Swiss Alps, miles and miles from home.

I was there when Ashley got married in her long, white gown trimmed with heirloom lace and small pearls, wondering what Callie would have looked like in a wedding dress. Over the years, I would take Megan, Ashley, and their children to a restaurant or a park. Watching the children play, I would often think about Callie. Would she have had children of her own?

Anthony finished college and moved out of town, and I got a full-time faculty position at the university. The house grew quiet with just Tom and me and the animals living there. The cedar chest remained in the back of my closet gathering dust, and Callie's prom dress hung forlornly in her otherwise empty closet.

I have learned to live with a broken heart, but the core essence of love that still exists between us keeps me strong. I've moved on with my life, but Callie will always be a part of me. Not a day goes by that I don't wistfully think about her, where she is and what she might be doing now in heaven. I suppose it will be this way until the end of my life.

I feel Callie's presence most often at the beach. I lie in bed and listen to the faint sound of the surf as a salt-tinged breeze drifts through my open bedroom window. In the early hours of morning, just before dawn, in that semi-drowsy state between wakefulness and sleep, I sometimes see Callie's face materialize behind my closed eyelids. Callie is always smiling, her blonde hair pulled back in a ponytail and her eyes a crystal blue.

I wander along the beach late at night, watching the flashlights blinking as tourists look for crabs scuttling along the shoreline. Phosphorescence lights the ocean waves, and sometimes a bolt of lightning shoots across the night sky, merging with the distant sound of thunder. An unseen presence often joins me as I walk along the beach. A soft voice mingled with the waves and sand calls, "Mama." And for an instant, I'm not alone.

Does Callie really watch over me? Will she stay until I, too, cross over? Will she reach down from heaven, arms outstretched, ready to bring me back home when I take my last breath? Is there really a Seraphiel? Did he send Tom, Joy, Kira, and the three girls to comfort me in my despair? Is this all part of my divine plan?

Is this my destiny?

Sometimes late at night, when Tom is at the gym and the house is still and I'm in my office grading papers, I lean back in my chair and let my mind drift. I imagine a cold winter night in mid-December. I'm at work in my office, a candle lit in my window to help Callie find her way home. I hear the faint sound of music with a heavy bass beat in the distance. The sleeping dogs scattered around my desk prick up their ears. Then I hear the purr of an engine as a cobalt-blue Mustang turns onto my street. The sound becomes louder and louder as the car makes its way into my driveway and then suddenly stops. Next I hear the clattering of high heels on the steps, the door opens, and Callie bursts into my office, long hair flowing, eyes sparkling, wearing a black leather jacket and jeans. "Mama," she exclaims as she walks into the room. "I'm home."

Acknowledgments

First to my daughter, Cassandra, my inspiration for writing this novel, thank you for never giving up on trying to communicate with me from beyond the veil. It truly has been a magical journey and I know without a shadow of a doubt that you are always with me, right by my side.

To my son Philip, you will see much of yourself in the character of Anthony. You possess tremendous strength and courage to have walked down this road with me. I love and honor you more than you will ever know.

In the beginning, when this novel was just a piece of stardust caught on paper, Yvonne Perry made me believe that I had all I needed inside me to write the essence of my experience with the afterlife.

To my first editor, Signe Pike, you were brave enough to take on the challenge of working with a purely academic writer. You showed me how to create beautiful word pictures and dialogue on paper, making my novel come more alive than I ever thought possible.

Roni Angel, and Micahael, I cannot thank you enough for being my mentors on this long journey through the shadow of death, gently guiding me towards the light when in my darkest moments I thought that I might drown in remorse, regret, and tears.

Terri Clemens, you helped restore my connection to Cassie and became my messenger in the days when I felt that she was lost to me.

Shawn Gallaway, my BFF, thank you for gently guiding me through my dance with love and fear on the way to publishing my novel and for the beautiful song, *Dancing Down the Dreaming Road*, that you wrote for me. Yes, I finally chose love.

Jan Salerno, the midwife for those who seek to overcome their fear of deep water so they can commune with the dolphins, thank you for introducing me to these playful and gentle sea creatures.

To Cassie's three BFF, Mallory Moffitt, Gina Sas-Zaloziecki, and Tiffany McKenzie, thank you for being the daughters of my heart and for your unwavering support in the months and years after Cassie's death.

To Angelique Moselle and Keith Coley, thank you for believing in me and the message in my novel.

To my fellow seekers of spiritual awareness in the Messages from Your Heart, Alchemy of the Soul, and Angel Awakening Classes as well as my pod on our Dolphin Tune Adventures, we have chosen quite a ride through this journey called life. I wish you Godspeed.

And finally, for those who have lost loved ones, especially to suicide, I hope, for you, that through understanding that life and love go on forever, the dawn will break and the sorrow will be washed away.